Dedicated to "Beautiful Word," Skawenniio Barnes of the Kahnawake Mohawk Reserve in Québec, whose passion and perseverance built a library for her community in 2003.

Contents

Acknowledgments

I am very grateful to the following people for their welcome encouragement, support, and advice: at Trent University, Professors Elwood Jones, Michele Lacombe, Jean Manore, John Milloy, Michael Peterman, Dale Standen, Thomas H. B. Symons, John Wadland, the staff of the Interlibrary Loans department at the Bata Library, and to many of the faculty, staff, and students associated with the Frost Centre for Canadian Studies and Native Studies; Professor Peter McNally at McGill University; the diverse group of scholars associated with the History of the Book in Canada project, particularly Joyce Banks, Patricia Fleming, Janet Friskney, Elise Moore, Laura Murray, Germaine Warkentin, and others who have offered insight; Professor Donald B. Smith at the University of Calgary; Professor J. R. Miller and David A. Smith at the University of Saskatchewan; for their interest and support, my friends Paul De Decker at New York University, Jeff Lilburn at Mount Allison University, Charles Frank, and Kevin Lee; and to my parents, Fred and Heather Edwards. I would also like to thank the anonymous readers who helped to shape and refine this text.

The research and coordination necessary to produce this work was in part made possible by financial assistance awarded by the T. H. B. Symons Trust for Canadian Studies. The author gratefully acknowledges the support of this award.

Brendan Edwards
Saskatoon, Saskatchewan
May 2004

We youngsters were playing tag nearby when someone called me. I stood still and hesitated to approach my elders until my grandfather, Panapin, called me by name.

As I stood before them, one of the elders pointed to the tattoo I had on my left cheek beneath the eye and said to my grandfather:

"Panapin, mark that tattoo on your grandson's cheek. You are fortunate indeed to have that mark of identification on your grandson's face. One of the redcoats at Fort Walsh told me that when the westward migration of the white-men begins in earnest, they will come in swarms like the grasshoppers in flight. They will occupy all of our buffalo country and will build centers like the anthills. When these things have come to pass the redcoats told me that we would not be able to identify our own people!

"And, furthermore," he continued, "our children and grand-children will be taught the magic art of writing. Just think for a moment what that means. Without the aid of a spoken word our children will transmit their thoughts on a piece of paper, and that talking paper may be carried to distant parts of the country and convey your thoughts to your friends. Why even the medicine men of our tribe cannot perform such miracles."

Dan Kennedy (Ochankuhage)
Recollections of an Assiniboine Chief (1972) 48.

Introduction

In 1959, Angus McGill Mowat, former head of the Public Libraries Branch of the Ontario Department of Education, established a public library for the Cree and Ojibwe community at Moose Factory. This library was credited as the first public library established on an Indian Reserve in Canada, and the second in North America.[1] The Moose Factory library was a post-retirement project for Mowat, and was one of his last significant public endeavors in the field of education and libraries. Mowat's career is documented by Stephen Foster Cummings in his 1986 doctoral thesis and by other histories of the public library movement in Ontario, but little emphasis is placed on his library endeavors among the Aboriginal peoples of the province. Mowat's library in Moose Factory, however, was not the first library designed with an Aboriginal population in mind. Libraries in Aboriginal communities emerged well before Mowat's endeavors in the late 1950s.

Western notions of the book and print culture were first introduced in Aboriginal communities simultaneously with the arrival of missionaries. As will be demonstrated in the discussion that follows, collections of print materials for conversion and language training purposes were first gathered by evangelical missionaries in Sunday schools among the First Peoples of Upper and Lower Canada as early as the 1820s, and Aboriginal peoples themselves began asking the federal Department of Indian Affairs to establish public and school libraries in their communities as early as 1901.

These early interests and initiatives in library development as they relate to Aboriginal peoples in Canada have been largely ignored. Considerable discussion has existed around Aboriginal library development post-Mowat, from 1960 onward,[2] but histories of library development in Canada in general have ignored the role these institutions played in the intellectual, religious, and social relationships of Aboriginal people and non-Aboriginal Canadians.[3] A 1980 study on the existing literature on libraries and Aboriginal peoples in Canada and the United States revealed that eighty-five percent had been published between 1969 and 1979, and most tended to be descriptive in nature rather than critically evaluative or problem-solving.[4] Much of the significant amount of literature published since 1979 has been overwhelmingly concerned with contemporary problems associated with developing and managing libraries in Aboriginal communities. No effort whatsoever has been made to explore the pre-1960 historical period when the introduction of print literacy and books cumulated in efforts by missionaries, government, and Aboriginal peoples themselves in establishing libraries well before Mowat's initiatives of the late 1950s. In part, such study has not been undertaken because it is has often been the assumption that Aboriginal peoples, who are understood as originating from oral cultures, had little concern with the Western printed word and books until the mid- to late twentieth century. The journalist, Michael Rose, however, has shown that among Aboriginal peoples in Australia, there has been a significant history of interest and activity in adapting the printed word as a tool in the development of political and social activism.[5] Many First Peoples in Canada have been similarly active and interested in employing Western understandings of print as a means of communication for at least the last one hundred years. Their interests in books and libraries serve to help illustrate this point.

If library historians have largely ignored the development of these institutions in Aboriginal communities, book historians[6] and bibliographers,[7] such as Joyce M. Banks, Bruce Peel, Germaine Warkentin, and John Murdoch have done a slightly better job in addressing the issues surrounding the introduction and relationships of print literacy, books, and First Peoples in Canada. Some of the more interesting and critical work that touches upon the fields of library and book history in relation to the experiences of Aboriginal peoples has been produced by linguists, anthropologists, literary, and other scholars writing from an interdisciplinary point of view. Writings by Walter D. Mignolo, Laura Murray, Bruce Greenfield, and Hilary E. Wyss, however, have not exclusively focused on the particular experience and relationships of First Peoples in Canada to the printed word, libraries, and education.[8]

In the contemporary world of library and information studies, there has often been an emphasis placed on mastering and keeping pace with new electronic resources—often resulting in the devaluing of library history. Celebrants of the so-called electronic revolution have at times envisioned a paperless society in the near future, and have identified the historical mission of the library as an obstacle to the professional project of librarianship.[9] But libraries are institutions that are embedded deeply within the cultural realm of Western society, and their structural and functional characteristics are determined by and large by their definition as institutions contrived to consume, preserve, transmit, and reproduce history.[10] As is true of all history, the history of libraries is a living part of our contemporary culture, capable of illuminating some aspect of the present with the light of the past. An examination of the history and development of library services by and for Aboriginal peoples serves to tell us much about the assumptions, motivations, and goals of those making the decisions in the establishment of these institutions, while also providing a venue for discussion on ideas surrounding theories relating to what constitutes knowledge, literacy, and methods of information dissemination.

Revisionist library historians, such as Bruce Curtis, Michael Harris, and Dee Garrison, have argued from the mid-1970s onward that the establishment and promotion of libraries in North America through the nineteenth and early twentieth centuries was motivated by intentions to employ libraries and the reading materials they embodied as instruments of social control.[11] Their theses, generally speaking, argue that libraries and the practice of careful selection and dissemination of books acted as agents of social control exercised by members of the upper classes, who sought to influence the behavior of those classes of society considered to be in need of improvement. In this view, library development projects were, in essence, political undertakings aiming to produce moral, peaceful, rational, hard-working, and loyal populations by directing patrons' reading practices into "improved" channels. Conceptualized as both a means of encouraging popular literacy, and regulating that literacy, early libraries, and librarians were aristocratic, elite, and authoritarian in nature, often seen to play the role of filling the void of "idleness" and repositioning leisure time into morally useful time.[12] This mind-set was particularly prevalent when it came to the role of the library and librarian in morally uplifting the lower, working, and immigrant classes of the population. Early library histories characterize libraries as stabilizing agents in society, assuming that the "common man," if properly motivated and rewarded, could learn and be uplifted in moral stature.[13]

The establishment of libraries and the employment of books among Aboriginal peoples in Canada in the nineteenth and early twentieth centuries by missionary and government representatives at first glance can be seen as falling in line with the arguments of revisionist library historians. Libraries and books were indeed conceptualized by church missionaries and government officials as tools to be employed in civilizing, converting, and assimilating Aboriginal peoples, but the story of library development and the uses of print among Aboriginal peoples in Canada is more complicated than this. Much of the evidence surrounding early publications produced with Aboriginal audiences in mind suggest that motivations behind the uses of print were complex, varying widely around issues of language and the ultimate efficacy of adopting Western-style literacy. While print and books had been employed by church missionaries as early as the seventeenth century among First Peoples, attempts in the early nineteenth century by missionaries to establish libraries for Aboriginal communities were largely unsuccessful. It is only at the turn of the twentieth century, and at the prompting of Aboriginal peoples themselves, that the federal Department of Indian Affairs began to take some conscious action in establishing libraries of printed materials.

The assumption that print culture was a Western political and cultural tool of conversion, civilizing, and assimilation is only partially correct. The history explored in the pages that follow is characterized by the efforts of some First Peoples to articulate and integrate print literacy, books, and libraries into the larger fabric of Aboriginal knowledge preservation and communication.[14] Some Aboriginal peoples in Canada were active and conscious participants in embracing print culture and in efforts to establish libraries. Print literacy and libraries, traditional Western-based tools of communication, knowledge transfer, and heritage preservation, were in these cases articulated and integrated by First Peoples in Canada as part of the larger Aboriginal processes of creating and inventing a common, mutually comprehensible world after the arrival and inevitable interaction of settlers and missionaries. In cultural studies terms, this process should be understood as a conjuncture–an historical moment when ideas converge and take meaning from one another. The imported Western reality of books and libraries were not strictly imposed, but rather negotiated, conceptualized, and adapted to Aboriginal systems of spoken and written communication as a creative blend of old and new in Aboriginal efforts to survive the present and prepare for the future.[15] Aboriginal efforts however, were often thwarted by the Department of Indian Affairs whose relentless single-minded vision of conforming Aboriginal populations to European ways applied libraries and print to assimilative purposes in the early twentieth century.

The stories employed in the telling of this history are by no means exhaustive in nature. In most cases, these are the stories of the pioneers of Western literacy, book distribution, printing, and library development among the First Peoples of Canada. With little or no work having been previously published in the field, the work that follows was drawn from a wide range of primary and secondary resources. Primary sources from which these stories were drawn were mainly archival and published primary resources, including the *Annual Reports* of the Department of Indian Affairs, published missionary and Aboriginal accounts, and various newspapers. A great number of secondary resources, from a wide range of disciplines and areas of study, including history, anthropology, and library, religious, and cultural studies, were also read and reread within the contexts of Aboriginal peoples and their relationships with print culture and libraries.

Of particular interest in the pages that follow are the efforts of Roman Catholic and Protestant missionaries, and the later efforts of the federal Department of Indian Affairs, whose primary tools of education in their attempts to convert, civilise, and assimilate Aboriginal peoples were often rooted in Western notions of literacy and the written and printed word. In seventeenth century Acadia and in the Gaspé region of Québec, Roman Catholic missionary attempts at reaching and converting the Mi'kmaq people resulted in their appropriation and use of traditional Mi'kmaq hieroglyphic writing forms in propagating the Christian doctrine. Also explored are the motivations of Protestant missionaries, particularly Methodists in Upper and Lower Canada, who in the early nineteenth century were effectively employing print materials and putting considerable creative efforts into translation work among Aboriginal communities for civilizing and religious conversion purposes.

In the early nineteenth century, American-born evangelist and Minister of the Gospel, Thaddeus Osgood, was widely promoting the benefits of libraries in fostering the social betterment of Aboriginal populations in his work with the Central Auxiliary Society for Promoting Education and Industry among the Indians and Destitute Settlers in Canada. Osgood worked among the Aboriginal peoples and settlers of Upper and Lower Canada as early as 1814, but was never successful in establishing libraries in Aboriginal communities.

The translation and self-printing work of the Methodist missionary, James Evans, in the 1830s and 1840s in Upper Canada and the north west, would lay the groundwork for the eventual establishment of libraries in Aboriginal communities at Sarnia, Rice Lake, and Moose Factory. Evans' missionary work among the Ojibwe and Cree people of these regions amounted to the so-called invention of syllabic characters, and the first printed books in Aboriginal languages that would effectively spur the interests of First Peoples in the Western mode of communication and knowledge transfer. Evans' effectiveness was rooted in his observation of the necessity of adapting Western print and book forms to traditional Aboriginal methods of communication, and in his close work (although largely uncredited) with Cree and Ojibwe translators and missionaries.[16]

Government education policies directed at civilizing and assimilating Aboriginal peoples into a Eurocentric notion of Canadian society employed by the Department of Indian Affairs did not make regular or conscious use of books and libraries until the very late nineteenth and early twentieth centuries. Initiatives taken on behalf of Indian Affairs in establishing such institutions appeared only after being prompted at the request of Aboriginal peoples themselves, particularly Charles A. Cooke, a Mohawk employee of the Department at the turn of the century. Cooke's initiatives would lead to the eventual establishment of an Indian Affairs departmental library in the late 1890s. These early missionary influences, the hesitation of government, and the interests of Aboriginal peoples in libraries and print material are at the center of the discussion that follows.

Several questions have guided this discussion, providing context and a frame within which the primary and secondary resources employed in the researching of this work were read. Why do libraries and/or discussions about libraries within the Department of Indian Affairs emerge when they do? For instance, in 1901 in Sarnia, and 1939 in Peterborough. Why does secondary literature on the subject seemingly overlook these earlier discussions and begin their studies in the 1950s? What relationships or ties can be traced between the work of Roman Catholic and Protestant missionaries in Aboriginal communities in the early nineteenth century and the proposed establishment of libraries or library services in the early twentieth century? What kind of materials are included in these libraries? Detailed lists of books from the libraries of all Indian day schools across the country between 1943 and 1947 exist. What do these materials tell us about the curriculum taught at these schools and the motivations and goals of educators? And what can we learn about how this curriculum was received and used by Aboriginal peoples?

Essentially, these questions may be summed up into one larger or overarching research question. What were the motivations and effects of introducing book literacy (or reading and writing the printed word) into Aboriginal cultures where orality and other variant forms of literacy already existed and had served the People well for many generations? The answers to this question reveal that print collections and libraries were employed by Aboriginal and non-Aboriginal peoples in different ways, and with varying degrees of success. Missionaries and government envisioned books and libraries as tools to assist them in their efforts to convert, civilise, and assimilate the First Peoples of Canada. Aboriginal peoples, on the other hand, through writing, alphabetic literacy, and the eventual formation of libraries, were taking steps to partially control the construction of their own identities within the contexts of colonialism and Western understandings of knowledge and communication.

Notes

1. Stephen Foster Cummings, *Angus McGill Mowat and the development of Ontario public libraries, 1920-1960.* Doctoral dissertation, University of Western Ontario, 1986; Prior to Mowat's accomplishments in Moose Factory, Ontario, the first public library established in an Aboriginal community in North America is credited to be that of the Colorado River Agency in Arizona, established in 1957. See: Dean C. Welsh, "Colorado River Tribes public library first in the nation" *Indian Historian* 2, no. 1 (Spring 1969): 8, 38.

2. Literature with an overwhelming historical focus on the post-1960 era of library development and First Peoples includes: Edith Adamson, "Public library service to the Indians of Canada" *Canadian Library Journal* 26, no. 1 (1969): 48-53; Jane Aspinali, "Library self-determination? Ontario Native task force backs separate system" *Quill and Quire* 58, no. 2 (1992): 10-12; Donna Bright, *The Provision of public library services to Native Canadians living on reserves in Ontario, Manitoba, Saskatchewan, Alberta, and British Columbia*, Master's thesis, School of Library and Information Science, University of Western Ontario, 1992; British Columbia Library Association First Nations Interest Group, *Library services for First Nations people: report on a workshop held in Penticton, British Columbia April 22, 1993* (Vancouver: BC Library Association First Nations Interest Group, 1994); Grace Buller, "Native peoples and library service in Ontario," *Ontario Library Review* 59, no. 1 (1975): 4-9; Judith Ann Carlson, *Library services for the Native peoples of North America: an examination of existing service in Ontario and recommendations for their improvement* (Toronto: Ryerson Polytechnical Institute, 1980); Grace Crooks, "James Bay Public Library, Moose Factory," *Ontario Library Review* 43, no. 1 (1959): 23-26; Earl Commanda, "Indian library and information services," *Ontario Library Review* 62, no. 4 (1978): 260-262; Stephen Foster Cummings, *Angus McGill Mowat and the development of Ontario public libraries, 1920-1960.* Doctoral dissertation, University of Western Ontario, 1986; Stephen Cummings, "On the compass of Angus Mowat: books, boats, soldiers and Indians" in *Readings in Canadian library history*, ed. Peter F. McNally (Ottawa: Canadian Library Association, 1986), 245-258; *Empowering people through libraries: conference proceedings* (Saskatoon: Library Services for Saskatchewan Aboriginal Peoples Conference, 1992); Nancy Hannum, "Do Native people use public libraries?" *BCLA Reporter*

39 (1995): 25-29; Gordon H. Hills, *Native libraries: cross-cultural conditions in the circumpolar countries* (Lanham MD: Scarecrow Press, 1997); Susan Hollaran, "Rural public library service to Native Americans" *Rural Libraries* 10, no.1 (1990): 31-48; Mary Land, "Double jeopardy: Native libraries face complex mandate with scarce resources" *Quill and Quire* 61, no. 2 (1995): 14-15; Native Information Services Task Force, *Report: empowerment through information* (Toronto: Ministry of Culture and Communications, 1992); Lotsee Patterson, "Native American library services: reclaiming the past, designing the future" *Wilson Library Bulletin* 67 (December 1992): 28-42, 119; Elizabeth Rockefeller-MacArthur, *American Indian library services in perspective: from petroglyphs to hypertext* (Jefferson NC: McFarland & Company, 1998); Stan Skrzeszewski, et al., "Bookmobile services to Native people: an experiment in Saskatchewan" in *The Book stops here: new directions in bookmobile service*, ed. Catherine Suyak Alloway (Metuchen NJ: Scarecrow Press, 1990) 312-321; June Smeck Smith, "Library service to American Indians" *Library Trends* 20, no. 2 (1971): 223-238; Task Group on Native Library Services, *Report to the Ontario Public Library Review on Native library services in Ontario* (Toronto: Obonsawin-Irwin Consulting, 1981); Charles Townley, "Encouraging literacy, democracy, and productivity: the current status of American Indian libraries" *Journal of Multicultural Librarianship* 5, no. 1 (1990): 26-32.

   3. There is very little or no discussion of library development as it relates to First Peoples prior to Mowat's endeavors in the following histories and discussions of library development in Canada. Any discussion that does arise is merely in passing: Lorne Bruce, *Free books for all: the public library movement in Ontario, 1850-1930* (Toronto: Dundurn Press, 1994); Elizabeth Colyer, "Library development in the Far North," in *Librarianship in Canada, 1946 to 1967: essays in honour of Elizabeth Homer Morton*, ed. Bruce Peel (Victoria BC: Canadian Library Association, 1968), 104-111; Tamara E. Grad, *The Development of public libraries in Ontario, 1851-1951.* Master's thesis, School of Library Science, The Drexel Institute of Technology, 1952; E. A. Hardy, *The Public library: its place in our educational system* (Toronto: William Briggs, 1912); Peter F. McNally, ed., *Readings in Canadian library history* (Ottawa: Canadian Library Association, 1986); Patricia L. Smith and Garth Graham, "Library service north of the sixtieth parallel: the Yukon and Northwest Territories" in *Canadian libraries in their changing environment*, ed. Loraine Spencer Garry and Carl Garry (Downsview ON: York University, 1977), 118-143; Madge Wolfenden, "Books and libraries in fur trading and colonial days," *British Columbia Historical Quarterly* XI, no. 3 (1947): 159-186.

   4. Richard G. Heyser and Lotsee Smith, "Public library service to Native Americans in Canada and the Continental United States" *Library Trends* 29, no. 2 (1980): 353.

   5. Michael Rose, ed., *For the record: 160 years of Aboriginal print journalism* (St. Leonards NSW: Allen & Unwin, 1996), xvii-xxxv.

   6. A small number of authors have addressed to some extent the role played by the introduction of print and books into Aboriginal communities in Canada. Among the most notable and important work done in this area of study includes

that of: Joyce M. Banks, *Books in Native languages in the Rare Book Collections of the National Library of Canada*. Revised and enlarged edition (Ottawa: National Library of Canada and the Ministry of Supply and Services, 1985); Joyce M. Banks, "The Church Missionary Society Press at Moose Factory: 1853-1859" *Journal of the Canadian Church Historical Society* XXVI, no. 2 (1984): 69-80; Joyce M. Banks, "James Constantine Pilling and the literature of the Native peoples" *Bibliographical Society of Canada: Colloquium III: National Library of Canada, 19-21 October 1978* (1978), 59-70; Bruce Peel, "Early mission presses in Alberta" *Alberta Library Association Bulletin* 11, no. 1 (1963): 3-6; Bruce Peel, "How the Bible came to the Cree" *Alberta Historical Review* 6 (1958): 15-19; Bruce Peel, "Rossville Mission Press: press, prints and translators" *Papers of the Bibliographical Society of Canada* 1 (1962): 28-43; David L. Schmidt and Murdena Marshall, *Mi'kmaq hieroglyphic prayers: readings in North America's first Indigenous script* (Halifax: Nimbus Publishing, 1995); Germaine Warkentin, "In search of 'The Word of the Other': Aboriginal sign systems and the history of the book in Canada" *Book History* 2, no. 1 (1999): 1-27.

7. Some notable bibliographies of books printed in Aboriginal languages in Canada, and for use among Aboriginal communities in Canada include: Joyce M. Banks, *Books in Native languages in the Rare Book Collections of the National Library of Canada*. Revised and enlarged edition (Ottawa: National Library of Canada and the Ministry of Supply and Services, 1985); Barry Edwards and Mary Love, *A Bibliography of Inuit (Eskimo) linguistics in collections of the Metropolitan Toronto Library* (Toronto: Metropolitan Toronto Library Board, 1982); Karen Evans, *Masinahikan: Native language imprints in the archives and libraries of the Anglican Church of Canada* (Toronto: Anglican Book Centre, 1985); John Murdoch, *A Bibliography of Algonquian syllabic texts in Canadian repositories* (Quebec: Project ASTIC, Gouvernement du Quebec, Ministeres des Affaires culturelles and Direction regionale du Nouveau Quebec et service aux autochtones, 1984); John Murdoch, *A Bibliography of Algonquian roman orthography texts in Canadian repositories* (Rupert House PQ: Project ASTIC, 1988); John Murdoch, *Bibliography of Inuktitut roman orthography texts in Canadian repositories* (Rupert House PQ: Project ASTIC, 1988); David H. Pentland and H. Christoph Wolfart, *Bibliography of Algonquian linguistics* (Winnipeg: University of Manitoba Press, 1982); James Constantine Pilling, *Bibliography of the Algonquian languages* (Washington: Government Printing Office, 1891); James Constantine Pilling, *Bibliography of the Eskimo language* (Washington: Government Printing Office, 1887); James Constantine Pilling, *Bibliography of the Iroquoian languages* (Washington: Government Printing Office, 1888).

8. Little of this discussion has focused its attentions on the experience of First Peoples in Canada, except for the work of Germaine Warkentin (see note 5) and Bruce Greenfield, "The Mi'kmaq hieroglyphic prayer book: writing and Christianity in Maritime Canada, 1675-1921," in *The Language encounter in the Americas, 1492-1800: a collection of essays*, ed. Edward G. Gray and Norman Fiering (New York: Berghahn Books, 2000), 189-229. On the other hand, some very insightful work has been done on the experience of Aboriginal groups with

print culture in the rest of the Americas, including: Elizabeth Hill Boone and Walter D. Mignolo, eds., *Writing without words: alternative literacies in Mesoamerica and the Andes* (Durham: Duke University Press, 1994); Walter D. Mignolo, *The Darker side of the Renaissance: literacy, territoriality and colonization* (Ann Arbor: University of Michigan Press, 1995); David Murray, *Forked tongues: speech, writing and representation in North American Indian texts* (Bloomington: University of Indiana Press, 1991); Laura Murray, "The Aesthetic of dispossession: Washington Irving and ideologies of (de)colonization in the early Republic" *American Literary History* 8, no. 2 (1996): 205-231; Laura Murray, "'Pray, Sir, consider a little': rituals of subordination and strategies of resistance in the letters of Hezekiah Calvin and David Fowler to Eleazar Wheelock, 1764-1768" *Studies in American Indian Literatures* 4, no. 2-3 (1992): 48-74; Laura Murray, ed., *To Do Good to my Indian brethren: the writings of Joseph Johnson, 1751-1776* (Amherst: University of Massachusetts Press, 1998); Hilary E. Wyss, *Writing Indians: literacy, Christianity, and Native community in early America* (Amherst: University of Massachusetts Press, 2000).

9. See for instance: F. W. Lancaster, ed., *The role of the library in an electronic society* (Urbana-Champaign: University of Illinois, Graduate School of Library Science, 1980); F. Wilfrid Lancaster, "Whither libraries? Or, wither libraries" *College and Research Libraries* (1978): 345-357; Patricia Molholt, "Libraries and new technologies: courting the Cheshire cat" *Library Journal* (1988): 37-41; Gregg Sapp, *A Brief history of the future of libraries: an annotated bibliography* (Lanham: Scarecrow Press, 2002);   Paul Schneiders and Pam Richards, "Some thoughts on the function of library history in the age of the virtual library," *IFLA Round table on Library History*, http://www.ifla.org/VII/rt8/1997/thoughts.htm, (1997); and James Thompson, *The end of libraries* (London: Clive Bingeley, 1982).

10. Michael H. Harris and Stanley Hannah, "Why do we study the history of libraries? A meditation on the perils of ahistoricism in the information era" *Library and Information Science Research* 14, no. 2 (1992): 128.

11. See for instance: Bruce Curtis, "'Littery merritt', 'Useful knowledge', and the organization of Township Libraries in Canada West, 1840-1860," *Ontario History* LXXVIII, no. 4 (1986): 285-311; Bruce Curtis, "The Speller expelled: disciplining the common reader in Canada West," *Canadian Review of Sociology and Anthropology* 22, no. 3 (1985): 346-368; Dee Garrison, *Apostles of culture: the public librarian and American society, 1876-1920* (New York: Free Press, 1979); Michael Harris, "The Purpose of the American public library: a revisionist interpretation of history," *Library Journal* 98 (1973): 2509-2514. The general lack of critical theorizing in library history, and a call for library historians to join with social and cultural historians in helping to locate the role of libraries within a larger context of social and cultural forces is outlined in: Wayne A. Wiegand, "American library history literature, 1947-1997: theoretical perspectives?" *Libraries & Culture* 35, no. 1 (2000): 4-34.

12. Bruce Curtis, "'Littery merrit', 'Useful knowledge', and the organization of Township Libraries in Canada West, 1840-1860," *Ontario History* LXXVIII, no. 4 (1986): 285, 287.

13. Philip Corrigan and Val Gillespie suggest that the upper-middle class and elitist origins of public libraries in England account for the modern day fact that library patrons are overwhelmingly drawn from a narrow band within the middle class. They put forth that working class people have always classified the Public Library in the same social architecture of state provision as the Town Hall, the Courthouse, School Board and so on–as part of a culture and a system within which the working classes have to live, but which is not their system. See Corrigan and Gillespie, *Class structure, social literacy and idle time: the provision of public libraries in England* (Brighton UK: John L. Noyce, 1978). A similar argument might be made to explain the contemporary relationship of Aboriginal peoples to the institution of libraries in Canada.

14. This theory of articulation is derived from the cultural studies work of Stuart Hall, which conceptualizes the conjunctures at which people knit together disparate and seemingly contradictory practices, beliefs, and discourses in order to give their world some semblance of meaning and coherence. Articulation theory describes how people attempt to make unity which is neither necessary nor previously determined. It is not so much an effort to find a middle ground between two paradigms, as it is to use the two paradigms themselves as limits and pressures on each other, as forms of reciprocal interrogation. See: Stuart Hall, "On Postmodernism and articulation: an interview with Stuart Hall," Ed. Lawrence Grossberg, *Journal of Communication Inquiry* 10, no. 2 (1986): 45-60; John Trimbur, "Articulation theory and the problem of determination: a reading of *Lives on the Boundary*," *Journal of Advanced Composition* 13, no. 1 (1993): 33-50; Similarly, a reading and understanding of Claude Lévi-Strauss' theory of "bricolage" is useful. See: Claude Lévi-Strauss, *The Savage mind* (Chicago: University of Chicago Press, 1966). See also: Terrence Hawkes, *Structuralism and semiotics* (Berkeley: University of California Press, 1977); Jarold Ramsey, *Reading the fire: the traditional Indian literatures of America* (Seattle: University of Washington Press, 1999). I am grateful to Paul De Decker for suggesting some of these readings.

15. I am grateful to Elise Moore for her guidance in conceptualizing this thesis. Her excellent paper outlining the story of the circulating libraries of the Manitoba and Saskatchewan Wheat Pools, "The Wheat Pool Libraries and the 'useful knowledge' movement," (paper presented at the History of the Book in Canada open conference for volume III, Simon Fraser University, Vancouver, BC, 16 November 2001) was of great value in providing theoretical context. Theories of Aboriginal accommodation of Western influences are outlined at length in: Colin G. Calloway, *New worlds for all: Indians, Europeans and the remaking of early America* (Baltimore: Johns Hopkins University Press, 1998); James H. Merrell, *The Indians' new world: Catawbas and their neighbors from European contact through the era of removal* (Chapel Hill: University of North Carolina Press, 1989); and Richard White, *The Middle ground: Indians, Empires and Republics in the Great Lakes region, 1650-1815* (Cambridge: Cambridge University Press, 1991).

16. The continued success of the Cree syllabics in the north west was in part assisted by the efforts of the Anglican missionary, Joseph Reader, who in the 1890s established a printing press at Oonikup, Saskatchewan, and printed books in the script. For more on Reader, see: Nan Shipley, "Printing press at Oonikup," *The Beaver* (Summer 1960): 48-53.

1

Contexts and Foundations

Placing this history:
literacy, books, libraries, and First Peoples

Knowledge systems, literacy, and the printed word

The existence of formal methods of written Aboriginal languages prior to European contact in what is today Canada is not an issue of debate–quite simply, the Aboriginal peoples of Canada employed unique and varying methods of written communication before contact. This work looks at the history of libraries and books–two predominantly Western-based knowledge tools–as they relate to the Aboriginal peoples of Canada. While there were no books or libraries as scholars of book history and print culture commonly understand them in any North American Aboriginal cultures prior to contact, the First Peoples certainly possessed elaborate forms of communicating knowledge through unique sign systems. The Aboriginal peoples of Canada have employed, both prior to and after contact, a number of sign-oriented levels of discourse in the material of wampum belts, pictographs and petroglyphs, birch bark scrolls, hieroglyphics, and winter counts. Book and library histories seek to document the histories of what are most often called written or print cultures, but as Germaine Warkentin has noted, discussion in this line of study, "fostered and developed as it has been by print-oriented scholars, has not always heeded either the significance of–or the problems inherent in–the term 'written.'"[1] Armando Petrucci in his definition of the history of writing, notes that such history

> must take into account every type of testimony produced in its period, from books to documents, from inscriptions to coins, from seals to graffiti, of writings in mosaic and carvings in ivory ... of writers and of users, of the processes by which writing is produced, and of those by which it is learned and archived.[2]

Histories concerned with the book and libraries are grounded in this same materiality, assuming the basic bibliographical requirement of "marks made upon a material base for the purpose of recording, storing, and communicating information."[3] By extension then, any history of print culture and Aboriginal peoples must in some way address the issue of Aboriginal sign-systems, literacy, and knowledge systems that both pre-dated and sustained themselves following the introduction of the Western book in Canada. This study, concerned with the establishment of libraries among Aboriginal peoples following the introduction of the book, would not be complete without some discussion of Aboriginal meanings of literacy and the assumptions of literacy and knowledge that were part and parcel of the reactions to the introduction of libraries and books by non-Aboriginal newcomers.

For a moment it may be of some value to ponder the meanings of libraries themselves. What is a library? A library is generally defined as a collection of books, periodicals, recordings, or other such materials for use by the public or by members of a group; a collection of books; or as a room or building containing a collection of books (for reading or reference rather than for sale).[4] The word itself derives from the Latin *libri*, meaning book, and as such, libraries are commonly thought of as collections of books or printed documents. Libraries, by their very nature, make assumptions based on Western notions of literacy and knowledge. Literacy, in a Western understanding, is defined in terms of language, script, culture, and the pedagogy of reading and writing. A moral consensus has abounded since at least the mid-nineteenth century that has represented literacy as the ability to read and write, and that one's ability or inability to become literate stands as a social explanation of success and failure within Western society. Obstructive dichotomies have become well established, such as literate versus illiterate, and print versus oral. If literacy is key to one's success or failure within Western culture, then it follows that literacy itself must be understood within a social and political context. J. Elspeth Stuckey, in her intriguing critique of the uses of literacy within North American culture notes that

> literacy, to be sure, is a powerful, unique technology. Yet literacy remains a human invention contained by social contract, and the maintenance of that contract in education betrays our ideas of humanity as surely as literacy enforces them.[5]

She asserts that literacy serves an ideology that entrenches a class and cultural structure in which those who have power have a vested interest in keeping it. Rather than engineering freedom, Stuckey argues that literacy, as it is defined within a Western understanding, corroborates other social practices that prevent freedom and limit opportunity:

> literacy education begins in the ideas of the socially and economically dominant class and it takes the forms of socially acceptable subjects, stylistically permissible forms, ranges of difference or deviance, baselines of gratification. Becoming literate signifies in large part the ability to con- form, or, at least, to appear conformist. The teaching of literacy, in turn, is a regulation of access.[6]

Thus, throughout the eighteenth, nineteenth, and most of the twentieth centuries, the book was often used as a symbol of status–though purportedly to educate, the book also identified the class of its owner. The possession of books could signify the extent to which an individual or family was literate and knowledgeable, and conversely, the absence of books could (although often falsely) imply illiteracy or a lack of knowledge. It is within this context that literacy was employed for hegemonic purposes by upper and middle class Canadians of west- ern European descent in their efforts to homogenize language, class, values, and culture. Economic leaders, government, and social reform- ers, particularly in the nineteenth century, grasped the vehicle of liter- acy and the uses of schooling for promoting the values, attitudes, and habits deemed essential to order, integration, cohesion, and progress. Throughout the last several centuries the acceptance of the primacy of print, and the abilities to read and write, have advanced to almost universality. While the uses of literacy have often been debated, its definition and basic value have not. Literacy, as the ability to read and write, has been seen as one of the many social reforms of the eighteenth and nineteenth centuries that sought to improve society and the human condition. Increasingly, through to the twenty-first century, to be literate and to spread literacy have been considered of great importance, where the ability to effectively read and write is seen as carrying bene- fits to individuals as well as to societies, nations, and states. Literacy has been conceptualized and assumed to be of value to the community, socioeconomic and self-worth, mobility, access to information and knowledge, rationality, morality, and orderliness. Within a dominant social understanding, the Western tendency to disseminate this defini- tion of literacy is associated with the triumph of light over darkness, of liberalism, democracy, and of universal progress. For these reasons, literacy and schooling have been assumed to be necessary for economic and social development, the establishment and maintenance of democratic institutions, and individual advancement.[7]

Literacy, however, narrowly defines alphabetic writing and print as devices designed exclusively for the transcription of speech. In this limited view, Aboriginal cultures did not, prior to contact, possess written forms of communication or literacy, since Aboriginal sign systems were understood to be largely graphic tools that did not literally transcribe speech, but rather acted as memory aids depicting concepts or specific events. Thus Aboriginal cultures have often been labeled as "pre-literate." If we look at writing instead as any graphic means of preserving and communicating information, then Aboriginal cultures have always employed their own unique forms of literacy. Further, Aboriginal cultures have also preserved and communicated information through orality, placing a far greater value on the ability of the spoken word to perpetuate knowledge than have contemporary Western cultures. Libraries, for their part, emerged out of Western cultures that have for at least the last two centuries come to understand writing and literacy through

> the Romantic notion that writing systems evolved through stages from primitive to modern with the inscriptions made by Aboriginal peoples around the world fixated at the primitive, pictorial stage. Only we in the West made it to the top, with the invention of the true alphabet.[8]

This view of literacy is rather simplistic–Aboriginal cultures in Canada have through pictorial inscriptions on rock, and numerous other sign systems, developed standard forms of written communication of oral cultures over many millennia, which in turn demanded a form of literacy in reading these sign systems.[9] Additionally, First Peoples viewed the land as text, deriving much of their education and knowledge holistically from experiences on the land. Western approaches to reading and learning, which are often linear and sequential and largely derived from books, therefore assume a different kind of literacy, one that ignores and often devalues traditional Aboriginal ways of knowing.[10]

Within a Western understanding, libraries are systematically acquired and organized collections of books and related materials that serve a purpose of preserving and communicating information and knowledge. Libraries, as such, were introduced into Aboriginal cultures (along with books and Western notions of literacy) after contact with Europeans. This monograph attempts to document the history of the establishment of such institutions. However, libraries introduced post-contact were not the first libraries employed by Aboriginal peoples, just as books were not the first medium of written communication to be employed by Aboriginal peoples. In forms largely unrecognizable to early missionaries and settlers, the First Peoples maintained their own libraries of materials ranging from wampum belts, winter counts, birchbark scrolls, hieroglyphics, petroglyphs, and pictographs. Further, orality and the remembering and perpetuation of stories constituted other kinds of libraries. Memory acted as a kind of living library, and this is perhaps no better stated than in the words of Luther Standing Bear, Lakota of the Oglala tribe in the United States:

> These stories were the libraries of our people. In each story there was recorded some event of interest or importance, happenings that affected the lives of the people. There were calamities, discoveries, achievements,, and victories to be kept. The seasons and the years were named for principal events that took place. There was the year of the 'moving stars' when these bright bodies left their places in the sky and seemed to fall to earth or vanished altogether; the year of the great prairie fire when the buffalo became scarce; and the year that Long Hair (Custer) was killed. But not all our stories were historical. Some taught the virtues—kindness, obedience, thrift, and the rewards of right living. Then there were stories of pure fancy in which I can see no meaning. Maybe they are so old that their meaning has been lost in the countless years, for our people are old. But even so, a people enrich their minds who keep their history on the leaves of memory. Countless leaves in countless books have robbed a people of both history and memory.[11]

Contemporary Ojibwe storyteller, Louise Erdrich, has described Ojibwe birchbark scrolls and rock paintings found in northwestern Ontario, for example, as constituting perhaps the first books and libraries in North America. Further still, she notes that information expressed through pictographs and birchbark scrolls hold the same meanings today to Ojibwe people as they did thousands of years ago.[12]

As Walter D. Mignolo has noted, when the modern world encountered the "other," alphabetic writing met oral traditions and pictoideographic writing or sign systems. European newcomers, in their one-sided understanding of literacy, viewed people without writing, without letters, as a people without enlightenment, as a people without history. Key to the process of effectively civilizing and Westernizing the North American First Peoples was the idea of colonizing the voice, whereby the domain of the letter took over the domain of the voice. Central to mainstream Western thought has always been the theory of the letter leading to a theory of writing that transcends the regionality of spoken languages and oral cultures. Thus, with contact began a process of colonizing Aboriginal languages (by writing their grammars) and the colonization of Aboriginal memories (by writing their histories).[13] Libraries, and the philosophies behind them, are institutions that inherently embody Western notions of literacy, language, memory, and knowledge dissemination, and from a non-Aboriginal perspective, have acted as colonizing tools from their earliest introduction into Aboriginal communities.[14] That said, however, this text will demonstrate that historically Aboriginal peoples were in some cases the initiators in establishing libraries of books and other printed materials in their communities. Why Aboriginal peoples have done so is one of the questions the telling of this history intends to address.

While missionaries, government, and school officials involved in Indian education undoubtedly used schooling and literacy as tools to impose Western values upon Aboriginal peoples, a number of First Peoples demonstrated agendas of their own, embracing Western measures for purposes unintended by their colonizers. Susan E. Houston and Alison Prentice have shown in their work on the nineteenth century emergence of public schooling in Ontario that the system there did not merely emerge from the minds of the political elite. The sensibilities of the people of that province at all levels had become "attuned to the need for schooling in the new industrializing economy," and "parental concerns undoubtedly played a significant part in the emergence of public as well as private schooling."[15] While school and government authorities saw public education as imposing themes of social discipline and moral regulation, the nature of schooling in the province would in the end be made up of multiple intentions and effects as students and parents alike shaped the system to suit their own purposes. Likewise, some Aboriginal peoples embraced the idea of Western education and demonstrated a degree of agency in its ultimate effects. John Tootoosis, a Cree leader born in 1899, recalled that although his father did not entirely like the idea of sending his children to school, he nonetheless "wanted them to learn to read, write, and count and be able to speak the language of the white men... that he did not have these skills himself, had often needed them and knew that Indian people would have a better chance in the future if they had them."[16] Some Aboriginal students became discriminatory and selective in what they chose to take away from their schooling, articulating the messages of Western education and literacy for their own political, social, and cultural purposes.[17] Cases of Aboriginal articulation of Western education are particularly evident in the efforts of some First Peoples to establish book collections and embrace the printed word, beginning at the very end of the nineteenth century. First Peoples across the country had their own unique ways of communicating, prior to and after European contact. With the introduction of a Western understanding of the printed word, some Aboriginal peoples recognized that there was value in becoming literate in the English and French scripts. First Peoples' interests in Western education and literacy were in part motivated by a desire to communicate more effectively with the emerging non-Aboriginal dominant order, to negotiate an Aboriginal place within the Dominion in ways that were more immediately understood.[18]

Relationships: what this history can tell us

The study of library history can tell us much about the cultural, social, political, and intellectual life of a people[19]–within the contexts of this monograph, the "people" are the First People of Canada and those individuals and groups behind the establishment of libraries and library services within a select number of their communities. An examination of the history and development of library services by and for Aboriginal peoples serves to tell us much about the assumptions, motivations, and goals of those making the decisions in the establishment of these institutions while also providing a venue for discussion of ideas surrounding theories relating to what constitutes knowledge, literacy, and mediums of information dissemination.

There are no other historical explorations of libraries within an Aboriginal context in Canada. Furthermore, what little study has been done concerning early translations and the publishing of books in Aboriginal languages has not been discussed within the contexts of library development. The study of library history and development as it relates to Aboriginal peoples in Canada fits well into current studies concerned with compiling histories of the book and print culture in this country. The book and libraries as they relate to Aboriginal peoples, particularly within a historical context, is an area of study with a number of possibilities and ample room for discussion. The print materials that libraries build their collections upon represent and provide access to an element of the past, or perceived heritage, and constitute important tools of learning and education. But what these books and printed materials also represent is the largely Western heritage of the printed word and approaches to education. It has been well documented that libraries (as thought of in a Western, book collecting context) are not well employed by Aboriginal peoples. Explanations for this are many, and a number of texts which focus their attentions on contemporary library issues as they relate to First Peoples offer insights ranging from a lack of Aboriginal librarians and input into libraries to collections that do not reflect the wide array of First Peoples' cultural and political concerns, languages, and writing.[20] Western understandings of libraries, and the purposes they endeavor to serve, have been challenged within the writing and researching of this monograph. Standing Bear's remarks on memory as a living library raise a number of key questions regarding the nature of knowledge, literacy, historical memory, and the role that "libraries" play in the promotion and understandings of these. Any historical and interdisciplinary approach to the subject of Aboriginal libraries must acknowledge and attempt to address these complicated ideas.

History, communication, and the construction of time and space

At the time of European arrival in the northern part of North America, newcomers did not recognize any traces of a formal or civilized expression of written language or printed materials in any Aboriginal cultures. What newcomers did see were pictorial inscriptions that they understood to be, at best, supplementary aids to a predominantly oral tradition of communication. Aboriginal peoples in fact had, and continue to employ, their own unique means of communicating and disseminating knowledge, and although not recognized as such by early settlers and missionaries, the First Peoples were highly literate in their own scripts.[21] Methods of knowledge transfer and communication within Aboriginal contexts included oral tradition, dances, "art," astronomy, and the spiritual. The oral traditions of the First Peoples are thousands of years old and most often take the form of stories passed down from generation to generation. These stories have practical, historical, spiritual, and entertaining purposes and are often referred to as the "life-blood" of Aboriginal knowledge. Oral narratives tell the People who they are, of important events, life lessons, and serve as cultural, philosophical and spiritual guides. Unlike the printed word, oral traditions rely heavily on, and disseminate much of their meaning, through performance. Outside of a performance context, stories can lose their meaning and strength when reduced to mere words on a page. In other words, orality demands life-long learning or literacy, if you will, on behalf of the listener, to fully comprehend and understand the message of the orator. Within an oral tradition, listeners are the students, while the storyteller is the teacher. Most often, it is the Elders of a community who are its principal storytellers, and stories are told not to just a few intellectual types, but are normally shared with the entire group. Hand-in-hand with oral narratives, and working similarly, is that of song as a means of knowledge transfer.

Petroglyphs and pictographs

Petroglyphs and pictographs are rock carvings and rock paintings respectively, and are found throughout Canada. "Rock art," as petroglyphs and pictographs are often referred to, are open to interpretation, where their meaning may only be known by their creators. Explanations for their existence include clan symbols, prayer rocks, recordings of important events, rituals and ceremonies, and shamanic purposes. Petroglyphs and pictographs are often termed "picture-words" by Aboriginal peoples today. Those found at Petroglyphs Provincial Park in Ontario are referred to as Kinomägewäpkong, "The Rocks that Teach," by the local Ojibwe Anishnabe who hold the site in reverence and continue to use it today for religious and spiritual purposes.[22] Another form of so-called "rock art" is that of the Inuit inukshux, found throughout the North. Inukshux are figures of humans made of stones which are used as markers to guide travelers and assist in caribou hunting. Today the image of the inukshuk has been adopted as a symbol to remind the People of their dependence on each other, and the value of friendship. It is also the image chosen for display on the territorial flag of Nunavut.

Wampum belts

Iroquoian nations, including the Mohawk, Oneida, Onondaga, Cayuga, Seneca, and Tuscarora, create and use wampum belts for

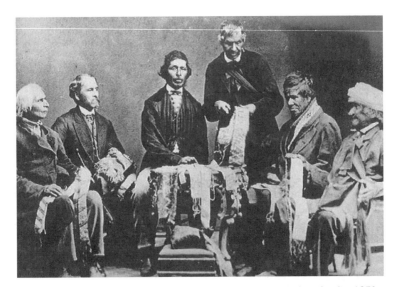

Iroquois Chiefs from Six Nations reading wampum sometime in the 1870s. From left to right: Joseph Snow, Onondaga; George Henry Martin Johnson (father of E. Pauline Johnson), Mohawk; John Buck, Onondaga; John Smoke Johnson (grandfather of E. Pauline Johnson), Mohawk; Isaac Hill, Onondaga; and John Senaca Johnson, Seneca. (Photograph courtesy of Electric Studio/National Archives of Canada/C-085137)

recording speeches, negotiations, treaties, and important events. Wampum are also used by the Wendat, Abenaki, Malecite, Mi'kmaq, and Algonkian. These belts are most often made of whelk shells and quahog clamshells, and usually depict abstract figures, like slanted lines, diamond shapes, hexagons, and representations of human figures. The belts are used to emphasize speeches, acting as memory-aiding devices, emphasizing the particulars of a treaty, for example. Acceptance of a wampum belt by another group or individual indicates that the message encoded on the belt is agreeable to both parties–likewise, if it is returned to the giver, it means the terms of the agreement are not acceptable. Wampum belts are used not only to remind one's self, but the other nations including European colonists, of the promises spelled out in the treaties.[23]

Winter counts

Winter counts are a form of communication used by the Aboriginal nations of the plains. These consist of paintings on deer or buffalo skins, and are created every winter, recording a chosen event either unique to the tribe or having affected all tribes, such as an eclipse or meteor shower. Winter counts are a kind of community chronicle, built on the rhythms of the annual cycle of winter and summer, recording structural time and representing a chronology extending over several generations, with each year associated with a memorable event. Time is not marked by a date or number cycle, but rather by the most significant event occurring between consecutive winter seasons.[24]

Mi'kmaq hieroglyphs

According to oral traditions, Mi'kmaq hieroglyphs or komqwejwi'kasikl (literally meaning "sucker fish writings"–the sucker fish being a river bottom feeder that in its quest for food leaves trails on the muddy bottom) were devised for inscribing maps and tribal records prior to European arrival. They are derived from a pictograph and petroglyph tradition, and are the closest comparable Aboriginal form to the European idea of a written language. While no physical evidence of any pre-contact scripts are known to exist, seventeenth-century reports by French missionaries testify to the existence of pictographic writing traditions among the Mi'kmaq and other eastern Algonkian speaking peoples.[25]

Birch bark scrolls

The Ojibwe people of the Great Lakes region employ pictorial birch bark manuscripts, which are most notably associated with the Grand Medicine Society, or Midewiwin–a graded fraternity devoted to physical and spiritual healing. The birch bark records are used at every stage of initiation to the society for instructional and guidance purposes, and are considered to be sacred liturgical documents. Birch bark scrolls comprise an array of pictorial representations finely engraved on the inner surface of the outer bark of the white birch tree. On occasion, lines are supplemented with red or blue pigment. Joan Vastokas explains that these bark records measure in length from centimeters to several meters. Longer examples can be found in the form of scrolls, consisting of up to six separate sheets of bark stitched together. The panels are framed at two ends by wooden sticks, and the bark naturally curls into tightly wrapped scrolls. The scrolls function on a number of levels, both historically and spiritually, describing the origins, history, and traditions of the Ojibwe people. Further, they are used by Mide members to record, narrate, and preserve the history and traditions of the people. Birch bark scrolls serve an important role as visual narrative texts and pictorial aids for the recitation of oral traditions, and as liturgical tools for Mide members. Further, the scrolls serve as both permanent visual documents and as teaching aids for the education of new members of the Midewiwin. As in a Western book printing tradition, scrolls were reproduced when worn out or when additional copies were required.[26]

Each of the above represents a unique communication form and demand a familiarity or literacy on behalf of their creator and the reader or listener. With the obvious exception of oral traditions, each of these represents a decipherable form of writing that acts as a means of preserving and communicating information. Newcomers did not recognize Aboriginal sign systems as other forms of writing equal to their own because within their Western understandings, writing was thought of as the transcription of speech.[27] Birch bark scrolls, hieroglyphics, winter counts, wampum belts, and petroglyphs and pictographs all act as historical documents and forms of writing, representing cultural expressions and events that were meant to be read by contemporary and future members of the community. These and other pre-existing Aboriginal systems of communication are equally valid to Western notions of the printed word in that they are relatively permanent and function for their communities as documents to establish and record ideas and events. Not recognizing these as writing forms, or as valid methods of communicating and preserving knowledge, settlers and missionaries assumed that the First Peoples were societies without history, and with no concern for recording their own histories. In part, this can explain the motivations of missionaries and settlers in introducing the Western notion of the book and printed word into Aboriginal cultures. But deeper still, Aboriginal and Western notions of communication and history are further complicated by cultural understandings of time and space.

Notions of time and space vary greatly depending on the society and era in which they are experienced. In his writing on history and communication in Canada, Gerald Friesen provides useful commentary on the relation of time and space as their implications to cultural ways of communicating.[28] Contemporary Western societies divide time into minutes, days, years, and centuries. We often experience time as an insistent, linear, and monetized unit of life, with the understanding that time is a fixed measure. Space, on the other hand, can be measured in kilometers, described in terms of shapes, or mapped by distance–in other words, it is a seemingly concrete and objective thing. Increasingly, however, our notions of space are becoming vague, as space has been made to appear less definitive. Technologies, from the steam engine to e-mail, have increasingly given us the sense that space can be transcended.[29]

A number of traditional Aboriginal societies, like contemporary Western societies, have organized their economic activities around ecological time, coinciding with the solar and lunar cycles and the seasons. These same traditional societies will often employ a second measure of time–that of structural time, marking the passing of generations and explaining the interaction of groups within them. Anthropologist and astronomer, Anthony F. Aveni explains:

> These people do not believe in history the way we do, though they do have a sense of history. As in events and relationships that comprise tribal life, there is a kind of immediacy to both cyclic ecological time and linear structural time among these tribal societies. Ultimate origins do not matter in their temporal time schemes. Interaction, with either nature or other people, is the real reason to keep time; and when things cease to interact or before they ever had interacted, there is no need of reckoning it.[30]

Societies such as these place great importance on continuity and duration, and do not separate the past from the future in the same way that Western societies often do. The past could, and often did, repeat itself. If one pays close enough attention to time, the past can be seen to already hold the future.[31] Friesen explains the significance of this conception of time to history:

> History in this sense was what had been foretold, a fact that both emphasized the importance of the event and made its telling worthy of contemplation by others. In this story-telling process, one's sense of time is subject to revision. Time is less fixed, less rigid and unbending, to the Aboriginal storyteller and to those who lend an ear to his or her narrative than it might seem to observers unaccustomed to this perspective or unsympathetic to such notions.[32]

Aboriginal perceptions of space as nature and land are as equally important notions as are perceptions of time in distinguishing between traditional understandings and Western cultural assumptions. In many oral traditions and stories, for example, the land and elements of nature provide many of the characters, denoting a specific and unique sense of place. Further, Aboriginal maps made at the request of fur traders customarily measured canoe routes and networks of rivers and lakes in time rather than in spatial units. An easy downstream paddle of twenty kilometers might occupy the same space on a map as a difficult five kilometer portage because they require equal time to traverse.[33]

Cultural conceptions of time and space are valuable to this discussion on libraries and Aboriginal peoples because such notions dictate our cultural understandings of history and what constitutes knowledge. Libraries are built upon assumptions of disseminating knowledge, and are commonly thought of as institutions supporting the study of history and maintaining community notions of heritage. There are generally two schools of thought on human understandings of knowledge.[34] The first subscribes to the notion that our understandings of knowledge are defined by culture. In this view, our conceptions of time and space are tied to social behavior and organization, thus the way people perceive time, or the way they reckon its passing, is closely tied to their world view of what constitutes knowledge and how knowledge is compartmentalized. The second view sees human knowledge as absolute, being entirely separate from culture. In this view, all human beings share in their understandings of what constitutes knowledge, where time is seen as a duration, either cyclic or linear in nature–otherwise human cultures could not even begin to communicate with each other. First Peoples' reactions to the book and libraries, and settler and missionary motivations for persuading Aboriginal peoples to adopt the printed word and in establishing libraries, are rooted in their cultural understandings of knowledge, communication, and time and space. However, Aboriginal and settler understandings of these notions should not be seen as constituting a dichotomy. Aboriginal reactions to the printed word and libraries should not be labeled as cut and dry. Rather, this history reveals that Aboriginal and Western understandings of knowledge, literacy, history, and time and space often meet on a middle ground. For the most part, Western societies have too often failed to recognize Aboriginal knowledge systems because they were so unlike that which they were accustomed to, and in part, due to cultural insensitivity. The idea, however, that First People did not embody their own unique and sophisticated ways of maintaining history and disseminating knowledge has been built upon simplistic notions of "us" and "other," based upon dichotomic understandings of culture and world views. While Aboriginal and Western ways of looking upon and understanding the world vary considerably, it is dangerous to label them simply as binary opposites. Further, the communication divide between the cultures was not unbridgeable. A means of communicating between Western and Aboriginal cultures, however, was largely one-sided, with the onus of understanding and articulation weighing heavily on First Peoples. It was in this light that some Aboriginal peoples chose to embrace Western notions of education and the printed word.

Libraries and heritage

Through their conscious collecting habits and intellectual control over books, printed materials, media, and now a growing number of electronic-based materials, libraries have always been institutions with an interest in preserving and perpetuating Western-specific approaches to learning, knowledge, and written heritage. By the nature of libraries' preservation practices and in providing access to materials, the collections embodied by public libraries constitute an important element of maintaining and acting as a guardian to a community's printed and recorded heritage. From about the 1930s onward, most public libraries have been steeped in the philosophy of acting as the guardians to the people's right to know, with the idea of facilitating the democratic process by making a wide spectrum of human knowledge, cultural heritage, and social intelligence readily available to all who might seek it. But libraries were not always conceptualized in this way. Prior to the 1930s, public libraries were largely conceived as deterrents to irresponsibility, intemperance, and rampant democracy, and were administered in an elitist and authoritarian fashion by librarians and trustees from the middle and upper classes.[35]

Even in the post-1930 era, problems relating to accessibility and administration have persisted. Libraries, in both the nineteenth and twentieth centuries, have been largely institutions of interest primarily to the middle classes, who have consistently made up the majority of library clientele.[36] Libraries therefore assume largely middle class, Western values and embody a cultural heritage that follows these values. The National Library of Canada, for example, since its formation in 1953 has reflected in its own development stages in the development of the Canadian nation itself. The National Library was estab-

lished in the context of a developing national consciousness, and has
continued to presume the existence of a national cultural conscience.[37]

The National Library is the most obvious example of a library
fulfilling the role of maintaining, promoting, and modeling a collective
(in this case national) identity through heritage. In a culture that values
the printed word, however, all libraries are hallowed institutions, and all
libraries embody a collective Western and largely middle class heritage.
American library historian, Jesse H. Shera, notes that public libraries in
the United States evolved from fulfilling a "narrowly conservational
function to a broad program directed toward the advance of popular
education," arguing that their objectives changed merely to reflect
larger transformations in society itself. The needs of society demanded
"the need of democracy for an enlightened electorate," and libraries
adapted to meet these changing social requirements.[38] Yet, as Shera
clearly notes, nineteenth century public libraries were supported from
public funds and worked as integral parts of local governments, with an
interest in improving citizens and through them society as a whole.[39]
Therefore, despite Shera's assertion that libraries followed, rather than
created social change, the founding intentions of early American public
libraries implied that their creators envisioned them as embodying and
promoting a specific middle class, literate heritage.[40] Libraries, for the
most part, like the societies they represent, are cultural and educational
tools that place literacy in reading and writing above all other means of
communication.

In fulfilling a heritage role within a national, regional, cultural or
organizational community, the study of libraries, their collections, and
their use can tell us much. Canadian library historian, Peter F. McNally
has noted that the study of libraries can constitute a significant litmus
test of the cultural and intellectual life of a society, and is an important
element in the historical study of any society.[41] Library history is
cultural history, thus in studying the motivations and conditions behind
the establishment of libraries, the make-up of their collections, and their
widespread or lack of use (thus determining the relevance or irrelevance
of the library to the community), we can gain some insight into the
perceived and/or practiced heritage of a people. The study of libraries
and their histories is an attempt at discovering the ways in which
libraries influence their coeval society, and conversely, is also an
exploration into the ways in which that society inhibits, encourages or
directs library growth. Historians generally agree that libraries have
emerged and prospered mostly in those societies where there is economic prosperity, urban concentration, government encouragement, and

where the population is literate and stable.[42] In other words, libraries are a direct window on the historical development and heritage of a society or community. The historical study of libraries within an Aboriginal perspective is all the more unique in that the cultural assumptions of libraries must be weighed against the cultural realities of the communities that embody them.

Library services for Aboriginal peoples have, for the most part, failed to act as culturally significant and supportive institutions. Library materials, while arguably well-intentioned, have too often been acquired with little or no thought in incorporating Aboriginal cultures, knowledge systems, languages, literacies, and heritage into their collections. Only recently have library programs incorporated Aboriginal input on services and collection development on a wide scale–this is most evident in recent moves to do input and needs assessments in Aboriginal communities, staffing libraries with community members, and creating Aboriginal library boards.[43] As will be demonstrated in the pages that follow, early initiatives in establishing libraries for First Peoples in the late nineteenth and early twentieth centuries recognized the necessity of incorporating Aboriginal heritage and ways of knowing. This opportunity was soon lost, however, as libraries took on traditional Western characteristics in Euro-Canadian attempts at employing these institutions as civilizing and assimilation tools, in the process largely alienating the Aboriginal communities they were meant to serve.

Notes

1. Germaine Warkentin, "In search of 'The Word of the Other': Aboriginal sign systems and the history of the book in Canada," *Book History* 2.1 (1999): 2.

2. Qtd in Warkentin, 3.

3. Warkentin, 2.

4. Katherine Barber, ed., *The Canadian Oxford dictionary* (Toronto: Oxford University Press, 1998), 825.

5. J. Elspeth Stuckey, *The Violence of literacy* (Portsmouth NH: Boynton/Cook Publishers, 1991), viii.

6. Stuckey, 19.

7. Harvey J. Graff, *The Literacy myth: cultural integration and social structure in the nineteenth century* (1979; New Brunswick NJ: Transaction Publishers, 1991), passim.

8. David R. Olson, "Aboriginal literacy," *Interchange* 25.4 (1994): 391; The point of view that traditional Aboriginal writing methods were "primitive" is highly flawed as the recent deciphering of the Mayan codes, for example, clearly illustrates. For more on the Mayan codes, see the work of Michael D. Coe.

9. Marie Battiste, "Micmac literacy and cognitive assimilation," *Indian education in Canada, volume 1: the legacy*, edited by Jean Barman, Yvonne Hébert, and Don McCaskill (Vancouver: University of British Columbia, 1986), 23-44; Annie York, Richard Daly, and Chris Arnett, *They write their dream on the rock forever: rock writings in the Stein River Valley of British Columbia* (Vancouver: Talonbooks, 1994), passim.

10. For more on Aboriginal approaches to learning from the land, see for instance: Jeannette C. Armstrong, et. al., eds., *We get our living like milk from the land: Okanagan tribal history book* (Penticton BC: Theytus Books, 1994); "School in the bush," *Native Reflections*, prod. Dennis Sawyer and Andy Thompson, National Film Board of Canada, 1996.

11. Luther Standing Bear, *Land of the Spotted Eagle* (1933; Lincoln: University of Nebraska Press, 1978), 27-28.

12. Louise Erdrich, *Books and islands in Ojibwe country* (Washington DC: National Geographic Society, 2003), 5.

13. Walter D. Mignolo, *The darker side of the Renaissance: literacy, territoriality, and colonization* (Ann Arbor: University of Michigan Press, 1995), passim; See also: Battiste, 25-35.

14. For discussion on the colonising effects of libraries among Indigenous populations in Africa, for instance, see: Adolphe O. Amadi, *African libraries: Western tradition and colonial brainwashing* (Metuchen NJ: Scarecrow Press, 1981).

15. Susan E. Houston and Alison Prentice, *Schooling and scholars in nineteenth-century Ontario* (1988; Toronto: Ontario Historical Studies Series & University of Toronto Press, 1991), xi.

16. Jean Goodwill and Norma Sluman, *John Tootoosis: as told by Jean Goodwill and Norma Sluman* (1984; Winnipeg: Pemmican Publications, 1987), 94.

17. Jean Barman, Yvonne Hébert, and Don McCaskill, "The Legacy of the past: an overview," *Indian education in Canada: volume 1, the legacy*, ed. Jean Barman, Yvonne Hébert, and Don McCaskill (1986; Vancouver: University of British Columbia Press, 1992), 10-11.

18. Some First Peoples may have also turned to adopting the written word because they felt their religious and spiritual cultures were under threat. Writing down oral text may have been conceived as a means of protecting Aboriginal knowledge and beliefs. See: Harold G. Coward, "The Spiritual power of oral and written scripture," *Silence, the Word, and the Sacred*, E.D. Blodgett and H.G. Coward, eds. (Waterloo: Wilfrid Laurier University Press for the Calgary Institute for the Humanities, 1989) 111-137.

19. Peter F. McNally, "Foreword," *Readings in Canadian library history*, Peter F. McNally, ed. (Ottawa: Canadian Library Association, 1986), iii-iv.

20. See for instance: Jane Aspinali. "Library self-determination? Ontario Native task force backs separate system," *Quill & Quire* 58. 2 (1992): 10-12; Judith Ann Carlson, *Library services for the Native peoples of North America: an examination of existing service in Ontario and recommendations for their improvement* (Toronto: Ryerson Polytechnical Institute, 1980); Nora T. Corley, *Resources for Native people's studies* (Ottawa: National Library of Canada, 1984); Gordon H. Hills, *Native libraries: cross-cultural conditions in the circumpolar countries* (Lanham MD: Scarecrow Press, 1997); Gene Joseph, "Library services to First Nations in British Columbia" http://web.ucs.ubc.ca/bcla/fnig/gene2.htm (Vancouver: University of British Columbia, 1994); Mary Land, "Double jeopardy: Native libraries face complex mandate with scarce resources" *Quill & Quire* 61.12 (1995): 14-15.; Deborah A. Lee, "Academic information needs and library use of a sample of Aboriginal students at the University of Alberta," Diversity Now conference: people, collections and services in academic libraries, University of Texas at Austin, 4 April 2000; Elizabeth Rockefeller-MacArthur, *American Indian library services in perspective: from petroglyphs to hypertext* (Jefferson NC: McFarland and Company, 1998).

21. The author adheres to what John DeFrancis labels as an inclusivist definition of writing and communication. Meaning that writing includes any system of graphic symbols used to convey some amount of thought. See: John DeFrancis, *Visible speech: the diverse oneness of writing systems* (Honolulu: University of Hawaii Press, 1989), 3-7.

22. *Kinomägewäpkong: the teaching rocks*, prod. Ontario Ministry of Natural Resources, dir. Lloyd Walton, Ontario Ministry of Natural Resources, 1987.

23. Tehanetorens, *Wampum belts* (Oshweken ON: Iroqrafts, 1983), passim.

24. See Hugh A. Dempsey, *Crowfoot: Chief of the Blackfeet* (Edmonton: Hurtig, 1972), passim.; *A Blackfoot Winter Count*, Occasional paper no. 1 (Calgary: Glenbow-Alberta Institute, 1965), passim.; Anthony F. Aveni, *Empires of time: calendars, clocks, and cultures* (New York: Kodansha, 1995).

25. For further discussion of Mi'kmaq hieroglyphics, see David L. Schmidt and Murdena Marshall, eds. and trans., *Mi'kmaq hieroglyphic prayers: readings in North America's first indigenous script* (Halifax: Nimbus Publishing, 1995).

26. Joan M. Vastokas, "History without writing: pictorial narratives in Native North America," *Gin Das Winan: documenting Aboriginal history in Ontario: a symposium at Bkejwanong, Walpole Island First Nation, September 23, 1994*, eds. Dale Standen and David McNab, Occasional papers no. 2 (Toronto: Champlain Society, 1996), 54-55; See also: Selwyn Dewdney, *The Sacred scrolls of the Southern Ojibway* (Toronto and Buffalo: University of Toronto Press for the Glenbow-Alberta Institute, 1975). Historically, the scrolls were collected into libraries of sorts. However, the scrolls were secret writings for Mide initiates only, and there were strict rules as to when and to whom the sacred narratives could be told.

27. Linguistic and literacy scholars now recognize that writing is not adequately thought of as the transcription of speech, but rather as a means of preserving and communicating information. See Elizabeth Hill Boone and Walter

D. Mignolo, eds., *Writing without words: alternative literacies in Mesoamerica and the Andes* (Durham: Duke University Press, 1994); Roy Harris, *The Origin of writing* (London: Duckworth, 1986); David R. Olson, *The Word on paper: the conceptual and cognitive implications of writing and reading* (Cambridge: Cambridge University Press, 1994).

28. Gerald Friesen, *Citizens and nation: an essay on history, communication, and Canada* (Toronto: University of Toronto Press, 2000). See also Anthony F. Aveni, *Empires of time: calendars, clocks, and cultures* (New York: Basic Books, 1989).

29. Friesen, 34-35.

30. Aveni, 183.

31. Aveni, 209.

32. Friesen, 36.

33. Friesen, 40-41.

34. Friesen, 34-44.

35. Michael Harris, "The Purpose of the American public library: a revisionist interpretation of history," *Library Journal* 98 (1973): 2514.

36. Harris, 2514.

37. Rebecca Kingston, "The National Library of Canada: a study in the growth of a nation," *Canadian Library Journal* 45.3 (1988): 170.

38. Jesse H. Shera, *Foundations of the public library: the origins of the public library movement in New England, 1629-1855* (1949; Hamden CT: Shoe String Press, 1965), v-vi.

39. Shera, 247.

40. Sidney H. Ditzion confirmed that public library development throughout much of the United States mirrored that which took place in New England. See: Ditzion, *Arsenals of a democratic culture: a social history of the American public library movement in New England and the middle states from 1850 to 1900* (Chicago: American Library Association, 1947).

41. Peter F. McNally, "Foreword," *Readings in Canadian library history*, ed. Peter F. McNally (Ottawa: Canadian Library Association, 1986), iii.

42. Michael H. Harris, *History of libraries in the Western world.* Fourth edition (Metuchen NJ: Scarecrow Press, 1995), 4-5.

43. See: Aspinali, 10-12; Hills, passim; Land, 14-15.

2

The Nineteenth Century

"Read, write, and worship God daily"
The Missionary's tools: the written word,
books, and education

> Do not believe that there exists anything more honourable to
> our or the preceding age than the invention of the printing
> press and the discovery of the new world; two things which I
> always thought could be compared not only to Antiquity, but
> to immortality.[1]

> As a missionary of civilisation and refinement, its power is
> potent; no matter how humble the roof, if books are scattered
> about, there is reasonable hope of finding conversible
> companions.[2]

Social expectations and assumptions of the printed word

Throughout much of the period under discussion, the printed word,
particularly as it gained wider and wider diffusion throughout the
eighteenth and nineteenth centuries, was a social instrument that wielded
great power and consequently required careful monitoring and often strict
control. Particularly in the context of First Peoples, but true also among
settler and non-Aboriginal populations, print by means of pamphlets,
books, and tracts was most often enlisted to work in the service of
government and religious purposes.[3] Print was a tool of social order, and
was employed in influencing and shaping ideas, morals, and ultimately
religious beliefs and cultural norms. In the case of the First Peoples of
Canada, non-Aboriginal missionaries and governments used print as an
important tool for religious and cultural conversion, civilizing, and
assimilative processes.

The traditional Western-based view of the time was that the purpose
of print was to "amuse and instruct," a conception with its origins in

classical literature.[4] Within this view, the assumption and expectation was that printed materials had to be both pleasing and instructive but also, and more importantly, morally correct. While opinions varied slightly along denominational lines as to what constituted correct morals, there was nevertheless a general agreement among the Christian denominations and state that virtue above vice was the first requirement of all printed works. Generally speaking, Western Euro-Canadian understandings of moral values in the eighteenth and nineteenth centuries assumed that virtue meant Christian piety, honesty, devotion to family, and acceptance of God and the state as sources of all order. Immorality, or vice, generally meant anything that could be interpreted as or be seen to be sympathetic to atheism, alcoholism, murder, sexual or economic profligacy, individualistic anarchy, or any form of political degeneracy.

Mary Lu MacDonald in her work on literature and society, in the two Canadas in the nineteenth century, notes that vigilance regarding the moral lessons of a literary work were usually expressed in terms of a regard for the general well-being of society. Except for the language in which it was written, MacDonald demonstrates that there was little to distinguish the content of literary criticism in the popular Roman Catholic newspaper *Les Mélanges Religieux* from the literary criticism in the Methodist equivalent, the *Christian Guardian*. Few individuals overtly disagreed with the churches in this period, which were unquestionably the most powerful social institutions in the land. MacDonald also notes that the overwhelming number of writers in this period, without a doubt, accepted the idea that correct morality as defined by the Christian churches was absolutely necessary to good literature. She also notes that Canadian literary criticism of the period, despite its incidental character and regional basis, displayed considerable unity of vision since it was based on a coherent system of accepted social values. Praise was given or withheld according to content. Did the work amuse and instruct? Did it teach good moral values? Did it express notions of national unity? Most of the available reading was morally acceptable, and thus received little attention or criticism in the popular press of the day. The shrill response of critics to works which violated the unwritten codes of moral behavior can give the impression that such transgressions were more common and significant than they actually were, since most critical railing was directed at the exceptions. There was little need to applaud the status quo.[5]

These notions of morality that most associated as necessary to "good literature" were influenced and rooted in the teachings and practices of the

The frontispiece of Daniel Claus' *A Primer for the use of the Mohawk children, to acquire the spelling and reading of their own, as well as to get acquainted with the English tongue*, in English and Mohawk, published in London in 1786.

Protestant and Catholic churches. Clergy and members of these churches were influential at both the cultural and practical level, and had been present in North America from very early in European experience on the continent. The churches made it their business to establish and maintain their influence throughout the new colonies to both Aboriginal populations and settlers. Among Aboriginal populations, Protestant and Catholic missionaries saw it as their duty to civilize and convert. Protestant missionaries believed that First Peoples should be "civilized" first, and by extension, religious conversion would follow. For this reason, education and literature were often greater concerns for the Protestant missions, since these were believed to bring about "civilized" behavior. Catholics, on the other hand, did not see "civilizing" as a necessary first step to conversion, and were thus not always as active in their promotion of a literary education. Communication, of course, between missionaries and the First Peoples was a challenge. In meeting unknown languages, both missionaries and Aboriginal peoples faced difficulties in effectively communicating, each having to learn, at least in part, the other's language. Early in the language relationship, it was the missionaries who had to do much of the language learning if they were to be at all successful in their attempts to civilize and convert. Missionaries used various techniques in learning Aboriginal languages–they listened to the new languages and tried to speak them; they worked with and through informants; and they started to collect words and phrases, ranging in small handwritten vocabularies for their fellow brethren to extensive published dictionaries. Later, Christian missionaries would employ the written word and print under the guise of education in their efforts to civilize, convert, and culturally assimilate Aboriginal peoples to Western moral standards.

Civilization and salvation: the goals of the Missions

Missionaries, from the very beginning of European contact in North America, were leaders of Euro-Canadian culture, blending Christianity and Western practices. Missionary rhetoric, both Catholic and Protestant, has proclaimed one goal from the beginning of the mission enterprise in Canada until well into the twentieth century. That is, to save the immortal souls of lost Indians from eternal damnation. However, conversion of Aboriginal souls alone was often insufficient. The conquest had to be more complete, requiring radical change in body as well as spirit, in all aspects of appearance and conduct. From the missionary perspective of most Protestant denominations, Aboriginal peoples could not be Christians until they abandoned Aboriginal ways of living and thinking and accepted "civilized" customs.[6] In this way, conversion meant the remaking of the Indian in the European image, the conquest of the Indian soul and civilizing the Indian mind. Cultural invasion in the name of "civilization and salvation" was the motivating philosophy of nearly every North American missionary. Civilization was generally defined as a mixture of sedentary agriculture, individualism, capitalism, routine labor, and the adoption of European style permanent settlements and family values. Missionaries sought nothing less than a revolution in Aboriginal social relations and basic values, and set higher standards of conduct for Aboriginal converts than for non-Aboriginal settler populations. "Commerce, Civilization, and Christianity" was the three-fold slogan for all the missions from their earliest days through the nineteenth century.

Although their methods differed over time and according to denomination, missionaries' three main means of conversion generally included the construction of mission towns, the establishment of Indian churches, and institutional education. In constructing mission towns, missionaries sought to develop environments that would foster the "civilization and salvation" goals of the mission. These environments featured many of the familiar Euro-Canadian institutions: monogamous family, sedentary agriculture, civil government, formal education, and organized churches. Mission towns reflected how Europeans defined civilization and were designed to foster new identities and allegiances in converts, while also serving to isolate converted First Peoples from their unconverted kinsmen, thus preventing the possibility of reversion to traditional beliefs. Through the establishment of Indian churches and congregations, missionaries hoped to spiritually nurture and culturally change Aboriginal peoples in a European image. The formation of successful churches and congregations were also positive visible signs, in the minds of missionaries, of civilization and salvation. Most important to the mission however, was the introduction of institutional education. From the sixteenth century onward, missionaries believed that the school, like the town and the church, was to be employed as a predominant tool in the quest for Aboriginal minds, souls, and bodies. Through education, missionaries endeavored to sever the First Peoples from their traditional values and redirect their minds along European and Western paths. Mission schools were influenced by the prevailing educational theories of the day. Vocational training was offered for the purpose of preparing students for employment in the trades, while the work of transforming Aboriginal peoples into "civilized" Christians was to be done by the "literary" curriculum. Some concentrated on Bible studies, and almost all gave highest priority to French or English-language instruction. Basic Western style literacy, or the ability to read and write alphabetic script, was a central element and goal of most mission schools in their efforts to culturally transform Aboriginal peoples and wholly remake them in the "civilized" image.[7]

The introduction of print literacy, and by extension libraries, were thus elements of missionary and Western attempts to colonize Aboriginal languages, cultures, and memories. The written word, and the idea of the book, were employed as warranties of truth. In basing much of their teachings around the Bible and related tracts and hymns, missionaries promoted the idea of the book as a human container and expression of knowledge and the divine word. Further, although writing does not presuppose the book, by the early nineteenth century missionary under-standings of literacy and celebrations of the letter did narrow down the relationship between the two to be almost exclusive. Aboriginal traditional literacies and alternative forms of writing were largely ignored and devalued in the eyes of Western colonizers. Further, non-book forms of writing were outward signs of an uncivilized people, who lived without order and reason. Celebrations of the letter and its partnership with the book were not only conceptualized as warranties of truth, but also were the foundations of Western assumptions about the relationship between alphabetic writing and history. Aboriginal people, a people largely without letters, were thought of as a people without history, and oral narratives and alternative forms of writing were seen as incoherent and inconsistent. Through institutional education, missionaries contributed to a process in which alphabetic writing was elevated as the most desirable system of communicating truth and history.[8] Through alphabetic literacy, access could be gained to Christianity, a religion seen to based on unchanging truths. Order and reason could be brought to the lives of perceived savage converts through providing access to reading and writing in a Western tradition, preferably in either English or French. From a missionary and later government perspective, there existed a clear connection between language, Western literacy, and cultural change. In fact, one could not be "civilized" if one spoke an Aboriginal language.[9]

The uses of print in early Missionary-First Peoples relations

The written word and books were translated as early as the seven-teenth century by Christian missionaries into Aboriginal languages. Among the earliest were those printed at Rouen, France for the Jesuit missionaries in 1630 as a means of encouraging support for the missions' activities in civilizing and converting the Aboriginal peoples of New France. Until the early twentieth century, the nature of printed materials in Aboriginal languages in Canada was almost entirely evangelical. With few exceptions, books for the use of the Aboriginal peoples of Canada were written or translated by missionaries and printed or published by religious orders and societies. The vast majority are translations of the Bible or devotional works, some include music, and some were printed—as were the first texts printed in Aboriginal languages—to encourage support for the missions. Besides religious works, other texts printed in Aboriginal languages were concerned with recording their languages in the form of vocabularies and dictionaries—but even these texts were most often translated or prepared by members of the missions, with their ultimate purposes lying in the proposed civilizing, education, and conversion of Aboriginal peoples. Some Aboriginal language texts were printed overseas as a means of providing an element of North American exotica for contemporary European readers of the day. A commercial interest was evident as well in such printed works as *A Dictionary of the Hudson's Bay language* in Cree, the trade language of Rupert's Land, printed in London, England in 1701.[10]

The first books printed in North America in Aboriginal languages, excluding Mexico, were those translated by the Puritan missionary, John Eliot, in colonial America beginning in 1654 with a primer or catechism printed at Cambridge. Scriptural translations followed, and in 1663 the "Eliot Bible" was published. Following these works, a slow but steady flow of books in Aboriginal languages emerged from American presses. The earliest books printed in Canada in Aboriginal languages were those printed for converts to Christianity, at Quebec in 1767, soon after the introduction of the printing press there. Prepared by Jean Baptiste de La Brosse, they included an alphabet and a primer and prayer book in the Innu language. The next known Canadian imprint, the first Aboriginal language work to be printed at Montreal, was a Mohawk primer of Roman Catholic prayers in 1777. This was followed by a bilingual edition of the Church of England Book of Common Prayer (1780) in Mohawk and English, printed at Quebec for Daniel Claus, Deputy Superintendent of Indians in Canada and paid for by Governor's warrant at the expense of His Majesty's Forces. This is the first known example of government support for Aboriginal language books. As well, it is evidence of a concern for the needs of Loyalist Indians faithful to the state church—or in other words, the Anglican response to Roman Catholic books in Aboriginal languages.

Further, this is the first instance of the Protestant and Roman Catholic rivalry that emerged thereafter over the printing of books for the use of Aboriginal converts. This rivalry was significant in its attempts to forge and maintain Aboriginal loyalties with the British and French, with books acting as agents of an imperial agenda in addition to a civilizing and Christianizing agenda. Such activity was particularly important in stimulating Aboriginal language publishing in Canada and abroad later in the nineteenth century.[11]

Rare Book Librarian at the National Library of Canada, Joyce M. Banks, has estimated that prior to the nineteenth century, fewer than ten books were printed in Aboriginal languages in Canada. With the turn of the century, Anglican and Roman Catholic missionaries were joined in their labors of translating and book production by the Moravian, Wesleyan, and Methodist missionaries, resulting in a great explosion of printed titles in Aboriginal languages. Thousands of titles in Aboriginal languages emerged in Canada during the nineteenth century, attracting the interest of collectors, linguists, and bibliographers.[12] The vast majority of these printed materials were religious in nature, constituting either translations of the Bible, hymns or sermons, or religiously motivated tracts or pamphlets. Any non-religious publishing that did occur in Aboriginal languages was in the form of dictionaries or grammars, which were most often intended for the benefit of fellow missionaries in language learning or employed in more general attempts at regulating perceived heathen and uncivilized languages within the frames of Christian culture and morals.[13] Conscious attempts to move beyond translations of religious literature to fiction were never rooted in Canada as they were in other parts of the British Empire until well into the twentieth century, by which point most printed materials presented to the First Peoples were in English or French. European fiction (*Robinson Crusoe* and *Pilgrim's Progress*), for instance, was widely translated and printed in the nineteenth century by missionaries and supported by the colonial government in New Zealand in Maori as part of an explicit government policy of Maori acculturation.[14]

Books printed in English and French for the use of Aboriginal peoples

The earliest communications between missionaries and Aboriginal peoples involved, usually to a significant extent as demonstrated in the wide array of vocabularies, dictionaries, and grammars, the learning of Aboriginal languages by missionaries. However, learning English and

French came to constitute a necessary and more important step in ultimately converting Aboriginal populations to the Christian faith. Within the missionary movement of the north west in the mid-nineteenth century for example, determining the language of instruction was a contentious issue for the Methodist, Anglican, and Roman Catholic missions. The first Anglican missionaries in the north west, with the exception of John West, made no attempts at learning Aboriginal languages because they believed the best way to Christianize was to teach in English.[15] Anglican James Hunter translated scripture into Cree at The Pas, but these were in roman script to facilitate later translation to English. The Methodists and Roman Catholics, on the other hand, were the most adamant in encouraging language study by missionaries, resulting in many valuable grammars, vocabularies, and dictionaries, and the development of a syllabic system of writing Cree attributed to the Methodist, James Evans. The Anglicans joined their Methodist and Roman Catholic counterparts following John Horden's adoption of Evans' syllabic in his work among the Cree and Inuit of Moose Factory after 1851. Henceforth practically every Protestant missionary in the north west used or adapted Evans' syllabic.[16] The efforts of Charles Pratt, Peter Jones, Peter Jacobs, and other members of an emerging Aboriginal ministry who sported impressive bilingual and bi-cultural skills, were also very significant factors in influencing the missions' usage of language. Pratt, for instance, who was a non-ordained Aboriginal teacher working with the Church Missionary Society, would translate his English Bible into Cree orally, adapting the scriptures to Assiniboine-Cree religious beliefs,[17] while Reverends Jones and Jacobs worked and translated extensively for the Methodists.

Not long after the turn of the twentieth century, however, when Christianity had achieved a firm foothold in many Aboriginal communities, the balance of power had shifted enough to ensure that translations of sermons and printed materials to Aboriginal languages were deemed less important or necessary. The conversion or civilizing process had taken on new forms and was being achieved largely through the English and French languages.[18] Missionary interests and motivations in learning Aboriginal languages and translating religious texts were part of a conscious effort on their behalf to propagate the Christian doctrine from inside. Such efforts were an attempt to appeal to some element of Aboriginal knowledge systems, better enabling Missionaries to effectively promote the Christian doctrine. By the turn of the twentieth century, many if not most Aboriginal populations were relegated to small reserves under the control of the federal Indian Affairs department, and residential and day school systems run by the various Churches were in place to complete what was perceived as the final step in civilizing and assimilating Indian populations into the larger Western European society, eliminating the so-called "Indian problem" that was seen to be hindering the economic and political development of the country.

Fathers Chrestien LeClercq, Pierre Maillard, and Mi'kmaq Hieroglyphics in the seventeenth century

The Récollet missionary, Father Chrestien LeClercq, is said to have discovered in 1677 an elaborate written method of communication among the Mi'kmaq people of the Miramichi River region in the French colony of Acadia. Mi'kmaq oral tradition indicates that the hieroglyphs were in fact developed for inscribing maps and tribal records well before the arrival of Europeans in the new world. David Schmidt and Murdena Marshall, in their work, *Mi'kmaq Hieroglyphic Prayers*, note that the hieroglyphic script was in fact "the first script developed and used in North America (excluding Mexico) for a Native language, it predates the Cherokee syllabary–usually accorded the distinction of being the continent's earliest indigenous writing system–by at least 144 years."[19] LeClercq's record of the Mi'kmaq hieroglyphic writing tradition in his 1691 publication, *Nouvelle Relation de la Gaspesie*, testifies to the existence and widespread use of this pre-contact North American script. LeClercq first arrived in the territory of the Mi'kmaq in October of 1675, resolving to go among the people of the region and impart to them "the most solid truths of Christianity."[20] By the 1670s, the Mi'kmaq people of the Gaspé Peninsula and Acadia were no strangers to Catholic missionaries–since the colony's founding in 1604, hopes of Christianizing the First Peoples of the region had drawn members of the Récollet, Jesuit, and Capuchin missions. LeClercq arrived in the Miramichi River region in February of 1677. Having heard reports of the local Mi'kmaq population's reverence for the Christian cross, he hoped that they would be amenable to conversion.[21] LeClercq explains that his first approach to converting the Mi'kmaq was to teach them to pray. Finding that they were slow to memorize scripture through oral repetition, LeClercq made the following observation in the second year of his mission:

A hand-drawn illustration depicting Father Chrestien LeClercq teaching prayers using the Mi'kmaq hieroglyphic script. The original illustration appears in LeClercq's *Nouvelle relation de la Gaspesie*, published in 1691.

Being much embarrassed as to the method by which I should
teach the Indians to pray to God, I noticed that some children
were making marks with charcoal upon birch-bark, and were
counting these with the finger very accurately at each word of
prayers which they pronounced. This made me believe that by
giving them some formulary, which would aid their memory
by definite characters, I should advance much more quickly
than by teaching them through the method of making them
repeat a number of times that which I said to them. I was
charmed to find that I was not mistaken, and that these
characters which I had formed upon paper produced all the
effect that I could wish, so that in a few days they learned
without difficulty all of their prayers.[22]

LeClercq, having stumbled upon a written form of communication
already well in place among the Mi'kmaq, made great use of this
observation, employing the hieroglyphic form of writing to great effect in
teaching the Christian doctrine. The Récollet explains that these "definite
characters" were written in charcoal on sheets of birch bark he called
leaflets or instructional papers. Multiple copies of these leaflets were made
and distributed to each Mi'kmaq family at Miramichi, and LeClercq also
painted the writing form on large bark sheets, which served as a kind of
blackboard for group instruction. Although LeClercq wrongly claimed that
he invented the writing form, through his encouragement at least, the
Mi'kmaq hieroglyphic writing style was given legitimacy from a Western
point of view (in LeClercq's time at least) as a recognizable form of
written communication, with these leaflets or instructional papers
constituting a form of the book clearly fostering a kind of recognizable
literacy:

The facility which I have found in a method for teaching the
prayers to our Gaspesians by means of certain characters
which I have formed, fully persuades me that the majority
would soon become educated; for, in fact, I should find no
more difficulty in teaching them to read than to pray to God
by means of my prayers, in which each arbitrary letter
signifies a particular word and sometimes even two together.
They have so much readiness in understanding this kind of
writing that they learn in a single day what they would never
be able to grasp in an entire week without the aid of these
leaflets, which they call *Kignamotinoer*, or *Kateguenne*. They
preserve these instructive papers with so much care, and they
have for them so particular an esteem, that they keep them

very neatly in little cases of birch-bark bedecked with wampum, with beadwork and with porcupine quills. They hold
them between their hands, as we do our prayer-books, during
the Holy Mass, after which they shut them up again in their
cases.[23]

LeClercq's *Nouvelle Relation* also illustrates that in the Récollet's
interpretation, reading and writing literacy fostered by the hieroglyphic
leaflets became a kind of competitive pastime among the Miramichi
Mi'kmaq people. LeClercq notes that

the principal advantage and usefulness which results from this
new method is this, that the Indians instruct one another in
whatsoever place they may happen to be. Thus the son teaches
his father, the mother her children, the wife her husband and
the children the old men; for advanced age gives them no
reluctance to learn from their little nephews, and even from
the girls, the principles of Christianity. Even some of the
youngest Indians, those who do not yet possess the entire use
of speech, pronounce, nevertheless, the best that they can,
some words from these leaflets which they hear spoken in
their wigwams when the Indians, by a holy emulation, read
them and repeat them together.[24]

And further, "I cannot express to you with what ardour these poor Indians
competed against one another, with an emulation worthy of praise, as to
which would be the most learned and most clever."[25]

Schmidt and Marshall suggest that this passion for learning and
teaching noted by LeClercq was probably widespread, accounting for the
script's rapid dissemination throughout Acadia and the Gaspé.[26] In visiting
the Mi'kmaq at Restigouche in 1678, LeClercq remarks that

How agreeably I was surprised, and what consolation I felt in
my heart, when, wishing to present some of my papers to
certain Indians who had come from a long distance on
purpose to be instructed, I found they could already decipher
the characters with as much ease as if they had always lived
among us. This was because some whom I had formerly
instructed had returned to their homes and had taught the
others, thus performing, in regard to them, the office of
missionary.[27]

It is just as likely however, that the script's seemingly widespread dissemination to other communities in the Gaspé and Acadia predated LeClercq, since the Récollet had admittedly only modified an existing Mi'kmaq writing form, and Mi'kmaq oral tradition supports this claim. LeClercq, rather than inventing and propagating the script alone, had merely stumbled upon an existing form of written communication among the Mi'kmaq and applied it to the Christian doctrine, encouraging its presentation in book form that was recognizable within the Western understanding of written communication.

LeClercq returned to France in 1687, but hieroglyphic writing and reading of the Catholic doctrine, as the people had construed it, persisted among the Mi'kmaq of northern Acadia and the Gaspé Peninsula. By the end of the seventeenth century, the script was in use for religious purposes throughout the entire territory of Acadia–in the southwest at Port-Royal, and to Malagawatch on Cape Breton Island. In part, diffusion of the script was assisted by LeClercq having shared it with Father Moreau's ministry at Beaubassin,[28] but as was the case with LeClercq's experience at Restigouche, it is more likely the Mi'kmaq themselves disseminated the script. Later, in 1735, a cleric of the Spiritan order, Pierre Maillard, would rediscover the hieroglyphics at Malagawatch, and continue to employ the script for religious purposes at the Cape Breton mission until 1748. Maillard designed a roman based Mi'kmaq orthography, but was reluctant to teach the Mi'kmaq parishioners to read or write their language (or French for that matter) in the alphabet.[29] In an early example of missionary censorship, Maillard feared that access to secular and political materials inscribed in the roman alphabet might foster anti-French sentiment among the Mi'kmaq. He says, if the Mi'kmaq "should be in a state to use, as we do, our alphabet, be it to read or to write, they inevitably would abuse this knowledge through this spirit of curiosity ... which hurriedly drives them to know bad things rather than good."[30] He continues, saying that "they would surely emancipate themselves ... if they could make use of our alphabet ...; they would not hesitate strongly to persuade themselves that they knew much more than those who are intended to instruct them."[31] Further, Maillard was certain "that to ... substitute the alphabet for the characters which the Indians use to read and write, this would work very badly, for them as for us."[32] Moreover, Maillard believed that alphabetic literacy could make the Mi'kmaq a strategic threat to the French influence in the region: "they would be capable of causing great harm among the people, as much with respect to religion and behavior as with respect to politics and government."[33]

Maillard discouraged the Mi'kmaq from learning alphabetic script in

A portion of the "Carte Generalle de la Nouvelle France" from LeClercq's *Premier Etablissement de la Foy* (1691) illustrating the region where the Mi'kmaq hieroglyphic script was in use in the seventeenth and eighteenth centuries.

French or Mi'kmaq by reinforcing his observation of the Aboriginal concept of writing as a sacred instrument: "The Micmacs believe that everything printed in the books are words of God or one of his servants and just written for the good of man.... Just because they deeply believe that only these kind of stories deserve to be written and printed ... because of their ideas about books, I think that we better use our hieroglyphics."[34] This conjecture implies that Maillard did not believe the Mi'kmaq script should be employed for anything more than a memory aid to scripture and spiritual practice. Bruce Greenfield notes that considering the motives and mentality of Catholic missionaries like Maillard and LeClercq, the use of Mi'kmaq hieroglyphics as an evangelization tool is understandable—they conveyed with near verbal precision key elements of doctrine and practice, which were an essential part of an alphabetic religion. But as a writing system unique to the Mi'kmaq language, the hieroglyphics also satisfied the Roman Catholic desire to limit access to the Bible and other sacred and secular writings. And most importantly, from a colonial viewpoint, they were an exclusive method of communication that was not likely to be used by any other power, and hieroglyphic literacy offered the Mi'kmaq very limited access to French society.[35] Maillard clearly understood that if the

Mi'kmaq were to learn to read and write in the alphabetic script, they could employ this knowledge in ways that might undermine the messages of the Catholic Church. In limiting Mi'kmaq literacy to the hieroglyphics, Maillard intended to limit their abilities to use the written word and the French language in ways that might empower the Mi'kmaq on social and political levels. This approach stands in stark contrast to the methods used later by Protestant missionaries, particularly Methodist, who would actively promote education and Western literacy among Aboriginal populations.

Maillard died in 1762, and with his death France's presence among the Mi'kmaq communities of Acadia and the Gaspé, for the most part, came to an end. Even without the presence of Catholic priests in their communities, the Mi'kmaq would continue to employ the hieroglyphic script for spiritual practices. Despite Maillard's earlier conjecture that the Mi'kmaq script only served as a memory aid to scripture, evidence suggests that the hieroglyphics were also employed to write original secular messages. The work of influential linguists that claim the script could not be used to write new information, but only as memory prompts, further complicate the matter.[36] But take for instance the evidence presented in the journal of John Knox, a captain in the Halifax garrison, who reports in October 1757 the use of the script by Clare Thomas, a Mi'kmaq hostage, in communicating original information: "Clare made a sign to me for a pen, ink, and paper; these I accordingly procured for her, and she instantly filled one side of it with writing, or characters, which are to me unintelligible; I have it now before me, and, though there are some letters in it apparently similar to part of our alphabet, yet it is utterly impossible to make any discovery from it."[37] Accounts by Father Maillard himself also suggest the script was used to transcribe a religious debate between an Anglican and a Catholic during his tenure.[38] Historical observations recorded by non-Aboriginals tend, for the most part, to assume that the hieroglyphics could not be used to record original thought, as the following report to the Department of Indian Affairs in 1880 by R. MacDonald, Indian Agent at Pictou, Nova Scotia, illustrates:

> This [speaking of hieroglyphic prayer books], I need not say, is the poor Micmac's greatest treasure on earth; father has explained to son, and son to grandson, this simple record.... Each Sunday evening, the head of the family with profound reverence, takes 'the book' into his hand, deciphers it from beginning to end, and then with great earnestness, impresses what he considers its most important truths on the minds of

his by no means inattentive hearers. Yet there are many
drawbacks to this mode of teaching. The volumes are hieroglyphic. Their perusal imparts no conception of a written
alphabet, or arithmetic, of secular history, of current events,
or of literature properly so-called. The world that lies outside
of personal observation is unknown to the ordinary Micmac.[39]

Thus, evidence that the Mi'kmaq script could be used to compose original
and secular information is contradictory. It is likely that Maillard's fears
of what the Mi'kmaq would be exposed to if they were to learn an
alphabetic script were fueled by a belief that the Mi'kmaq were only using
the script for religious purposes. This raises the question of Maillard's own
literacy in the hieroglyphic script–given the evidence presented in the
journal of Captain John Knox, it is conceivable that the Mi'kmaq
employed the script regularly for purposes beyond the Catholic scripture.
Unfortunately early examples of the hieroglyphics from LeClercq and
Maillard's tenures are unavailable, leaving the question of whether or not
the script was employed to record original thought unanswered. Ruth
Holmes Whitehead, however, points out that the missionaries' glyph
signifying the sun is the same sign as a petroglyph in Bedford, Nova Scotia
that most definitely predates the time of LeClercq.[40] While the exact
purposes of the hieroglyphics in pre-contact and contact times are not
entirely clear, it is without a doubt that indigenous picture-writing practices
pre-existed the Catholic missions, and it is entirely likely that the texts
served the Mi'kmaq in ways that the missionaries did not envision.

    Use of the hieroglyphic script, at least for religious purpose, persisted
throughout the eighteenth and nineteenth centuries. Schmidt and Marshall
report that the Mi'kmaq's wide use and loyalty to the script was a
significant detour in distancing them from the influences of Anglo-
Canadian Protestantism. Baptist minister, Silas T. Rand, for instance in his
unsuccessful bid to dissuade the Mi'kmaq from Catholicism between 1840
and the 1880's, blamed the hieroglyphic script for his failures.[41] The script
was first published in Western book form only in 1866, when Father
Christian Kauder had 2,700 copies of a hieroglyphic manuscript of prayers
printed at Vienna under the title, *Buch das gut, enthaltend den
Katechismus, Betrachtung, Gesang (The Good Book, Containing the
Catechism, Meditations, Hymns)*. This work would be reprinted in 1918
by the Capuchin missionary, linguist, and historian, Father Pacifique, at the
request of Mi'kmaq families who wished to send copies of Kauder's prayer
book to their men serving in the Canadian army in Europe. As the
twentieth century continued, however, efforts to maintain and preserve

hieroglyphic literacy floundered among the Mi'kmaq in large part due to the establishment of reserve schools where the sole language of instruction was English, and the Catholic Church adopted a policy of teaching new catechumens to read prayers exclusively in English and alphabetic Mi'kmaq. In the late twentieth and early twenty-first centuries, use of the script is increasingly limited to the Mi'kmaq communities of Cape Breton Island, but is still considered to be a unique expression of Mi'kmaqness.[42]

The "Good" Intentions of Thaddeus Osgood

Discussion around the use and establishment of organized collections of print materials, or libraries, among Aboriginal communities first emerged in the early part of the nineteenth century. The earliest promoter and thinker along these lines was Reverend Thaddeus Osgood (1775-1852). Reverend Osgood expresses his ideas and plans to establish schools, bible study groups, and free lending libraries for the Aboriginal peoples in Upper and Lower Canada in his published work *The Canadian Visitor* (1829?) and in the *Annual Reports* of the Central Auxiliary Society for Promoting Education and Industry among the Indians and Destitute Settlers in Canada (1828-1829).[43] Had Reverend Osgood been more successful in his endeavors, the establishment of libraries in Aboriginal communities may have emerged nearly one hundred years sooner, but conversely Osgood's ideas were never fully fulfilled. Nonetheless, a discussion of Osgood is valuable in painting a picture of early nineteenth century Protestant approaches to civilizing and converting.

A Congregational minister and educator, Osgood was born in Massachusetts, but his early work as a traveling preacher brought him to the Canadas in 1807, and he adopted the two colonies as his main missionary focus for the rest of his life. Although he remained a Congregationalist, Osgood was a religious oddity of sorts in his time, continually stressing the non-denominational aspects of his work. From the early to the mid-nineteenth century, Osgood's name came to be known, in both Upper and Lower Canada, with the development of day and Sunday schools, the education of Aboriginal populations, the temperance movement, Sabbatarianism, the organization of Sunday school unions and tract societies and actions against urban poverty and vice. Included in this work among the inhabitants of the rural frontiers and urban slums for the edification of humankind and in teaching the "plain truths of the Bible" and the greater glory of God was the establishment and promotion of libraries. Though initially Osgood focused on the distribution of religious tracts in propagating his religious messages, his interests increasingly turned to education and in developing literacy in reading and writing the printed word.[44]

Osgood emerged from a Congregationalist tradition in northern New England at the turn of the nineteenth century that constituted an early Protestant effort to mold moral character through religious education. Congregationalist missionaries in these parts promoted grammar schools, subscription libraries, and numerous short-lived proto-public libraries as part of their efforts of spiritual regeneration in the republic. Osgood and other missionaries sharing similar convictions "placed a heavy emphasis upon book distribution as a necessary adjunct to preaching."[45] Books and religious tracts were promoted by missionary societies of the region as a means of reaching the populations at frontier posts left vacant by too few suitable evangelists. The number of communities in northern New England far exceeded the number of evangelists, and in many places settlers had to wait for months and even years between visits from Congregationalist missionaries. Thus, in the absence of organized churches or ordained clergy, books and religious tracts were distributed widely as a means of perpetuating and promoting Euro-Christian religious traditions and teachings. Printed materials were employed as replacements of sorts for missionaries, evangelists, and ordained clergy. Despite the shortage of ministers, Congregationalist societies urged settler communities to "let your gravest and most able men lead in social prayers and praises, and let them read the best printed sermons they can obtain."[46] Thus, Osgood would have well understood the benefits of promoting print materials in his efforts to educate destitute settlers and Aboriginal peoples in the Canadas, and he recognized the use of books and tracts as tools of education and as vessels well-suited to embodying Western cultural and religious messages.

Very early in his Canadian experience Osgood set about raising money and traveling to isolated settlements, preaching, and bearing bibles, tracts, alphabet cards, and other teaching devices of particular appeal to children. As early as 1808, he called upon settlers in the isolated communities he visited to collect bibles and religious tracts and build up "moral libraries" so that such literature could be shared widely. Following a visit to a Brockville Sunday school in 1812, Osgood thereafter promoted the establishment of Sunday schools as a means of encouraging and promoting literacy and religion. Bibles and tracts served as texts in these Sunday schools where children and adults alike were offered the opportunity to be instructed. When the war of 1812-1814 broke out between the United States and England, Osgood remained in the Canadas, regarding the

English colonies as his special missionary field. Around this time he petitioned the Governor of Lower Canada, Sir George Provost, for funds to establish a free school for the poor in Montreal, to be open to children of all religious denominations and that would also act as a training center for teachers and as an example for other cities to follow. Governor Provost provided the Reverend with funds and free passage to England, where he could appeal to charitable people there to finance the project.[47]

Reverend Osgood was a shameless and successful fund-raiser, always seeking out the affluent in the towns he visited and begging for funds to perpetuate his work. With the free passage to England secured from Governor Provost, Osgood traveled for eighteen months in England, persuading some very well-known philanthropists to establish a society for the education of the poor in the Canadas. The Reverend succeeded in securing sufficient funds to establish a school, with monies to spare for a proposed house of refuge for the poor of Montreal. Osgood returned to England in 1825 to again obtain support for the promotion of non-denominational schools for the poor. This time he was successful in securing the support of none other than the Duke of Sussex, and the Bishop of Durham. His success in this endeavor was likely assisted in part by the presence of Aboriginal Chiefs who attended the organizational meeting of a new society formatted by Osgood for promoting education and industry in the Canadas. Whether intended to or not, the presence of the Chiefs in full dress had the effect of channeling English interest, and thus Osgood's, into supporting the promotion of education for the Aboriginal peoples of the Canadian colonies. As was common during the period, the teaching of reading, writing, arithmetic, and spelling was interspersed with useful manual labor, and students were to read and recite portions of the Scriptures that express support of such social duties and point the way to a happy eternity.[48]

Osgood's endeavors in educating Aboriginal peoples appear to differ from the efforts of later missionaries and government officials in that his approaches in educating First Peoples are very similar to those he practiced among the poor and destitute settler populations. Further, Osgood and the societies he established and represented encouraged the training and employment of Aboriginal teachers in their educating endeavors. At schools established in 1825 in Aboriginal settlements at Lorette, near Quebec City, and in the Mohawk village of Caughnawaga, a number of Aboriginal youths were trained as teachers.[49] At Mohawk communities on the Bay of Quinte in Upper Canada, Osgood expressed that "this blessed work of reformation appears to be going forward, and mostly through the instrumentality of the Native Teachers, in conexion with the Methodist Society."[50]

As a key agent and motivating member of the Sunday School Union of Canada, the Bible Society, the Tract Society, and the Central Auxiliary Society for Promoting Education and Industry among the Indians and Destitute Settlers in Canada, Osgood traveled extensively in the colonies, the United States, and to England, begged for funding, and carted books in his efforts to establish schools, Sunday schools, and juvenile libraries in each township and settlement in the Canadas:

> The books and tracts brought by the Agent from Great Britain and Ireland, as well as those received during the past and present year, from benevolent individuals in the United States, were by order of the Governor, for the time being, admitted free of duty, and have been parcelled out to destitute places in both Provinces, more particularly with the view to encourage the formation of Sunday School Libraries. The Bishop of Quebec, as our Agent reports, having lately consented to unite in forming a Lending Library, it is to be hoped that these excellent Institutions, (Lending and Circulating Libraries,) will soon become general throughout the settlements, wherever practicable.[51]

In speaking more directly in regards to the First Peoples of Upper Canada, in particular the communities at Grape Island and Rice Lake, Osgood notes:

> The first mentioned place is about six miles from Belville, and fifty four miles from Kingston. It is very gratifying to see two hundred of these once drunken and degraded people, now become sober and industrious, attempting to copy all that they see worthy of their imitation, from their white brethren–but shunning their errors. Here is a handsome village rising, with a good School-house, which serves as a Chapel.... Here is a Miss Hubbard, from the United States, who is very useful in teaching the Indian Children how to read, write, and worship God daily. This young woman was introduced to Canada by a Miss Barnes, now teaching at the Rice Lake.... Miss Barnes is employed here in a manner similar to what Miss Hubbard is at the other station.... There are about sixty [Indian] scholars at this station.[52]

But disappointment would plague Osgood's intentions throughout his life, and his efforts to establish schools, distribute books, and build libraries in the Aboriginal communities of the Canadas was short-lived and sparse in accomplishments. While he would continue to promote literacy and education among the settler populations of the colonies for the remainder of his life, as early as 1829 Reverend Osgood lamented that "in consequence of the impoverished state of funds, many applications for assistance, in destitute places, have been unavoidably refused, and what is most painful, the board and education of Indian children must be suspended, until increased means can be obtained."[53] Although rooted in what were considered good intentions, Osgood's lifelong commitment to the well-being of the destitute and education of Aboriginal populations amounted in few of his endeavors becoming permanent achievements or overwhelming successes. Osgood was an eccentric of sorts, and his tendency to jump obsessively from one good cause to another was in part to blame for his failures. Further, his status as a non-denominational Congregationalist did not sit well with members in particular of the Roman Catholic and Anglican faiths, who could not give approval to the religious curriculums of his proposed and realized schools. In Osgood's own words regarding the frustration he felt towards the only moderate successes of the Central Auxiliary Society and the inhibitions and reluctance of the Catholic and Anglican churches to provide their support, he offers, "And when it shall be better known, it will, undoubtedly, receive greater support, and become more extensively useful. It cannot be otherwise, when it is found that perfect freedom of conscience is allowed to all." Yet, Osgood was an eternal optimist, and he remained positive about even the moderate successes he had helped to achieve: "We have assisted in building several schoolhouses, and supporting a number of schools and libraries, without asking inhabitants of those places to what party or denomination of Christians they belonged."[54]

During an unusually lengthy visit to England between 1830 and 1835, unconfirmed rumors surfaced that Osgood had been jailed for improperly giving account of the use of monies he had collected on earlier visits. On his return to the Canadas five years later in 1835, the Reverend resigned his agency and the Central Auxiliary Society was permanently dismantled.[55] Osgood's talents and endeavors for the rest of his life remained committed to similar educational causes, but he never again turned his attentions towards the First Peoples of the colonies, and his efforts to establish libraries and distribute bibles and tracts among Aboriginal populations were never fully realized within his lifetime. Nonetheless, Osgood's legacy lies in his influence, rather than in his successfully completed projects. As W. P. J. Millar has observed, Osgood's

> appeals to the conscience of nineteenth century evangelical-
> ism tapped a growing awareness in Britain and the colonies
> that religious feeling might legitimately be manifested in new
> forms of humanitarian action. His career, moreover, shows the
> variety of instruments to which nineteenth century benevo-
> lence turned. The success of philanthropic causes he adopted
> reflects the gradual development of institutionalized social
> concern within Canadian society.[56]

Although by no means could Osgood be called a leader, many of his ideas and concerns were similar to those initiated, for example, by the influential Methodist leader, Reverend William Case, and by Anglican missionaries at Six Nations. It would be several decades, however, before any success-ful establishment of libraries in Aboriginal communities would commence.

The Religious Tract Society: for the spiritual welfare of the Indians

The efforts of Thaddeus Osgood in distributing religious tracts and publications among First Peoples and his plans to establish libraries were inspired by similar efforts and the mandate of the British organization, the Religious Tract Society. The Society was formed in 1799 following the Evangelical revival in the interests of publishing and disseminating Christian literature throughout the United Kingdom and the British colonies abroad. Published materials were Anglican and other Protestant denominations in their origins, scope, and contents, and these were distributed primarily among the lower and middle classes and settler populations. The Society promoted what it called the benefits of books, claiming that "books contained in libraries have frequently been the means of awakening the minds of the readers to the importance of religion."[57] A good number of missionaries representing the various Protestant denomi-nations in the British colonies in North America subscribed to the beliefs of the Society and distributed its books for the perceived betterment of the colonies and their populations.

Among the Aboriginal populations of the colonies, the Society's influence was significant in the early part of the nineteenth century, despite the comments of William Jones in 1850 who asserted that "the Society has much regretted that so little has been done for these interesting people: it has always been prepared to meet the applications of friends who are interested in the spiritual welfare of the Indians."[58] Further efforts by the Society in reaching Aboriginal audiences may not have been necessary, as First Peoples like the Ojibwe Methodist missionary Peter Jones, or Kahkewaquonaby, were already proponents of reading and writing, although perhaps not for the same reasons as those envisioned by the Society. Reverend Peter Jones was among those Protestants who touted the benefits of the Society's efforts and the benefits of writing and books generally. The Society quoted the Ojibwe Reverend in 1850 as proof of their progress and good will among Aboriginal peoples:

> Before the gospel entered the hearts of some of the people, there was no book in the Chippeway tongue–there was no written or printed language among us; but since we have found the Great Spirit–the True God–we have tried and succeeded in making books. It makes the heart of the poor Indian rejoice to see his child read in a book; to see him put the talk upon paper, and to see the talk go to a distance, makes him rejoice. I will give you one instance. At the river Credit we have a station. A chief had a son who was instructed in our Mission-school; afterwards he was employed as a teacher in another school, and went away more than a hundred miles from his father. After a time, he wrote a letter to his father in the Indian tongue, which he did not know how to read; the father brought it to me to read it for him, and while I read the tears ran down his eyes, and he rejoiced to hear the talk of his son on the paper coming from a distance, and he blessed and praised God that his son was instructed in reading and writing.[59]

Peter Jones' comments were less a praising of the Society than a telling example of his perceptions of Western methods of reading and writing in general. As a convert to Methodism, Jones was also a convert and believer in Western modes of communication. The Ojibwe Reverend's comments bare a similar resemblance to his contemporary non-Aboriginal missionary colleagues in perceptions on the civilizing values of reading and writing. Jones however, and other First Peoples who worked in the service of the Christian faiths, like Charles Pratt (Askenootow), a Cree Church Missionary Society catechist, understood the political and social benefits that could be gained for their people in publicly praising the perceived values of Western literacy. Articulating Western methods of communication for their own purposes, Jones and other Aboriginal peoples hoped that these efforts would establish First Peoples as contemporaries and equals in the eyes of the colonial governments and settlers who had invaded their territories and cultures.[60]

The publishing efforts of the Religious Tract Society, and similar groups like the Upper Canada Bible Society, resulted in a great number of religiously oriented publications being distributed throughout the English-speaking colonies of North America. While these efforts were not immediately or distinctly aimed at Aboriginal populations, through missionary contact some First Peoples were inevitably exposed to the Society's literature. The tracts' effectiveness among Aboriginal populations in meeting the goals of the Society–being that of religious and moral conversion–however, is difficult to gauge. The Society reported in 1850 that grants were made to friends at Niagara some twenty-five years earlier in 1825, noting that "the poor Indians were visited, a school established in the midst of them, and even a village library formed. The Indian chiefs took much interest in these efforts."[61] Unfortunately, further evidence to support the existence of this library at Niagara and its relative importance and place within the unnamed Aboriginal community is elusive. The community itself in question is not known to be Ojibwe or Iroquoian, but may have been New Credit or Ohsweken, the most likely missions within the Niagara region. If a library indeed existed, it undoubtedly was built in the interests of housing the publications of the Religious Tract Society, and would have been employed in the service of the Christian mission. Further, the Society in the early part of the nineteenth century published almost exclusively in the English language, meaning any library furnished in the Society's interests among Aboriginal peoples would not have included many works in Aboriginal languages. The likelihood of this library's continued use by First Peoples at the time is very difficult to gauge, and it would appear that the collection, if it even existed, did not survive.

The Methodist influence: committed to moral transformation

Thaddeus Osgood, in his failures to establish fully non-denominational schools and lending libraries among Aboriginal communities, noted in 1829 that were Aboriginal peoples themselves in a reasonable position to financially support their own communities, his endeavors might yet take root. Osgood, in establishing schools and libraries in non-Aboriginal communities often worked on the principle of securing funding with the promise that the community in question would match any donation with a comparable sum of funds. In the case of Aboriginal communities, he notes, "in relation to what may be given towards Schools of Industry among the Indian Tribes, it would be difficult to obtain an equal sum, for very few of them can do any thing more than what is necessary for their own subsistence."[62] Yet, Osgood also observed that the desire of some of the First Peoples of Upper Canada to provide their children with a Euro-Christian education was very great, and he expressed his opinion that it was important to lend a little assistance towards Schools of Industry, which were to be established in communities at the River Credit, Lake Simcoe, and at the Thames under the direction of Methodist missionaries. Funds were secured for the benefit of these communities, "to be laid out in promoting a knowledge of Agriculture and the useful arts..., under the care of Messrs. Case, Jones, Ryerson, and Jackson, who are connected with Indian Affairs at those places. It is very important that these zealous friends be encouraged."[63] While Osgood's efforts to secure funds for books and schools for Aboriginal populations in the Canadas following 1830 would cease, Methodist missionaries to whom he offered funds in trust, along with Reverend James Evans and others, would play a significant part in the spread of Western print culture, literacy, and later libraries in the Aboriginal communities of Upper Canada.

Canadian Methodism emerged from existing traditions in England and the United States. A denomination of Protestant origins, Methodism first emerged in Newfoundland in the 1760s and was less than one hundred years old at the time of its introduction into the Canadas by the turn of the nineteenth century. As Neil Semple illustrates in his encyclopedic historical work on Canadian Methodism, *The Lord's Dominion* (1996), Methodists saw in Canada the denomination's destiny of supplying and shaping the spiritual and moral characteristics of national life: "Canadian Methodists intended to spread evangelical Christianity throughout the length and breadth of the country and to build Canada into the site of Christ's earthly kingdom."[64] In their attempts to transform and create in this land a highly moral, just, and Christianly spiritual country, Methodists saw no greater tool than education, and gave a high priority to mission work, particularly to new immigrants and Aboriginal populations. Fostering literacy in reading and writing played a key and foremost role in educating settlers, new immigrants, and Aboriginal peoples. Similar in approach to the New England Congregationalist tradition from which Reverend Osgood emerged, Methodists distributed religious tracts and books widely in their crusades to Christianize the Canadas. In 1829 the

Methodist Episcopal Church in Canada founded the weekly denomina-
tional newspaper, the *Christian Guardian*, under the editorship of Egerton
Ryerson. The newspaper quickly became one of the most widely distributed and influential newspapers in Upper Canada. In that same year,
Methodists also established their own book and publishing house, the
Methodist Book Room, which complemented the *Christian Guardian*, and
in addition to distributing religious publications from the United States and
England, began publishing a distinctly Canadian literature.[65] Among the
first of these published materials was a collection of hymns translated into
the Ojibwe language by the Ojibwe-Methodist missionary, Reverend Peter
Jones.

Education played a central role in the Methodist missions, and it is
impossible to overstate its significance as the denomination attempted to
disseminate its broader social message. This desire and reliance on
education was influenced by the evangelical belief in humanity's natural
depravity and also in its ultimate perfectability. Through education, wilful
sinfulness could be prevented, rather than reforming the sinner later in life.
It was thus no coincidence that Egerton Ryerson, an influential Methodist
minister, was instrumental in developing what would later become the
Ontario provincial public education system. Methodists also understood
that knowledge could be either good or evil, depending on how it was
learned and utilized, thus the goal of education from a Methodist
perspective was to stimulate knowledge that could help to reveal God's
purpose and works–not to undermine religion. The denomination took
great care to essentially block perverse inquiry from weakening the
foundations of Christianity, which would lead to the destruction of
humanity and eternal damnation. If true progress was to be made,
education would have to develop a strong moral character, and intellectual
attainment would have to be secondary to establishing an intimate
relationship with Christ. The ultimate role of education was to fulfill the
Lord's command to revere God and love humanity.[66] In this regard, the
role of print and books was to emphasize morality and create well-
balanced men and women and personal piety. The Bible was the indispensable textbook in influencing Christian progress. Further, from a purely
Methodist perspective, stimulating literacy and utilizing Methodist-
published books, tracts, and periodicals was central to defining and
defending the place of Methodism, particularly within Upper Canada.

Methodists felt a particularly strong obligation with regard to children
in their commitment to make disciples of all and create a highly moral
social order. Sunday schools, which were also employed by Thaddeus

Osgood and missionaries representing other Christian denominations, were an important tool for Methodists in their attempts to morally transform and bind the children of settler and Aboriginal populations to institutional religion. Sunday schools were developed through the late eighteenth to the nineteenth centuries from non-sectarian community organizations run by dedicated lay men and women interested in basic moral and educational training, to semi-independent church auxiliaries, finally to departments of local churches with highly organized clerical and denominational control with the goal of bringing young people into a direct relationship with the church. Their early popularity came from the desire to provide the poor and so-called immigrant classes (which also included Aboriginal peoples) with a means to acquire basic literacy skills, although in Protestant Canada the secular educational role of Sunday schools was displaced by an evangelizing function. The teaching of reading and writing, however, was retained for the very young and in areas where common schools were not operating and among new immigrant and Aboriginal children who often missed the opportunity to attend day schools.[67]

What is most significant about Sunday schools, however, was their supplying of reading materials to the communities they served. Before the establishment of public library systems in Canada or the availability of inexpensive publications for the general public, Sunday schools were the main resource for reading materials among both adults and children. Sunday school libraries supplied Bible tracts, hymnals, temperance material, magazines, religious biographies, and general stories. Further, Sunday school libraries offered a moral alternative to trashy novels and the secular press. Growing out of the schools' early role in literacy training, these libraries reinforced the ideas and values taught in the schools, and disseminated evangelical literature. Sunday school promoters recognized that the libraries did more than provide reading material, and that their very presence attracted students and their parents.[68]

The Sunday school was the ideal agency of evangelical proselytism and social reform, and although not alone in fostering such institutions, the Methodist church led the way in this movement. Methodist Sunday school libraries boasted nearly 400,000 books and pamphlets by the end of the nineteenth century.[69] Sunday schools were among the earliest schools established by missionaries in Aboriginal communities, and there is considerable evidence to suggest that such schools existed across the country, representing the Protestant denominations, mainly Methodist, Anglican, and the Church of England and the Roman Catholic church.[70] It is less clear, however, that all Sunday schools established in Aboriginal communities in the early nineteenth century had libraries, but evidence suggests that many did. The earliest report of a library in any Aboriginal community arising in the annual reports of the Department of Indian Affairs emerges in that department's very first report. This is a Sabbath school library within the Chippewas of Saugeen community at French Bay on the Bruce Peninsula in Ontario, reported in 1864. Operated by the Methodist Wesleyan Society, the school was overseen by Reverend Mr. Cooley, and included a collection of some 150 volumes.[71] Further, the earliest printing endeavors in Aboriginal languages by missionaries were works that would have fit well into the Sunday school curriculum. Joyce M. Banks, Karen Evans, and James Constantine Pilling, in their extensive bibliographies of books printed in Aboriginal languages in Canada, note that the nature of this literature until the mid-twentieth century was mainly evangelical. With very few exceptions, books printed for the use of Aboriginal peoples in Canada were mainly Bible translations or devotional works written or translated by missionaries and printed by religious societies.

In his account of missionary work among the Ojibwe of the Algoma District of Lake Superior in the 1880s, Reverend Edward Wilson notes that a library of 500 volumes was lost when the mission school house was destroyed by fire.[72] Writing for a Methodist audience in the late nineteenth century, John McLean recounts the stories of missionaries in the Red River settlement and in settlements on the Saskatchewan, which include the acknowledgment of schoolmasters making use of Sunday school hymn books and "Sabbath School libraries."[73] Methodist missionary Egerton Ryerson Young also makes reference to books employed in the mission Sunday school at Rossville and at other missions to the Cree and Saulteaux in the Northwest in the 1890s, and notes the degree to which the Cree were literate and apparently eager to get their hands on more books.[74] That Sunday schools included libraries in this region is of no surprise, given the efforts of Reverend James Evans in translating and printing evangelical works in Cree syllabics in the 1840s.

"What our Indians call paper talk": the legacies of Reverend James Evans

Methodist missionary James Evans, under the influence of William Case, presiding elder of the Upper Canada District of the Methodist Episcopal Church, accepted an appointment to the Ojibwe communities at Rice and Mud Lakes in Upper Canada in 1828. While leading the mission at Rice and Mud Lakes, Evans developed an understanding of the Ojibwe language and began translating and writing, and with Case's encouragement proposed the publication of a vocabulary and dictionary of Ojibwe. Evans continued his work in translating after his appointment to the St. Clair Mission near Sarnia in 1834. It was here, with the encouragement of other Methodist missionaries, that Evans progressed rapidly in Ojibwe linguistics, becoming involved in a committee appointed to prepare an orthographic system for the language by the Canada Conference of the Methodist Church. This committee was composed of Evans, his brother Ephraim, Joseph Stinson, Ojibwe missionary Peter Jones, and William Case. By 1836 Reverend Evans had devised an Ojibwe syllabary of eight consonants and four vowels that was printed in New York in 1837 in the form of translated hymns and scripture and his *Speller and interpreter, in Indian and English, for the use of the mission schools.*[75] Early correspondence with William Case discusses Evans' work in translating the Ojibwe language at Rice Lake and the Credit Mission, and these also include discussions on the use of books in the schools. Case praised Evans' work, and his translating and use of the printed word were seen as a great benefit to religious instruction and conversion to the Methodist faith.[76] Evans' intentions however, like all other missionaries of the period, were rooted not only in religious instruction and conversion, but also to civilize Aboriginal peoples in efforts to transform them into a Western "civil and Christian society," as is demonstrated in a letter to Evans from Reverend Jonas Dodge in 1835:

> I have often thought with interest upon the condition of the natives of the vast western wilderness, and have asked the question in my own mind, is it *probable* that they will ever become a *civilized, intelligent, Christian* people? I would be pleased to know your mind on this subject, and whether you entertain the hope that they will become ultimately a civilized *community*, enjoying the advantages of civil and Christian *society*, or whether it is your principal object to preach the gospel to them in their present wandering state, imparting such instruction as you may be able, with the expectation only, of being instrumental in bringing them to the enjoyment of the blessings of the gospel in their *souls*, while as it respects *society* then may continue about the same.[77]

A response to a similar query from John Beecham in early 1836 when Evans is leading the mission at St. Clair offers some insight into the Reverend's thoughts on the subject of civilizing in addition to propagating

Christian values. Following three full pages describing in detail the perceived former drunken state of the Ojibwe at St. Clair, Evans responds "I might Sir write a volume in answer to your first Query, but I have said sufficient to shew that they were in the strictest sense, a poor, degraded people, untill they became *Christians* altho a Government agent and a Missionary resided among them some time previous to this late reformation...."[78]

By 1840 Evans had been appointed as the first Methodist missionary to the Cree community at Rossville, near Norway House in the Hudson's Bay Company territory, as part of a wider strategic Methodist ploy to restrict the activities of Anglican and Roman Catholic missionaries in the Red River country. Other Methodist missionaries were placed at Moose Factory, Rainy Lake, and Fort Edmonton. At Rossville, Evans worked with the Ojibwe preachers Peter Jacobs and Henry Bird Steinhauer in developing a syllabary for the Cree language. The earlier development of the Ojibwe syllabary had enabled the trio to develop the basic structure of the Cree syllabary (another Algonquian language) within two months of their arrival in the northwest. The Cree syllabary drew on shorthand, as well as symbols already in use among the Cree, and these were adapted to the language.[79] Each symbol was devised to stand for a syllable rather than a single letter, and nine symbols in four different positions encompassed the whole language. Use of the Cree syllabary spread so quickly among the Aboriginal population that Evans and company could not produce enough hand-written copies. An application to the Hudson Bay Company for a proper printing press was made, but was turned down with the reason given that it would be too heavy to transport. Nonetheless, using type made from the lead lining of tea chests melted down and molded in clay, with ink concocted from sturgeon oil and soot, and a modified jack-press used for bundling furs, Evans and company designed their own printing press and printed their first book, a hymnal, in syllabics at Rossville on 15 October 1841. In addition to this feat, the syllabic hymnal was the first book printed in western Canada.[80]

Evans' syllabic was employed by other Methodist missionaries in the north west, including George Barnley among the Cree and Inuit at Moose Factory, and Robert Rundle at Fort Edmonton and Rocky Mountain House among the Woodland Cree, Assinboine, Piegan, Sarcee, and Blood First Nations. The wide dissemination of the syllabic system attributed to Evans also coincided with a unique religious movement that swept the Hudson Bay Cree in the early 1840s. The syllabics played a special role in this movement, along with the spreading impact of Evans' preaching. This

movement combined Christian and traditional Cree elements, and gave rise
to the prophet Abishabis ("Small Eyes") and his associate Wasitack ("The
Light").[81] An articulated response to the presence and teachings of Evans
and others like him, this movement clearly illustrates the creative
responses of Aboriginal religions in synthesizing new Christian teachings
with their own traditional beliefs.

The syllabic-Cree system was highly adaptable to other Algonquian
languages, such as Ojibwe and Innu. It also proved adaptable to the needs
of other unrelated Aboriginal languages, such as Inuktitut, and is still
widely used by the Inuit today. Although the system was not generally
adopted by speakers of the Athapascan languages, or the peoples of the
Pacific coast, the Oblate Charles Ovide Perrault used an Athapascan
syllabic in 1856, and the Oblate Adrien Gabriel Morice designed a rather
successful syllabic for the Carrier language in 1890. Cree chiefs prepared
their acceptance speeches for Treaty nine in syllabics in 1906, and use of
Cree syllabary continues into the twenty-first century.[82] Like the religious
influence from which Evans' syllabic system emerged and was designed
to serve, the script was articulated and synthesized by the Cree of the north
west and by other First Peoples whose languages adopted similar scripts
in Aboriginal efforts to employ a Western writing tradition to their own
means and practices.[83]

Methodist missionary at Moose Factory, George Barnley

In the same wave that sent James Evans to the Hudson Bay Company
territory in the northwest, the Wesleyan Methodist Missionary Society
placed the young and inexperienced missionary George Barnley in Moose
Factory on James Bay, following George Simpson's invitation to the
Methodists to move into the company's vast territory. At the Moose
Factory post, Barnley was commissioned to spread Christian civilization
to the Inuit and Swampy Cree, which compelled the missionary to travel
extensively across the largely inhospitable James Bay region, his circuit
included Abitibi, Albany Post, and Rupert House. Throughout his stay in
the region (1840-1847), Barnley was aggravated by the trouble of
overcoming a strong commitment on behalf of the Crees and Inuit to their
own spiritualities and a local indifference to Christianity and Western
ways. Ultimately, Barnely would have a limited effect in influencing the
Crees and Inuit of the region, but it was during his tenure that the First
Peoples of Moose Factory in particular would be introduced to the

Western tradition of the written word and book form, although largely and indirectly through Evans' efforts at Rossville.[84]

In an attempt to effectively indoctrinate Methodist teachings, Barnley employed interpreters, assigned memory work, provided those interested with a system of writing, and planned to collect the Aboriginal population together in a village, in the hopes that the children would one day form a captive audience in a residential school. For the most part, Barnley spent much of his time in the region ministering only during the brief visits by the Cree and Inuit to the trading posts. He noted that without a printing press, ministering to the Aboriginal population was largely fruitless, since in his opinion, the written word could act as an "authority for constant reference where memorys report solicited confidence in vain, or more probably pointed out the path of error from that of truth, and it would prove an antagonist to Popery."[85] In 1842, Barnley observed members of the Cree nation making notes on his teachings of the Ten Commandments using an apparently traditional form of writing. He remarked, "their method of remembering is very curious, a number of hiroglyphics being marked with the finger nail on a piece of birch bark," demonstrating that evidently an indigenous form of the written word was already in existence in the territory, or that Evans' syllabic system had quickly spread to the Moose Factory region.[86] In any case, Barnley shortly after attempted to teach his own version of the alphabet based on Byron's stenography, but was largely unsuccessful. In October of 1842, two Cree from Fort Severn arrived at Moose Factory with samples of James Evans' syllabic writing. It has been speculated that these travelers may have been Abishabis and Wasitack, the key figures in the syncretic religious movement that would sweep the region only a short time later.[87] Regardless of their identities, Barnley abandoned his own system of the alphabet in favor of adopting Evans' syllabary for the sake of maintaining uniformity in translations. In a similar tradition to Evans, Barnley manufactured his own printing press of sorts, experimenting with casting lead type, carving small blocks of wood and inscribing nuggets of plaster made from nearby gypsum, eventually succeeding in producing Cree primers in syllabic. Shortly afterwards, William Mason, who had succeeded Evans' at Rossville in 1846, arranged to have a proper printing press and sent Barnley fifty prayer books.[88]

Barnley departed Moose Factory in 1847 and the mission remained largely vacant, with only scattered visits from Oblate priests, until 1851 when Anglican missionary John Horden moved in to continue efforts in civilizing and making Christians out of the Aboriginal population of the region.[89] Barnley's overall influence on the Cree appears to have been slight, and it is clear that Evans' syllabic was introduced into the Moose Factory region by the Cree themselves. Nonetheless, the records of Barnley's involvements in the north west are insightful in providing a glimpse into the origins of the introduction of the written word and Western book form. His successor John Horden acknowledged Barnley's modest accomplishments in the region, but incorrectly attributed the spread of the syllabic system among the James Bay Cree to the Methodist missionary. The First Peoples of the region maintained strong ties to their traditional beliefs throughout Barnley's tenure, adopting only superficial elements of Christianity while actively articulating Evans' syllabic writing forms.

Anglican missionary, John Horden, and the Moose Mission Press, 1853-1859

With the departure of George Barnley from Moose Factory in 1847, the James Bay region was without a permanent missionary influence until the Church Missionary Society dispatched John Horden to the region in 1851. Following Barnley's departure, and for the four years without a permanent missionary influence in the region, some of Barnley's Aboriginal converts moved to Norway House or to the American side of the Sault to maintain Methodist ties.[90] In the meantime, Roman Catholic Oblate missionaries made occasional visits to the region, but the Hudson's Bay Company would not allow them to establish a permanent mission.

In the autumn of 1853, John Horden, Anglican missionary at the Moose Church Missionary Society Station in Moose Factory, Ontario, began a program to print scriptural translations, devotional works, and other Anglican aids to worship for the Aboriginal peoples of the James Bay region. By the spring of 1859 he had produced a body of scriptural and devotional works, including twenty-three books, in an estimated 7,500 copies in the languages of the Moose and East Main Cree, Ojibwe, and Inuit of Little Whale River. These were meant to serve the needs of over 3,900 Cree, Ojibwe, and Inuit people living in scattered groups throughout a five hundred mile wide land mass around James Bay. Horden translated and printed all these religious works using the syllabic characters attributed to James Evans. Evans' syllabic had been reluctantly adopted as the approved Church Missionary Society syllabarium, and Horden's printing program was undertaken in accordance with an Anglican missionary policy developed by Henry Venn, Honorary Secretary of the Church Missionary

Society.[91]

Henry Venn's policy encouraged the Church Missionary Society missionaries to learn the languages and dialects of the region as quickly as possible, believing that it was impossible to effectively evangelize through an interpreter. He also advised missionaries to translate the Bible and devotional works into the languages of those among whom they served, for literacy was considered to be essential in successful evangelizing. Missionaries were thus instructed under Venn's policy to educate their audiences to read and write and use the translations provided.[92] Under Venn's instructions, "the missionary should be known as a man of the book."[93] The spread of Western-style literacy throughout the north west among the Aboriginal populations depended, without a doubt, upon the use of syllabic characters. Henry Venn was a strong proponent of the syllabic system and encouraged its use among the Church Missionary Society missions in the north west. Even before his arrival at Moose Factory, Horden was familiar with the syllabic method of writing and was prepared to use it, fully expecting to become a missionary-printer. In his first letter to Venn, Horden wrote: "Many of the Indians know something of the syllabic characters and I have seen some beautiful writing in which they are used written by an Indian. I think that if the Committee could grant me a printing press and a stock of syllabic type a great deal of good would come as they all have a great desire for learning to read."[94] Horden requested a printing press from the Church Missionary Society but was initially turned down on the grounds that the Society did not originally plan for him to remain at Moose Factory for more than a year, and further, David Anderson, Anglican Bishop of Rupert's Land, was at the time opposed to the use of syllabic characters in the diocese. For two years, between 1851 and 1853, Horden thus relied upon his own pen or sent translations to England for printing. The delay in having translations sent to England to be printed resulted in Horden disseminating most of his translations in hand-written manuscript form—a slow task that could not keep up with demand. In 1852, Bishop Anderson visited the Diocese of Rupert's Land and was favorably impressed by the degree to which the syllabic characters were disseminating throughout the region, resulting in his support of syllabics. Thus, with Anderson's change of heart and the slow progress of sending translations overseas to be printed or prepared by hand, an Albion typographical press with syllabic types was sent to Moose by the Church Missionary Society in August of 1853.[95] Horden began printing on the press by the end of November of 1853, and by the spring of 1857, he had printed sixteen books in less than four years in each linguistic tongue of the James Bay region, culminating in the printing of his first complete translation of the Book of Jonah from the Bible. By the end of 1859, he had printed translations of the Gospels of Matthew, Mark, Luke, and John in eight-hundred copies each. Many of these were sold to Aboriginal peoples through the Hudson Bay Company shop at Moose for two shillings a copy[96]–the Church Missionary Society having had a policy of charging for books where the recipients were able to pay, while those who could not afford the expense received copies at no cost.

Although Horden's imprints were widely used in the region, the number of books printed did not suffice in serving the needs of the people there. By the missionary's own accounts, the Cree, Ojibwe, and Inuit people of the Moose Factory region made widespread use of his printed books and demanded more copies than he could supply. Horden's accounts are believable considering the extent to which syllabic literacy spread throughout the James Bay region from at least the time of James Evans. Further, the Church Missionary Society expected that from Moose Factory, John Horden would supply the entire Aboriginal population of the Diocese of Rupert's Land with syllabic books. With Bishop Anderson's blessing, Horden concluded his printing at Moose in 1859, finding the task of supplying the entire James Bay region with books too much of a burden on his health, time consuming, and expensive. Thereafter, the task of supplying Rupert's Land with printed syllabic religious works was once again passed to the missionary societies' presses in England.[97]

The arrival of the Anglican press and the appearance of Horden's syllabic printed books prompted the Roman Catholic Oblate missionary André Marie Garin to beg a printing press from his superiors in Montreal. Action was swift—by March 1854, the Roman Catholics in the James Bay region had their own press, and Aboriginal Roman Catholic converts were thus "protected" from the influence of the Anglican books. Once the Roman Catholics established a press and started printing in syllabic characters, the Anglicans were thereafter forced to continue printing. Catholic and Anglican missionary groups in the region from this point forward vigorously competed for the attentions and conversion of First Nation's people in Rupert's Land, with printed books acting as powerful tools.[98] The adoption and success of the syllabic system within both Protestant and Catholic missions in the north west demonstrated that formulas of disseminating Christianity and civilization among First Peoples that had been deemed traditional until this point could not be applied without modification and accommodation. In the early years of missionaries adopting the system, non-Aboriginal critics complained that the syllabics made the learning of English less urgent among Aboriginal populations, thus isolating them from Western society, inhibiting assimilationist policies. More recently, Aboriginal critics have noted that the use of syllabics entirely for the propagation of Christian values and religious literature in part served to damage oral traditions and inhibited the emergence of Aboriginal languages as instruments of secular culture.[99]

A legacy of print

The Western technology of the printed word and an understanding of literacy as reading and writing alphabetic or syllabic script would be two of the more enduring and influential legacies to emerge from the missionary experience for most Aboriginal populations in the new world. Most Aboriginal groups in Canada were introduced to the Western book and notions of reading and writing through the various missionaries that visited their homelands in attempts to convert and civilize. Literacy became firmly identified with religion in the eyes of many First Peoples. This is not to say, however, that Aboriginal peoples did not have their own understandings of literacy and disseminating knowledge through written forms. Through a number of different and complex sign systems, be they Mi'kmaq hieroglyphics or Algonkian syllabics, or such media as petroglyphs, pictographs, wampum, and birch bark scrolls, Aboriginal peoples from the east to the west employed their own means of disseminating and perpetuating knowledge through written formats that in many cases supplemented oral traditions. Newcomers did not recognize or acknowledge these means of communication as having any relation to Western notions of literacy or the written word. However, as was discussed at greater length in chapter one, these Aboriginal methods of communicating constituted forms of "writing without words."[100] Each demanded a kind of literacy on behalf of both the "writer" and the "reader."

With the arrival of Europeans on the North American continent, however, and inevitable contact with the newcomers, particularly missionaries who had predetermined plans of education and civilizing, most Aboriginal peoples in Canada by the mid-nineteenth century would be exposed to, and in some cases well-practiced in employing Western forms of writing. Print is a powerful technology, and the early influence of missionaries in First Peoples' understandings and relationships to this technology cannot be overemphasized. The strata from which Christian missionaries in the new world emerged was that of religious conversion and exclusion. The Protestant and Catholic faiths, being religions of conversion and religions of exclusion, were also religions of the book. As "literate religions," they are characterized by their fixed points of reference, or "true" interpretations of the Bible, and are thus characterized as less tolerant to change. They are characteristically salvationist, placing great emphasis on individual paths to righteousness, which links these Christian denominations directly with the "individualizing" tendencies of the Western literate technology upon which they are built.[101]

James Axtell has argued that the Roman Catholic Jesuits best capitalized on print's potential for religious conversion among the people of the Eastern Woodlands region, beginning in the seventeenth century. In large part he argues that the Jesuits were successful in impressing Aboriginal converts with the printed word because the First Peoples of this region believed that print (and the Jesuits themselves) had shamanic qualities. Peter Wogan, on the other hand, disputes Axtell's thesis, finding little evidence to support the view that Aboriginal peoples in the seventeenth century perceived the French missionaries' writings as especially powerful, and challenges the notion that this reaction was typical and constituted a continent-wide automatic response to Western literacy.[102] Wogan asserts that we should expect that the Jesuits would have exaggerated the importance of European writing, and they also likely exaggerated or even misinterpreted Aboriginal reactions to the printed word since they generally saw writing as one of the main benefits they could bring to the Aboriginal peoples of North America. Thus, the Jesuits would have been inclined to see Western literacy as a central symbol of their own identities, which would have influenced their accounts of Aboriginal cultures.[103] Furthermore, in that Aboriginal cultures of the Eastern Woodlands and other regions employed their own complex sign systems and forms of writing before and after European contact, it seems less likely that "supernatural powers" would have been attributed to Western writing as Axtell asserts. Adjusting to Western literate tradition would have been less of a "radical change" than it is often characterized.[104] Assuming radical change and attributing supernatural powers to Western writing implies a dichotomy between literacy and illiteracy that revisionist literacy historians and social scientists in recent years have begun to debunk. Harvey J. Graff, for instance, notes that literacy scholars are increasingly connecting literacy to the larger network of communicative competencies, rather than contrasting them dichotomously and developmentally.[105]

If Axtell is correct, however, in saying that the Roman Catholics were more successful than their Protestant counterparts in employing writing as a tool for religious conversion in the seventeenth century, it would have to be for reasons more complex than his shamanic thesis.[106] That the Protestant denominations were not as organized as the Catholics in the region at the time must certainly account for the significant difference in their number of converts. Following the British conquest in 1759, the supply of Catholic recruits to missions was cut off, and the Protestant denominations were slow to show interest in Aboriginal missions and were generally not successful in their efforts among Aboriginal peoples until the early nineteenth century. By the nineteenth century, however, it would be the Protestant missionaries who were more determined, if not successful, in their use of the printed word. Even if seventeenth-century Eastern Woodland peoples were impressed by the Jesuit's books and thus converted to Catholicism, the Protestant, particularly Methodist and Anglican missions in the nineteenth century, were more determined in employing print as a tool of not only conversion, but perhaps more importantly, education. Protestantism, characterized in large part by an emphasis on veneration of the Bible, is often seen as fostering Western notions of literacy and popular education. While Catholics first began printing books in Aboriginal languages, Protestant missions would by the mid-nineteenth century be far more successful in reaching Aboriginal populations through the use of syllabics and alphabetic literacy. John Webster Grant notes that although accidents of geography were often in part responsible for the religious allegiance of many First Peoples, there was also some indication of conscious selection. This was particularly evident in the north west, where he notes that Protestant missionaries were easier to assimilate, being similar in appearance and manners to Hudson's Bay Company merchants and, even Roman Catholics admitted, could offer greater opportunities for education. This said, however, Protestants and Catholics were equally successful in their own ways in finding constituencies to which its approach was most congenial.[107] The Protestant approach, in the nineteenth century at least, (regardless of the actual number of converts gained as a result) was by nature more determined and enduring in employing the printed word. The Protestant missions' tendency and general willingness to employ Aboriginal catechists and missionaries, like Charles Pratt, Peter Jones, and Peter Jacobs, was central to their success in encouraging print literacy among Aboriginal populations.[108]

The nineteenth century was also a period where the output of publishing in Aboriginal languages would reach an unprecedented level. The seventeenth and eighteenth centuries produced books in Aboriginal languages of groundbreaking importance, but as Joyce Banks has noted, the total product of these centuries would give no intimation of the sheer volume of material that would appear in the nineteenth century.[109] Like those printed in the seventeenth and eighteenth centuries, these materials would also be overwhelmingly evangelical in nature. The increased output of printing in Aboriginal languages reflected also the nature of Aboriginal communities and their interactions with missionaries in the nineteenth century. It was in this period that missionary efforts would truly begin to succeed in maintaining some semblance of control or influence over the communal living arrangements of Aboriginal communities, particularly in Upper and Lower Canada and the British Maritime colonies. Early missionary efforts were frustrated by the inability of maintaining any consistent educative influence because many Aboriginal communities were characterized by frequent transiency. A complex mix of economy, the continual increase of settler intrusions on traditional lands, and colonial government interests in treaty making meant that many Aboriginal communities in the nineteenth century found themselves increasingly limited to living in one place, usually on Reserves. Here, missionaries could exercise increased amounts of influence, particularly in the realms of education. This also meant that missionaries themselves could become more stationary, and bulky items like printing presses could be more easily accommodated in the missions. Methodist missions in Canada West under the direction of William Case, for instance, were particularly interested in the prospects of developing mission towns as environments that could foster familiar Western institutions. Grape Island, in the Bay of Quinte near Belleville, was one such community. Established by Case in 1827, the planned community was meant to serve some 200 Ojibwe inhabitants, and was modeled after similar long-established villages in Canada East. Inhabitants were officially Christian and lived sedentary lives, an achievement the Methodists and colonial government hoped to emulate throughout the colonies. In 1836 the residents of Grape Island were moved to a more suitable location at Alderville on Rice Lake, south east of Peterborough. Similar settlements would be launched across the country under the auspices of the Indian Department, and under the direction of mainly the Protestant missions.

Protestant and Roman Catholic missionaries wrote and translated books for the use of Aboriginal peoples, in the process producing a number of vocabularies and dictionaries that have since become invaluable in the contemporary study of Aboriginal languages. Linguist Even Hovdhaugen notes that the majority of Aboriginal languages got their first and, in many cases, only linguistic descriptions from missionaries. Further, missionary influence was profound in the development of literary and sometimes even oral norms of languages.[110] Roman Catholic efforts in this mode of printing are particularly telling. Following the British conquest, Roman Catholic missionary efforts among Aboriginal populations stagnated outside of Québec and Lower Canada until the mid-nineteenth century. After 1843, the Roman Catholic influence reemerged in Upper Canada and spread throughout the west. Printed works produced by Catholic missionaries were often in the form of vocabularies, dictionaries, and grammars. These, however, were printed more for the benefit of missionaries and non-Aboriginal scholars than for Aboriginal peoples, as is demonstrated in correspondence between David Laird, Minister responsible for Indian Affairs, and the Oblate Emile Petitot. Father Petitot, who would subsequently become renowned as a linguist and ethnographer of the Dene people, wrote to the Minister in February of 1875 requesting monetary assistance to publish a dictionary and grammar. He states that "such a work could not fail, in view of the opening up of the North West, to be of great value not only to learned societies and to missionaries but also to Indian Agents and other persons employed by Government among the Indians speaking any of the dialects in question.... This work is not one which would be of any practical value [to] the Indians."[111] A decade later, Father Hugonnard, Oblate missionary and principal of the Industrial school at Qu'Appelle, wrote to the Indian Commissioner at Regina, Edgar Dewdney, requesting funds to assist in publishing a Cree-English vocabulary. This time the work in question was meant to assist Aboriginal students at the school, but notably for the purposes of learning the English language in the eventual hope of eliminating their mother-tongue. Hugonnard notes: "With reference to the difficulty in teaching the pupils of the Industrial schools to speak the English language, I have commenced to write a Manual of Cree and English Conversation which I think if used in the schools will facilitate the instruction very much."[112] Funding was approved for Hugonnard's endeavor, as was a similar project by Reverend Father Lacombe. However, the Commissioner notes that in reference to printing books in Aboriginal languages: "All Indian children are prone to use their own tongue in preference to English and the less it is used in teaching the quicker will the child be inclined to adhere to English solely in order to express its views. Having books in which the vernacular is found would foster its use and the more the mother tongue is kept alive the more is the child diffident in using the English language...." The consequence of a student maintaining his or her mother tongue, rather than learning English, is characterized by the Commissioner as, "to shrink more or less from whites and an unfitness to battle life." Further, printing in syllabics, held in esteem only forty years previous, was discouraged by claiming the method of writing to be "not necessary to their advancement."[113] The dictionaries, vocabularies, and grammars produced by missionaries, particularly the Roman Catholics, were thus meant to serve as temporary instruction tools for the benefit of the missions and government in converting, civilizing, and eliminating the use of Aboriginal languages. Further, language is clearly conceptualized as an explicit indicator of Aboriginality, and the printing of books by the later part of the nineteenth century is devotedly meant to encourage the assimilation of Aboriginal peoples to the predominant language of the colony. Missionary grammars, dictionaries, and vocabularies were thus, in most cases, employed in colonial efforts to regulate and control Aboriginal languages by grammatical rules, as part of a wider attempt at regulating perceived heathen and uncivilized societies within the contexts of Western-Christian culture and morals. In the words of Linguist, Rüdiger Schreyer, "before they could conquer the devil in the souls of these poor deluded savages they had to conquer their languages."[114]

The missions, by the late nineteenth century, also began asking government to supply their efforts with books, rather than printing and distributing works solely on their own. Demonstrated in an 1888 appeal to the Department of the Interior to furnish Industrial schools with books, Indian Commissioner to the Northwest Territories, Hayter Reed, recognized the opportunity print could present as a tool of cultural assimilation. The Commissioner before Reed's tenure had apparently refused the schools' requests for "bibles, hymn books, prayer books, and other religious works," on the grounds that their cost would be too significant and set a precedent for other such requests to the Department. Reed, on the other hand, notes: "I find ... that it is advisable to obtain returns from the schools of the advancement in religious instruction of the pupils ... and as it is stated that such instruction cannot be imparted without the necessary books, I should like the views of the Department as to whether or not the Government should bear the expense of their purchase." The Department in turn responded positively to the idea, and Reed ordered several catechisms, hymn books, and bibles for the Qu'Appelle, Battleford, and St. Joseph's Industrial schools.[115] Books and print then, from the perspective of the missions and government, were not simply aids to religious instruction, but were clearly conceptualized as tools of cultural assimilation.

Notes

1. Loys Le Roy, *De la vicissitude ou variété des choses en l'univers* (Paris: 1579), 98-99, cited in Cornelius J. Jaenen, *Friend and foe: aspects of French-Amerindian cultural contact in the sixteenth and seventeenth centuries* (New York: Columbia University Press, 1976), 10.

2. Mrs. Holliwell, "Holiday musings of a worker: no. II - the love of reading," *British American magazine: devoted to literature, science, and art* II (1864): 271.

3. Mary Lu MacDonald, *Literature and society in the Canadas 1817 - 1850* (Queenston ON: Edwin Mellen Press, 1992), 67.

4. MacDonald, 67.

5. MacDonald, 69-70.

6. Roman Catholics and conservative Methodists believed that conversion could take place before "civilizing." Missionaries following these beliefs understood Christianity and civilization to be one in the same–in other words, conversion to Christianity would lead to eventual civilization. Most Protestant denominations and liberal Methodists, however, looked upon conversion and civilization rather differently. For a good number of Protestant missionaries, civilization was a necessary first step before full conversion to Christianity could take place. For these missions, the establishment of schools and educating First Peoples were the means of full conversion. Through education and gradual "civilizing" it was believed that First Peoples would eventually come around to seeing the benefits of Christianity. Missionaries from the Anglican faith, like William Duncan and John Horden, placed a great emphasis on reforming First Peoples through education. In the Anglican view, perceived ignorance was the general cause of social problems, and unless Christian Indians were taught in both labor and learning, they would not rise above the status of heathen. For more discussion on mission methods, see: Jean Usher, "Duncan of Metlakatla: the Victorian origins of a model Indian community," *British Columbia: historical readings*, compiled and edited by W. Peter Ward and Robert A. J. McDonald (Vancouver: Douglas & McIntyre, 1981), 127-153.

7. James P. Ronda and James Axtell, *Indian Missions: a critical bibliography* (Bloomington: Indiana University Press, 1978), passim.

8. Walter D. Mignolo's excellent discussion of the role of language and the book in colonial relations in Latin and South America provides a unique context through which similar relations in North America can be framed. See: Mignolo, *The Darker side of the Renaissance: literacy, territoriality, and colonization* (Ann Arbor: University of Michigan Press, 1995); and Elizabeth Hill Boone and Walter D. Mignolo, eds., *Writing without words: alternative literacies in Mesoamerica and the Andes* (Durham: Duke University Press, 1994).

9. See: John S. Milloy, *"A National crime": the Canadian government and the residential school system, 1879 to 1986* (Winnipeg: University of Manitoba Press, 1999).

10. Joyce M. Banks, *Books in Native Languages in the Rare Book Collections of the National Library of Canada*, revised and enlarged edition (Ottawa: National Library of Canada and the Ministry of Supply and Services, 1985), i-iii.

11. Banks, i-iii.

12. Banks, i-iii. The greatest bibliographer of North American Aboriginal language texts was James Constantine Pilling, who published nine major bibliographies and one huge preliminary study between 1885 and 1894, covering the literature of nine linguistic families. No previous bibliographies, or none since, have approached the size, range, and scholarly quality of Pilling's works. For discussion on Pilling, see Joyce M. Banks, "James Constantine Pilling and the literature of the Native Peoples," *Bibliographical Society of Canada: Colloquium III: National Library of Canada, 19 - 21 October 1978* (Toronto: Bibliographical Society of Canada, 1979), 59-70.

13. Even Hovdhaugen, "Missionary grammars–an attempt at defining a field of research," ... *and the Word was God: missionary linguistics and missionary grammar*, ed. by Even Hovdhaugen (Münster, Germany: Nodus Publikationen, 1996), 15-16.

14. Shef Rogers, "Crusoe among the Maori: translation and colonial acculturation in Victorian New Zealand," *Book History* 1.1 (1998): 182-195.

15. John Webster Grant, *Moon of wintertime: missionaries and the Indians of Canada in encounter since 1534* (Toronto: University of Toronto Press, 1984), 111-112.

16. Grant, 111-112.

17. Winona L. Stevenson, "'Our man in the field': the status and role of a CMS Native catechist in Rupert's Land," *Journal of the Canadian Church Historical Society* 33.1(1991): 65-78.

18. David Murray, *Forked tongues : speech, writing, and representation in North American Indian texts* (Bloomington and Indianapolis: Indiana University Press, 1991), 5-7; Joyce M. Banks, "The Church Missionary Society Press at Moose Factory: 1853-1859," *Journal of the Canadian Church Historical Society* XXVI.2 (1984): 69.

19. David L. Schmidt and Murdena Marshall, eds. and trans., *Mi'kmaq hieroglyphic prayers: readings in North America's first Indigenous script* (Halifax: Nimbus Publishing, 1995), 4.

20. Father Chrestien LeClercq, *New relation of Gaspesia: with the customs and religion of the Gaspesian Indians*, trans. and ed. by William F. Ganong, The Publications of the Champlain Society V (1691; Toronto: The Champlain Society, 1910), 80.

21. Schmidt and Marshall, 5.

22. LeClercq, 131.

23. LeClercq, 126.

24. LeClercq, 126-127.

25. LeClercq, 131.

26. Schmidt and Marshall, 6.

27. LeClercq, 130.

28. LeClercq, 132 (note 3).

29. Schmidt and Marshall, 10-11.

30. Translations of Maillard from Bruce Greenfield, "The Mi'kmaq hieroglyphic prayer book: writing and Christianity in Maritime Canada, 1675-1921," *The Language encounter in the Americas. 1492-1800: a collection of essays,* ed. Edward G. Gray and Norman Fiering (New York: Berghahn Books, 2000), 198; "S'ils étoient une fois en état de se servir comme nous de notre alphabet soit pour lire, soit pour écrire, ils abuseroient infailliblement de cette science par cet esprit de curiosité, que nous leur connaissons, qui les domine pour chercher avec empressement à sçavoir plutôt les choses dans leurs mémoires" Pierre Antoine-Simon Maillard, "Lettre de M. L'Abbé Maillard sur les missions de l'Acadie et particulièrement sur les missions Micmaques," *Les Soirées Canadiennes: recueil de littérature,* troisieme annee (Quebec City: Brousseau Frères, 1863), 358.

31. Greenfield, 198; "Mais s'ils s'émanciperoient bien ... s'ils pouvoient faire usage de notre alphabet, soit pour lire, soit pour écrire; ils ne tarderoient pas à se fortement persuader qu'ils en sçavent beaucoup plus que ceux qui sont faits pour les instruire" Maillard, 360.

32. Greenfield, 198; "De vouloir substituer notre alphabet aux caractères don't nos sauvages se servent pour lire et pour écrire, ce seroit fort mal travailler et pour eux, et pour nous" Maillard, 362.

33. Greenfield, 198; "Seroient-ils capables de causer de grands maux parmi la nation, tant par rapport à la religion et aux bonnes moeurs, qu'au gouvernment politique" Maillard, 361.

34. Maillard, 362-363, cited in Schmidt and Marshall, 11.

35. Greenfield, 199-200.

36. See for instance, Ives Goddard and William Fitzhugh, "A statement concerning America B. C.," *Man in the Northeast* 17 (1979): 166-171; and Allan Ross Taylor, "Nonverbal communications systems in Native North America," *Semiotica* 13.4 (1975): 329-374.

37. Captain John Knox, *An historical journal of the campaigns in North America for the years 1757, 1758, 1759, and 1760,* ed. by Arthur G. Doughty, The Publications of the Champlain Society VIII (1769; Toronto: Champlain Society, 1914), 90.

38. Maillard, 410.

39. *Annual Report of the Department of Indian Affairs for the year ended 31st December, 1880* (1881): 45-46.

40. Ruth Holes Whitehead, "A New Micmac petroglyph site," *The Occasional* 13.1 (1992): 7-12.

41. Schmidt and Marshall, 13-14.

42. Schmidt and Marshall, 14-15.

43. Thaddeus Osgood, *The Canadian Visitor, communicating important facts and interesting anecdotes respecting the Indians and Destitute Settlers in Canada and the United States of America* (London: Hamilton and Adams, 1829?); Central

Auxiliary Society for promoting Education and Industry among the Indians and Destitute Settlers in Canada, *The Second Annual Report of the Central Auxiliary Society for promoting Education and Industry among the Indians and Destitute Settlers in Canada: submitted to the Public Meeting held in the Masonic Hall Hotel, Montreal, April 8, 1829* (Montreal: Montreal Herald and New Montreal Gazette Office, 1829).

44. W. P. J. Millar, "Osgood, Thaddeus," *Dictionary of Canadian Biography*, volume VIII, 1851 to 1860, 665-667; and Millar, "The Remarkable Rev. Thaddeus Osgood: A study in the evangelical spirit in the Canadas," *Histoire sociale - Social History* X.19 (1977): 59-76.

45. James R. Rohrer, "The Connecticut Missionary Society and book distribution in the early republic," *Libraries & Culture* 34.1 (1999): 18.

46. Missionary Society of Connecticut, *The Constitution of the Missionary Society of Connecticut* (1800) qtd. in Rohrer, 19.

47. Nathan H. Mair, *An Account of the deeds of Thaddeus Osgood, beggar Doing Good 2* (Montreal & Ottawa: The Archives Committee of the Montreal and Ottawa Conference of the United Church of Canada, 1986), 4-5.

48. Mair, 12-14.

49. Mair, 14.

50. Central Auxiliary Society, 29.

51. Central Auxiliary Society, 16.

52. Central Auxiliary Society, 27-28.

53. Osgood, 54.

54. Osgood, 5.

55. Mair, 19-20.

56. Millar, "Osgood, Thaddeus," *DCB*, 666.

57. William Jones, *The Jubilee memorial of the Religious Tract Society: containing a record of its origins, proceedings, and results. A. D. 1799 to 1849* (London: Religious Tract Society, 1850), 199.

58. W. Jones, 582.

59. Peter Jones qtd. in W. Jones, 581.

60. See: Winona Stevenson, "The Journals and voices of a Church of England Native catechist: Askenootow (Charles Pratt), 1851-1884," *Reading beyond words: contexts for Native history*, edited by Jennifer S. H. Brown and Elizabeth Vibert (Peterborough, Ontario: Broadview Press, 1996), 304-329; and Hilary E. Wyss, *Writing Indians: literacy, Christianity and Native community in early America* (Amherst: University of Massachusetts Press, 2000).

61. W. Jones, 578.

62. Central Auxiliary Society, 30.

63. Central Auxiliary Society, 30.

64. Neil Semple, *The Lord's Dominion: the history of Canadian Methodism* (Montreal & Kingston: McGill-Queen's University Press, 1996), 3; For an excellent discussion on the central role that Methodist missionaries played in the shaping of nineteenth century Canadian Indian policy relating to education and civilizing, see: Anthony J. Hall, *The Red man's burden: land, law, and the Lord*

in the Indian affairs of Upper Canada, 1791-1858, Doctoral thesis, University of Toronto, 1984.

65. For more substantial discussion of the early history of the Methodist Book Room, see Janet B. Friskney, "Beyond the shadow of William Briggs part I: setting the stage and introducing the players," *Papers of the Bibliographical Society of Canada* 33.2 (1995): 121-163; and *Towards a Canadian "Cultural Mecca": the Methodist Book and Publishing House's pursuit of book publishing and commitment to Canadian writing, 1829-1926*, M.A. thesis, Trent University, 1994.

66. Semple, 239-240.

67. Semple, 367-368.

68. Anne M. Boylan, *Sunday school: the formation of an American institution 1790-1880* (New Haven: Yale University Press, 1988); Allan Greer, "The Sunday schools of Upper Canada," *Ontario History* 67.3 (1975): 169-184.

69. Semple, 368.

70. Legislative Assembly of the Province of Canada, *Report of the Special Commissioners appointed on the 8th September, 1856, to Investigate Indian Affairs in Canada* (Toronto: Stewart Derbishire & George Desbarats, 1858); John McLean, *The Hero of the Saskatchewan: life among the Ojibway and Cree Indians in Canada* (Barrie ON: Barrie Examiner Printing and Publishing House, 1891); John McLean, *The Indians: their manners and customs* (Toronto: William Briggs, 1889); National Council of Women of Canada, *Women of Canada: their life and work* (National Council of Women of Canada, 1900); Rev. John H. Pitezel, *Lights and shades of missionary life: containing travels, sketches, incidents, and missionary efforts, during nine years spent in the region of Lake Superior* (Cincinnati: Western Book Concern, 1860); Eugene Stock, *Metlakahtla and the North Pacific Mission of the Church Missionary Society* (London: Church Missionary House, 1880); S. Tucker, *The Rainbow in the North: a short account of the first establishment of Christianity in Rupert's Land by the Church Missionary Society* (London: James Nisbet and Co., 1851); Henry S. Wellcome, *The Story of Metlakahtla* (London and New York: American News Co., 1887); Rev. Edward F. Wilson, *Missionary work among the Ojebway Indians* (London: Society for Promoting Christian Knowledge, 1886); Egerton R. Young, *On the Indian trail: stories of missionary work among the Cree and Saulteaux Indians* (Toronto: Fleming H. Revell Company, 1897); Egerton Ryerson Young, *Stories from Indian wigwams and Northern camp-fires* (Toronto: William Briggs, 189?).

71. Indian Affairs, Province of Canada, *Report for the half-year ended 30th June, 1864* (Quebec: Hunter, Rose & Co., 1865), 25.

72. Wilson, 135.

73. McLean, *The Hero of the Saskatchewan*, 25, 45.

74. Young, *Stories from Indian wigwams and Northern camp-fires*, 104-108, 287-288; and Young, *On the Indian trail*, 87, 187; High literacy rates among the Cree in the nineteenth century are confirmed in: J. A. H. Bennett and J. W. Berry, *Cree Syllabic Literacy: cultural context and psychological consequences*. Tilburg University Monographs in Cross-cultural Psychology. (Tilburg: Tilburg University

Press, 1991); and Olive Patricia Dickason, *Canada's First Nations: a history of founding peoples from earliest times* (Toronto: McClelland and Stewart, 1994), 241.

75. Gerald M. Hutchinson, "Evans, James," *Dictionary of Canadian biography,* electronic edition; Further biographical information on Evans can also be found in: John Flood, editor, "The Diary of James Evans, July 11 - August 30, 1838: part one," *Northward Journal* 44 (1988): 4-26; John Flood, editor, "The Diary of James Evans, September 4 - November 20, 1838: part two," *Northward Journal* 45 (1988): 4-20; and Fred Landon, "Selections from the papers of James Evans, missionary to the Indians," *Papers and records* (Ontario Historical Society) XXVI (1930): 474-491; James Evans' papers are located in the archives of the J. J. Talman Regional Collection, D. B. Weldon Library, the University of Western Ontario; and the archives of the Pratt Library, Victoria University (University of Toronto).

76. J. J. Talman Regional Collection, D. B. Weldon Library, University of Western Ontario, Reverend James Evans letters 1829 - 1877, files 1-8.

77. J. J. Talman Regional Collection, D. B. Weldon Library, University of Western Ontario, Reverend James Evans letters 1829 - 1877, file 30, "Rev. Jonas Dodge, Lyons [New York], to Rev. James Evans, Fort Gratiot, Michigan Territory, 20 April 1835."

78. J. J. Talman Regional Collection, D. B. Weldon Library, University of Western Ontario, Reverend James Evans letters 1829 - 1877, file 52, "Rev. James Evans [to John Beecham, London]. Report re: St. Clair Indians in answer to Beecham's letter of 3 December 1835. Incomplete draft. [1836]."

79. Cree oral traditions indicate that the syllabic characters attributed to James Evans were actually a gift from Kisemanito (Creator) to the Cree people. It is said that Kisemanito gave the characters to the Elders Mistanaskowew and Machiminahtik. Mistanaskowew, or Badger Bull, was from the west, while Machiminahtik, or Hunting Rod, was from the east. The two Elders received the gift of syllabics at the same time, but independently of each other. Evans is said to have learned about the syllabics through the teachings of Mistanaskowew and Machiminahtik. For more, see: Samson Cree Nation, "Plains Cree language website," http://www.wtc.ab.ca/nipisihkopahk/ (Samson Reserve AB: Samson Cree Nation Reserve, 2000?) Accessed 10 June, 2002.

80. Hutchinson electronic edition; The Cree translations and syllabary prepared and printed by Evans at the Rossville Mission Press are listed and discussed at length in: John D. Nichols, "The composition sequence of the first Cree hymnal," *Essays in Algonquian bibliography in honour of V. M. Dechene,* edited by H. C. Wolfart (Winnipeg, 1984), 1-21; Bruce Peel, "Early mission presses in Alberta," *Alberta Library Association Bulletin* 11.1 (1963): 3-6; Bruce Peel, "How the Bible came to the Cree," *Alberta Historical Review* 6 (Spring 1958):15-19; Bruce Peel, "Rossville Mission Press: press, prints, and translators," *Papers of the Bibliographical Society of Canada* 1 (1962): 28-43; Bruce Peel, *Rossville Mission Press: the invention of the Cree syllabic characters, and the first printing in Rupert's Land* (Montreal: Osiris Publications, 1974); and David

H. Pentland, "The Rossville Mission dialect of Cree," *Essays in Algonquian bibliography in honour of V. M. Dechene*, edited by H. C. Wolfart (Winnipeg, 1984).

81. Jennifer S. H. Brown, "The Track to Heaven: the Hudson Bay Cree religious movement of 1842-1843," *Papers of the Thirteenth Algonquian Conference*, edited by William Cowan (Ottawa: Carleton University, 1982), 53-63.

82. Dickason, 241.

83. For examples of Aboriginal usages of syllabic characters for their own uses, see: Brown, "The Track to Heaven"; and Willard B. Walker, "Native writing systems," *Handbook of North American Indians, volume 17: languages*, edited by Ives Goddard (Washington: Smithsonian Institution), 158-184.

84. John S. Long, "The Reverend George Barnley and the James Bay Cree," *The Canadian Journal of Native Studies* VI.2 (1986): 313-331; Semple, 174-176.

85. United Church Archives, Wesleyan Methodist Missionary Society correspondence, "Barnley to Society, 20 January 1846."

86. National Archives of Canada, George Barnley fonds, "Barnley's Journal, 10 August 1842."

87. Brown, "The Track to heaven," passim.

88. Long, 317-318.

89. George Barnley's departure from Moose Factory in 1847 coincided with a general Methodist withdrawal from the north west as a whole. By the early 1850s the once strong Methodist influence in the region was erased. James Evans had left Norway House/Rossville in 1845 and his replacements, William and Sophia Mason, joined the Anglican Church Missionary Society in 1854. Robert Rundle, who had been stationed at Fort Edmonton and Rocky Mountain House among the Woodland Cree and First Nations of the plains, departed for England in 1848. For further discussion on the Methodist influence in and departure from the north west, see: John Webster Grant, *Moon of wintertime: missionaries and the Indians of Canada in encounter since 1534* (Toronto: University of Toronto, 1984), 96-118; and Neil Semple, *The Lord's dominion: the history of Canadian Methodism* (Montreal & Kingston: McGill-Queen's University Press, 1996), 148-178.

90. Grant, 114.

91. Joyce M. Banks, "The Church Missionary Society Press at Moose Factory: 1853-1859," *Journal of the Canadian Church Historical Society* XXVI.2 (1984): 69.

92. Wilbert R. Shenk, "Henry Venn's instructions to missionaries," *Missiology: an international review* 5.4 (1977): 474.

93. Shenk, 475.

94. *Church Missionary Gleaner* II.2 (February 1852): 24.

95. Horden's press is today on display in the Rare Books and Special Collections Division of the McGill University Libraries, in Montreal, Quebec.

96. Approximately £5.46 or $13.45 CAD in today's currency.

97. Banks, 75-76.

98. Banks, 73-74.

99. Grant, 111-112.

100. I borrow this expression from Elizabeth Hill Boone and Walter D. Mignolo, eds., *Writing without words: alternative literacies in Mesoamerica and the Andes* (Durham: Duke University Press, 1996).

101. Jack Goody, "Introduction," *Literacy in traditional societies*, ed. Jack Goody (Cambridge: Cambridge University Press, 1968), 2-3; Goody also asserts that Western Christianity is based on the notion that historical sensibility cannot exist without permanent written records. In societies without the written word, myth and history are seen as merging into one, where conceptualizations of the past are inevitably governed by the concerns of the present. In this understanding, "historical truth" cannot exist in societies without the written word (See Jack Goody, "The Consequences of literacy," *Literacy in traditional societies*, ed. Jack Goody (Cambridge: Cambridge University Press, 1968), 27-68). This understanding is flawed however, failing to recognize that understandings and interpretations of written records are inevitably influenced, to some degree, by contemporary cultural concerns and ideologies.

102. James Axtell, "The Power of print in the Eastern Woodlands," *The William and Mary Quarterly* S3-44 (1987): 300-309.

103. Peter Wogan, "Perceptions of European literacy in early contact situations," *Ethnohistory* 41.3 (1994): 407-429.

104. See Goody, 10-11.

105. Harvey J. Graff, *The Labyrinths of literacy: reflections on literacy past and present* (London: Falmer Press, 1987), 4-5.

106. Wogan insists that Axtell's shamanic thesis may begin to explain the phenomenon, but ethnographic approaches to literacy are needed in the investigation into the complexities of Aboriginal perceptions of Europeans. Also, Grant notes that the reasons Aboriginal peoples converted to Christianity are varied and complex. First Peoples were far from passive recipients in their relationships with missionaries that led to conversion. Factors influencing an Aboriginal community's desire to convert or resist conversion involved a complex intertwining of the state of economy and trade, settler relations, treaty negotiations, and the relative strength and ability of traditional beliefs within this mix to address the hardships of sickness and changing relationships with the land. Grant also notes that conversion took three forms: articulating and adopting Christianity to supplement traditional beliefs; fully assimilating to Christianity; and merely "saying yes, but meaning no," or accommodating Christianity so as to not humiliate the missionaries. See Grant, 239-241, 248-251.

107. Grant, 114-115.

108. This is not to say that the Catholic missions were unsuccessful in encouraging print literacy. David Pentland discusses an Ottawa letter written in 1845 to Algonquin chiefs at Oka, which was most likely written by a Catholic convert who had been schooled by French missionaries. See: David H. Pentland, "An Ottawa letter to the Algonquin chiefs at Oka," *Reading beyond words: contexts for Native history*, edited by Jennifer S.H. Brown and Elizabeth Vibert

(Peterborough: Broadview Press, 1996), 261-279.

109. Banks, *Books in Native languages*, x.

110. Even Hovdhaugen, ed., *... and the Word was God: missionary linguistics and missionary grammar* (Münster, Germany: Nodus Publikationen, 1996), 7.

111. NAC RG10, vol. 1936, file 3704, "Headquarters–Reverend P. E. Petitot of Montreal requesting monetary assistance to publish a dictionary and grammar of the Dene-Dindjie (Indian) language, 2 February 1875."

112. NAC RG10, vol. 3599, file 1536, "Printing and publishing of Cree and English and Blackfoot and English vocabularies, compiled by Reverend Fathers Hugonnard and Lacombe (Indian Commissioner for Manitoba and Northwest Territories), 1886-1891."

113. NAC RG10, vo. 3599, file 1536.

114. Rüdiger Schreyer, "Take your pen and write: learning Huron: a documented historical sketch," *... and the Word was God: missionary linguistics and missionary grammar*, Even Hovdhaugen, ed. (Münster, Germany: Nodus Publikationen, 1996), 87.

115. NAC RG10, vol. 3805, file 51372, "Northwest Territories–correspondence regarding the provision by the Department of Bibles and other religious books for the pupils of the Industrial schools, 1888."

3

First Quarter of the Twentieth Century

Books in the schools and Aboriginal literary initiatives

The Indian Affairs department and wider educational contexts

By the late nineteenth century, the Dominion government was beginning to take an active role in the education of Aboriginal peoples. Much of the task of cultural transformation and education had been placed in the hands of the missionary churches. Money and personnel at the disposal of the missionaries was limited, however, and progress in assimilating was as a result rather slow. In 1860 the Indian department was officially transferred to colonial control in the Canadas. It was one of the last services to be transferred, and the Canadian authorities accepted the responsibilities reluctantly, demonstrating the relative unimportance placed on the matter of Aboriginal affairs. Only following Confederation in 1867 was a clearly identifiable branch of the public service created for dealing with Indian affairs, granting the federal government responsibility for "Indians and lands reserved for the Indians." Rather than developing original or innovative initiatives, however, the Dominion chose to continue with existing policies and to build upon those which had been established before Confederation in the Canadas.

The Indian Act of 1876 served to consolidate existing legislation and allowed for its uniform application across the country, continuing with the tradition developed in Upper and Lower Canada of placing Aboriginal peoples in a distinct legal category and under the specific legal control of the federal government. Regarded as minors, Aboriginal peoples were conceptualized as wards of the federal government and deprived of the privileges of full citizenship. The Act of 1876 also granted considerable powers to the superintendent general (and later the minister) responsible for Indian Affairs and his representatives, ensuring that Aboriginal peoples were subjected to centralized bureaucratic regulation. Education, long understood as an effective instrument for transmitting new habits and beliefs key to the cultural transformation of Aboriginal populations, was in the decades that followed Confederation accelerated to accomplish these ends. The schools, however, continued to be run in conjunction with the Christian missions. For the department, this was seen as a way to save substantial funds. Funding, in fact, dictated in many ways most of the department's decisions through the late nineteenth and early twentieth centuries more than any legitimate concern for the affairs of Aboriginal peoples. Successive governments' budgetary allocations reflected the relative insignificance attached to the department, and also the widespread conviction among those in the public service that gratuitous aid should never be granted to able-bodied Aboriginal peoples, hoping to spur an incentive of self-sufficiency through the adoption of Western economic practices.[1]

Government policies on the schooling of First Peoples began systematically focusing on assimilation through residential education in this period, and within this context language training in English and French was pushed in a conscious attempt to suppress and eliminate Aboriginal languages. This language training, however, was effectively limited by the nature and range of the books and print materials available. The vocabularies, grammars, dictionaries, and religious literature employed by the missionaries and school teachers in their efforts to promote language training were intended to work in the interests of conversion and assimilation, but most books and textbooks presented to Aboriginal peoples were titles lifted from the provincial education curricula. Other texts were written with missionary audiences in mind, and were therefore poorly suited to Aboriginal students who came from widely different cultural and linguistic backgrounds.

Schooling in Aboriginal languages had been opposed for the most part from the onset of the education relationship, and training made available in English or French was utilitarian in nature, designed to promote conversion and civilized manners but little more. The Mohawk community at Tyendinaga (on the Bay of Quinté, east of Belleville), for instance, in 1843 made a request to Reverend Bishop John Strachan to be allowed to have a school where the Mohawk language would be used. The Mohawks even offered to pay for the cost of printing books in their language for use in the school, but the predominant ideology of the day dictated that First Peoples be schooled solely in the colonizers' language. Reverend Strachan had appealed earlier to the Church Missionary Society suggesting that his proposed university, King's College, extend its program to Aboriginal peoples, but with the idea that they be trained as missionaries who could return to their people and teach. The Church Missionary Society responded favorably, but such a program failed to emerge at King's College.[2]

In settler communities throughout the Dominion, the establishment of libraries that served the general public had become commonplace by the late nineteenth century. Most notably, Mechanics Institutes developed in this era to serve the educative and leisurely needs of skilled and working men, and by the later part of the century, many of these Institutes had been transformed into public libraries throughout English Canada. It was also in this era that joint library projects between schools and townships emerged in Ontario and later other provinces. But as library historian Peter F. McNally has noted, the school/township and Mechanics Institute libraries were problematic in their admitted attempts to collect only those books deemed "worthy." Their policies were rooted in the notions of literary merit and useful knowledge, and thus excluded popular literature and novels that were of interest to most readers. Unless works were written by canonically sanctioned writers such as Dickens, Thackeray, or Bunyan, popular works and novels were rarely included in such libraries, ultimately making them of little interest or attraction to a great number of people. The comparatively uneducated population for whom such libraries were designed, being the lower, middle, and immigrant classes, were particularly uninterested in such collections.[3]

Philosophies of formal education in the nineteenth century were rooted in elevating and assimilating the population through the structured provision of literacy, with the intention of ensuring peace, prosperity, and social cohesion.[4] Bruce Curtis has noted that township and school libraries in Canada West were similarly conceptualized by the province's Education Office in the 1840s and 1850s as political undertakings. Aimed at producing a "moral, peaceful, rational, and loyal population," these early public libraries were seen as tools in directing people's reading habits and abilities into "improving channels." Reading was recognized as influencing the formation of individual character and behavior, and these were seen to ultimately affect the larger social order. Regulated reading was conceptualized by the upper and middle classes as an instrument to morally uplift and educate the lower and immigrant classes, drawing them away from such deplorable hobbies as drinking and gaming.[5] Egerton Ryerson, a Methodist minister, was largely responsible for formulating and putting into practice these ideas of libraries and reading in the province.

The idea of regulating and managing the reading habits of the general population through libraries was undoubtedly influenced by Ryerson's Methodist beliefs and training. Such ideas were not limited to Methodists–Ryerson had a wide range of Canadian supporters and counterparts, as well as European and American, each sharing the view that the whole of the population could be brought to experiencing desirable middle class behavior and come to see it as pleasurable. As Curtis notes, "If the urge to read could be fostered in the colony, the provision of sound libraries would direct reading into safe and productive channels."[6] Underlying such notions were understandings of literacy as a promotional tool for the values, attitudes, and habits deemed essential to order, integration, cohesion, and progress. The mid- to late nineteenth century was a period that ideologically saw a number of "moral" and "liberal" reforms, such as popular schooling and institution building, of which libraries were a part. These established a network of educational, social, political, cultural, and economic relationships that would be central to the dominant ideologies and their theoretical and practical expressions characteristic of the late nineteenth and twentieth centuries. As Harvey Graff has noted, "Schooling, with its transmission of morally leavened and often qualitatively low levels of skills, became more and more a vital aspect of the maintenance of social stability–particularly during times of massive if confusing social and economic transformations–and a regular feature of the life course of the young."[7] Literacy, libraries, and schooling were the integrative and hegemonic tools of the social and economic leaders and social reformers of the nineteenth century, whose influence would be remarkably resilient. The Canada West example, however, demonstrates that the general public's interests in reading were not easily swayed to the notions of useful knowledge, nor were they immediately receptive to the Education Office's official catalogs of suggested books.

On a practical level, the general public whom the government hoped to reform considered useful knowledge to be "dull, boring, laborious and unpleasant," resulting in little use of the province's early public libraries.[8] Nonetheless, if they were not immediately successful, public libraries would eventually catch on, even if the philosophies behind them did not change much in the coming decades and new century. The province of Ontario adopted the country's first public library legislation in 1882, followed by British Columbia in 1891, Manitoba in

1899, Saskatchewan in 1906, Alberta in 1907, New Brunswick in 1929, Newfoundland (which did not enter Confederation as a province until 1949) and Prince Edward Island in 1935, Nova Scotia in 1937, Quebec in 1959, and the Northwest Territories in 1966. The very presence of books–be they in schools, public libraries, or people's homes—was seen as a weapon against levity and impropriety. Books were considered as important as their contents, having the potential to humanize and refine the minds of readers. Following 1900, public library development in Canada was spurred (as it was in the United States) by philanthropists, particularly Andrew Carnegie, who donated sufficient funds to the construction and maintenance of numerous libraries. Harvey Graff has demonstrated that one use of alphabetic literacy was to unite heterogeneous peoples and to eradicate or minimize the distinctions that separated classes and cultures.[9] Public libraries, in the late nineteenth and the first half of the twentieth century, served to foster Western understandings of literacy, and in doing so contributed to homogeneous notions of nation building in the name of unity, progress, and dominant perceptions of morality.

Libraries meant to serve Aboriginal populations first emerged in roughly the same era and within similar ideological contexts, although their development was complicated to a great extent by cultural complexities and federal-provincial jurisdictional differences surrounding education, library development, and the affairs of Aboriginal peoples. One might expect, considering the civilizing and assimilatory purposes of print used earlier by missionaries and government, that First Peoples' libraries would also be designed solely for the purposes of disseminating useful knowledge and furthering the acculturation process. This may have been the intention of government and missionaries, but from an Aboriginal perspective, libraries were articulated as serving quite different purposes.

Reading and writing for recreation, and the emergence of libraries in the Indian schools

It is in the late nineteenth century that libraries began to emerge in the Indian schools, constituting the first recognizable collections of the Western book devoted to serving Aboriginal audiences. Missionary-run schools had made use of the printed word and books for educative and assimilative purposes from the schools' very beginnings in the late eighteenth century. A great number of grammars, dictionaries, and vocabularies written and translated into Aboriginal languages by missionaries, although largely written for a missionary audience, were used in the schools with the intent of assisting the instruction of the English and French languages and exposing young children to Biblical literature for the purposes of religious conversion and "civilizing" Aboriginal populations.

One of the earliest schools established for Aboriginal children was at Fairfield on the Thames River in Upper Canada. Opened in 1793 among the Delaware by the Moravian missionary, Reverend David Zeisberger, the school instructed in both the English language and Delaware. Books in both languages were in use at the school, including Reverend Zeisberger's own work, *Essay of a Delaware-Indian and English spelling book*, first printed in Philadelphia in 1776.[10] Titles used in other schools and communities, like *A Primer for the use of Mohawk children to acquire the spelling and reading of their own*, with alphabetic text in Mohawk and English, printed in 1786 at Montreal by Daniel Claus, Deputy Superintendent of Indians in Canada (1760-1787), demonstrate that even if most titles were intended for missionary and non-Aboriginal audiences, an intent was certainly present in the missions and government to expose Aboriginal children to the written word from the very earliest experiments of printing in Aboriginal languages in Canada. Undoubtedly these titles were used in the schools and would have had an indelible effect on their students, both in terms of language and cultural means of communication.

Collections of books, however, that might be termed "libraries" were not conceived in the schools until the second half of the nineteenth century. The earliest concrete evidence of libraries emerging in the schools surfaces in 1884, when T. P. Wadsworth, Inspector of Indian Agencies in the North West Territories for treaties 4, 6, and 7, recommended for the Battleford Industrial School "that a children's library be established, containing interesting tales for boys; for the larger boys, the 'Boys Own Annual'; for the smaller, 'Chatterbox,' and similar books, in which they would, during the long winter evenings, be able to find both amusement and instruction."[11] Wadsworth's recommendation at the Battleford school alone is curious, considering that as Inspector for the whole of the treaties 4, 6, and 7 region, he was responsible for a number of schools. However, his initiative is spurred by the "large and, at present, cheerless room" that the school amounted to in 1884, suggesting that student spirit and interest in learning to read, write, and spell in English may have been waning in the present environment. Nine years later, in 1893, the library was finally established at the Battleford Industrial School. The Inspector noted: "There is a library in connection with the school, containing 111 volumes of useful reading; and the pupils are reported as making good use of the books. Rev. Mr. Clarke obtained these books from friends in England."[12] The Battleford school was under the missionary direction of the Anglican Church, but fully funded by the Dominion government. Reverend Clarke's efforts in procuring books from England almost certainly guarantees a religious and moral leaning to the volumes, but it is also of note that the government, while quick to recommend a library be established in 1884, was not involved in the selection or purchasing of the books, leaving that responsibility fully in the hands of the Anglican missionary. A reluctance on behalf of the government in procuring books or establishing libraries, either within the schools or without, is an important characteristic of the establishment of libraries for Aboriginal peoples. It would be well into the twentieth century before the federal government through the Department of Indian Affairs would take an active interest in libraries and books as "civilizing" and educative tools. Libraries emerging in the late nineteenth and early twentieth centuries resulted through the efforts of the missions, individual philanthropists, or Aboriginal peoples themselves.

Throughout the late 1890s, numerous schools began reporting the emergence of libraries, seemingly following the lead of the Battleford Industrial School. C. W. Whyte, Principal at the Crowstand Boarding School, North West Territories in 1896, reported "We have a library of upwards of one hundred and fifty volumes, containing many of the very best and latest publications for children." Two years later the Crowstand library was reportedly the same size, and was said to be most popular during the winter months.[13] Also in 1896, A. J. McLeod, Principal at the Round Lake School in the North West Territories, reported "school libraries are used to advantage outside of school hours," and noted that it is one of the intentions of the school to "foster a love for reading." Students at the Round Lake School, under the direction of a teacher, also issued a semi-monthly school newspaper, significantly entitled *Progress*, of which a thousand copies were regularly printed: "The paper continues to be edited by Mr. Munro. It is eagerly read by the children, and brings us about sixty exchanges, most of which are also read and appreciated."[14] Newspaperman P. G. Laurie provided equipment and instruction in typesetting and printing for a time during the 1890s at the Battleford school, and in other western and northern schools the literary trade was taught. Students at Port Simpson published *Na-Na-Kwa*; at Alert Bay, *The Thunderbird*; at Blue Quill's, *Mocassin Telegraph*; at Kootenay, *The Chupka*; at Alberni, *Western Eagle*; and at Chooutla, *Northern Lights*.[15] At the Kitimaat Residential

School, some of the girls were taught aspects of the printing trade and produced a six or eight page quarterly which included local news with "printed historical sketches, Indian legends, church news, shipping news, births, marriages, deaths, and railway surveys."[16]

The Regina Industrial School in this same period boasted skilled trade instruction for boys as printers. A photograph of some of these Regina pupils appeared in the Indian Affairs department's *Annual report* for 1896.[17] The Industrial School in Regina reported two years later that "The daily papers are made use of and an interest fostered in present history. The books of the school library, all carefully selected, are in demand, especially during the winter."[18] In the midst of reporting on enforcement of English as the sole language of instruction in his school in 1897, Principal A. Naessens of the High River Industrial School in Alberta notes that "weekly newspapers are used for supplementary reading" and "A library has been founded.... Good use has been made of the books purchased, and it has created a love for reading among the pupils ... some of them subscribe on their own account for the Calgary papers on their discharge, and others 'club' their earnings to subscribe to papers for next winter."[19] The Wikwemikong Industrial School on Manitoulin Island in Ontario reported the founding of a library also in 1897; while the Kootenay Industrial School at the St. Eugene Mission in British Columbia noted that students "have a library of choice books, and delight in reading or listening to interesting stories."[20] The Mohawk Institution industrial school at the Six Nations community in Ontario and the St. Mary's Mission Boarding School at Mission City, British Columbia came on board with libraries in 1899, while in that same year the Qu'Appelle Industrial School in the North West Territories, noted that library books are "well patronized."[21]

At the turn of the century in 1900, the Pine Creek Boarding School at Winnipegosis, and the Birtle Boarding School at Birtle, Manitoba, reported libraries followed by the Shingwauk and Wawanosh Homes at Sault Ste. Marie, Ontario and the Crooked Lake School in the North West Territories in 1901. The Lytton (St. George's) Industrial School at Lytton, British Columbia, and the St. Albert Boarding School near Edmonton, followed suit in 1903.[22] Also in 1903, there is clear evidence of philanthropic support in the establishment of a school library at the Port Simpson (Crosby) Girls' Home at Port Simpson, British Columbia. The Principal, Hannah M. Paul reported, "Through the donation of a friend we have started a library for the home besides the books owned by individual pupils."[23] Paul's report also constitutes a unique occasion where the students are noted to own their own books. It is of interest to

A group of students reported to be in training as printers at the Regina Industrial School in 1896. (Photograph from Dominion of Canada, *Annual report of the Department of Indian Affairs for the year ended 30th June 1896*, page 350)

note that while the emergence of libraries was common in the schools in this period, the only school to repeatedly and consistently report expenditures relating to their library was the Mohawk Institute. In 1905, the Lytton Industrial School would also report modest expenditures relating to their library, but at no other time in the late nineteenth and early twentieth centuries would any other Indian schools report having spent any funds on the maintenance of their libraries.

In almost every case where books and libraries are reported by the Indian agents, superintendents, and school officials from the 1890s onward, their use is framed in the context of reading for recreation and during leisure time. The winter season is repeatedly cited as the most likely time for the students to use school libraries, pointing to the notion that reading and books were deemed as recreational and leisurely pursuits when outdoor activities and instruction were limited. From the missions' and school officials' perspectives, it was important that Aboriginal children (much like their non-Aboriginal working, immigrant, lower and middle class contemporaries) be busily involved in "useful" and "morally acceptable" recreational pursuits that would supplement the goals of their classroom instruction. Reverend O. Charlebois, Principal at the Duck Lake Boarding School in Saskatchewan notes, "A children's library, of the very best literary and moral character, has been added to the class equipment. The children are very fond of reading, and we notice a marked improvement in their oral expressions and written compositions"; while Reverend Arthur Barner at the Industrial School in Red Deer, Alberta reports that reading is "one of the favourite forms of recreation" of the pupils at that institution.[24] Evidence of Aboriginal children reading and showing interest in books and libraries for recreational purposes within the controlled setting of the schools were cited by Indian Agents, superintendents, and school officials as proof of the progressive and lasting effects of an education curriculum whose purpose was that of assimilation. As tools of Western understandings of literacy, knowledge, history, communication, and religion, books and libraries were seen to be central in the civilizing, assimilatory, and conversion endeavors of the mission and Dominion government schools. That Aboriginal children were seemingly self-motivated to read and employ libraries compiled by missionaries within a school setting outside of the classroom experience was positive proof to the missions and government that these colonial endeavors were taking root.

That the relatively new schools of western Canada appear to have been the first and most commonly found institutions to build libraries in the late nineteenth and early twentieth centuries is of some interest. Clearly these schools were built by the missions and Dominion government with some awareness of the nature and quality of Indian education in the eastern parts of the country. Further, their emergence in this period also coincided with conscious efforts by non-Aboriginal education planners in most provinces to develop and include libraries within their institutions, and the education of Aboriginal children from a curricular perspective was often based on provincial models.[25] Relatively new schools, like the Battleford, Crowstand, and High River (Dunbow) Industrial schools, would have been built with space enough to accommodate small libraries, whereas the older schools in eastern Canada would have had more difficulty from a spatial point of view.

In part these reasons explain the regional differences in the development of libraries for Aboriginal peoples, but of some significance to the fact that the western schools first reported their establishment and recreational use it must also be considered that the Western book form and understandings of literacy were generally more firmly rooted and culturally understood by many of the First Peoples in the west. This was most clearly illustrated in the sixty years preceding the founding of the Industrial schools with the spread of the syllabic system attributed to Reverend James Evans. Evans' syllabic form of recording the Cree and Ojibwe languages was likely derived from existing forms of Aboriginal written communication practices in the north west, which in large part explained the dramatic speed at which literacy in the syllabary spread throughout the region following Evans' arrival in 1840. A familiarity with the notion of written forms of communication, similar to those being perpetuated by the European-educated missionaries and government officials demonstrated in Evans' relationship with the Cree, must be considered as factoring into turn of the century reports by Indian Agents and school officials that Aboriginal children in western Canada took first to recreational reading and library use. The pre-existing cultural practices and understandings of First Peoples in the west may very well have facilitated what came to be understood by missionaries and government educators as "civilized" practices of recreational reading.

Aboriginal literacy in the Western script, colonialism, and libraries

One of the earliest references to a recognizable library within any of the schools in the eastern part of Canada is that of the Mohawk Institution industrial school at the Six Nations community on the Grand River in Ontario. In a report by the school's superintendent, R. Ashton, dated August 1898, it is noted that the school clearly has a library, and an upper story of the boys play-house contains a reading room: "Those who prefer to read are furnished with magazines and books from the school library, the boys have daily newspapers sent to their reading-room."[26] By the late nineteenth century, the Mohawk Institute had been in operation for several years and reading had come to be defined in recreational as well as educational terms. This encouraged the establishment of libraries containing reading materials not limited to religious instruction and the teaching of English grammar and vocabulary. Earlier reports of the establishment of a library for the use of Aboriginal peoples in the region in 1825 by individuals associated with the Protestant-based Religious Tract Society may also have been influential in the later efforts at the Mohawk Institute.[27] The Religious Tract Society's library, if it existed, is not known to have survived as late as the 1890s, but it may have laid some of the groundwork for the Institute's library.

The Mohawk Institute at Six Nations produced one of the first Aboriginal scholars and professionals, by Western standards, in one Oronhyatekha, M.D., also known as Peter Martin. Oronhyatekha attended the Institute between 1851 and 1854, where he reportedly learned to read and write in English. The Institute at the time was run and supervised by the Anglican Reverends Nelles and Elliot, who were also quite influential in the general operations of the Six Nations community. Oronhyatekha, after leaving the Institute, pursued a medical degree at the University of Toronto and Oxford University, becoming a medical doctor in 1866. In 1878 he was admitted to the International Order of Foresters, a fraternal society, and in 1881 became the first Canadian director of the Order, a position he held until his death in 1907. In his educational endeavors and professional career, Dr. Oronhyatekha challenged the racial barriers of his time and articulated in his own way the Victorian values of his professional colleagues, all the while maintaining a clear sense of his Mohawk identity.[28] As a writer, Dr. Oronhyatekha was widely published, often promoting the Mohawk people as a part of contemporary Victorian society. He also collected a wide array of Aboriginal items that emphasized the equality of First Peoples and non-Aboriginal colonizers. In a 1904 catalog of his historical, museum-like collection and library, he states: "In looking at all these specimens ... we must not forget when and by whom they were made and estimate the implements at their value to their original owners, as the product of their industry and patient skill."[29]

Dr. Oronhyatekha, in his academic, professional, and leisurely pursuits, illustrated an example of an Aboriginal person who demonstrated the means to articulate, select, and invent from the materials and practices most often associated with the increasingly dominant and influential non-Aboriginal Victorian culture of the nineteenth century while at the same time carefully maintaining and asserting his Aboriginal identity. This feat is most obviously illustrated in Oronhyatekha's persistent use of his Mohawk name, which is evident in almost all correspondence and reference to the Doctor throughout his lifetime. Oronhyatekha's successes also demonstrate the potential available in the Protestant-based education provided at the Mohawk Institute and similar institutions. Regrettably however, the Doctor's successes were also the exception, rather than the rule, as the great majority of students of the mission and government-run schools did not match Oronhyatekha's successes in integrating Aboriginal cultures and the culture of the colonizers. Nonetheless, on occasion, students like Oronhyatekha would emerge from the schools, employing their training in Western literacy and knowledge systems to their benefit as Aboriginal peoples.

Prior to the late nineteenth century, the possession of books by First Peoples was heavily influenced and limited by the interests of missionaries and readers' language capabilities. Further, their literacy rates in reading, writing, and comprehending alphabetic text did not fully develop overnight. Except in such cases as hieroglyphic and syllabic writing, the alphabetic literacy rates of most First Peoples in Western modes of knowledge transfer had only begun to emerge at a functional level by the late nineteenth century. D. F. McKenzie has noted that the use of books and literacy rates in alphabetic text among the Maori in nineteenth century New Zealand, for example, were greatly exaggerated by missionaries in that colony. McKenzie notes that English missionaries in New Zealand reported to their superiors in London precisely what they wanted to hear, and what they themselves wanted to believe–that the Maori had, in a mere twenty-five years, reduced their speech to alphabetic forms, achieved literacy in reading and writing alphabetic text, shifted their mode of communication and record keeping from memory to written record, accepted the mark of a signature as a sign of full comprehension of a legal commitment, and surrendered their notions of time, place, and person in an oral culture to the presumed permanency of the written or printed word. Realistically, however, most Maori had achieved only minimal competency in reading and writing alphabetic text in the time that the missionaries reported they had achieved full literacy and comprehension of the script.[30]

As was the case among the Maori in New Zealand, book ownership or perusal outside of the classroom and church experience by most First Peoples in the Canadas throughout most of the nineteenth century was sparse because literacy rates in the Western mode of knowledge transfer were minimal and still in the midst of developing. Missionary accounts of Aboriginal abilities to read and write and an eagerness to possess books were tainted by the missionaries' own wishes and misreadings of what they understood to be fully functional and comprehending literacy in the Western script. The teaching of reading and writing in alphabetic text that most Aboriginal peoples were subjected to in the mission schools and church settings was elementary at best. Given that elementary instruction in reading is primarily oral/aural, rather than visual, because it involves pronouncing and repeating letters, syllables, and words, it is not hard to imagine how oral repetition from memory might be misinterpreted as reading. With a knowledge system traditionally based in part on oral traditions, most First Peoples would have had retentive memories. Furthermore, the schools, with limited numbers of books at their disposal, relied predominantly on group teaching, which would have reinforced the use of memory rather than facilitating what the missionaries perceived as literacy.

Cultural complexities of communication aside, considering the nature of most reading material available at the time, it is not likely that many Aboriginal individuals or families possessed or encountered more than one or two titles at the absolute most. Ojibwe Methodist missionary, Reverend Peter Jones, in his description of the success of the Mississauga Credit River settlement in 1836, notes that the families there had comfortable houses and furniture, including "small shelves fastened against the wall for their books," although he does not mention the existence of any actual titles.[31] The choice of books available to Aboriginal peoples at the time in their own languages were entirely evangelical in nature and presented in the Roman alphabet. Any titles in their possession would have been Bibles or religious literature recommended to them by resident or visiting missionaries, and their presentation in alphabetic text likely meant that without schooling, few Aboriginal people would have taken an interest in such books. Furthermore, the nature of the education provided at the missionary and government-run schools was not very literary in nature. Although a good number of Aboriginal children were sent by their parents willingly to schools in order to learn "the whiteman's magic art of writing,"[32] the schooling they received was not geared to this sort of learning. Mike Mountain Horse, a day school student in the north west in the late 1890s recalled, "I do not remember any book learning acquired there."[33] With their focus more firmly rooted in religious, mechanical, and agricultural training suited to assimilate through preparing the boys to work as tradesmen, and the girls to be efficient housewives or domestic workers, the reading abilities of most graduates would have been questionable at best. Low quality education did not produce many highly skilled readers–in any language. An 1810 report from the Six Nations community notes the difficulty faced by teachers and readers alike in procuring adequate reading material:

> many who have learnt to read and write are not better for it unless they continue to read after they have left school. This is an objection of a nature which I fear is but too common; for they cannot have any great number of Books: & it is needless to add that the improvement of those who cannot get access to these few, must necessarily be inconsiderable & ... their writing can be of little use unless they read to furnish materials for writing: the principal Books which they have are Milton Popes Homer [sic] & a bible [sic] And in general they are very few....[34]

It is thus doubtful that any significant number of Aboriginal peoples did much reading beyond the scriptures, religious translations, and perhaps newspapers at school or elsewhere, as little more was made available to them and there would have been little incentive to do so. As the missionary John West observed in 1822, "Reading and writing will gain them but little credit ... [but if one] ... has learned to mend a gun, he will be highly respected."[35]

Reading and books were explicitly tied to Christianity and Western notions of civilizing in the eyes of most First Peoples. While a good number of Aboriginal children were sent to schools willingly, others were reluctant, seeing Western literacy in book reading and its ties to Christianity as a highly suspicious activity. Culturally, Western notions of books and reading were often suspected by Aboriginal elders and community leaders to undermine traditional methods of knowledge transfer and maintaining history and memory.[36] This resulted in instances of reluctance to send children to missionary and government-run schools, as is illustrated in the following example from the Six Nations community:

> there is a School in Mohawk village. when the hunting season is over some send their children to it; they are merely taught to write & read; ... many of the old men are not certain whether this School is of use or not–for some by learng. [sic] to read not only become idle, but contracts habits of Idleness which prevent them from excelling in the [...?] They also object & this is a remarkable objection, that while they are under the care of the Schoolmaster their manners are neglected;...[37]

Elders and community leaders had good reason to be suspicious of the missionary and government officials intentions of educating Aboriginal children, as the assimilative and conversion mandates of the schools has been well documented.[38] The school curriculums were clearly designed in the interests of recreating and reshaping the ontology of Aboriginal children, resocializing them to become "civilized" citizens. Maintaining and encouraging student attendance at the schools was difficult throughout their histories, as parents were sometimes known to resist sending their children to school and many children would run away from the schools if they attended at all. Within this educational environment, a willingness to become literate in English and French and master Western modes of communication was absent in a great number of First Peoples. The schools became increasingly successful at devaluing traditional Aboriginal cultural practices, but failed miserably to provide any significant or constructive cultural alternative.

Aboriginal writers who emerged out of the nineteenth century, such as George Copway,[39] Peter Jacobs,[40] and Peter Jones,[41] wrote in a Christian tradition as converts to Western religious and cultural traditions. Educated as Methodists, Copway, Jacobs, and Jones wrote almost exclusively for non-Aboriginal audiences in English, and their subject matter (with the possible exception of some of Copway's writing) was evangelical in nature. Their writings served to tell the history of the Ojibwe nation within Christian contexts that were understandable and marketable to European audiences. Hilary E. Wyss notes that such writing was employed by some Christian Indians as a means of recording thought and identity–at once participating within the structures of colonial society, but at the same time remaining rooted in traditional identity and spirituality. Wyss notes, "Literacy was for many Natives the means through which they acknowledged their participation in the larger colonial world. By writing their own narratives of conversion, Natives were defining their place in a newly forming colonial structure, positioning themselves simultaneously as Native Americans and as colonial subjects."[42] Such activity constituted an act of articulating and integrating the Western colonial technology of alphabetic writing for the purposes of engaging on the coloniser's terms, while at the same time maintaining a sense of Aboriginal identity. Copway and Jones, in their writings for instance, voice subtle yet powerful assertions of First Peoples' conceptions of their inherent rights to the land. Copway notes in the case of the Ojibwe, "The hunting grounds of the Indians were secured by right, a law and custom among themselves. No one was allowed to hunt on another's land, without invitation or permission."[43] Similarly, Jones asserts, "Each tribe or body of Indians has its own range of country, and sometimes each family its own hunting grounds, marked out by certain natural divisions ... all the game within these bounds are considered their property.... It is at the peril of an intruder to trespass on the hunting grounds of another."[44] Both Copway and Jones, understanding that their audience would be largely, if not solely, non-Aboriginal, included such commentary throughout their writings interspersed with descriptions of their people's conversions to Christianity. And through the very format of their testaments, in book form, Copway and Jones explicitly demonstrated to Western audiences the progress and fruits of civilization, seen to be brought to them through mission work and schooling. Writing became a central means of negotiating with European colonialism. Through writing, alphabetic literacy, and the eventual formation of libraries, some Aboriginal peoples took steps to control in part the construction of their identities within the contexts of colonialism and Western understandings of communication.

By the late nineteenth century and the early part of the twentieth century, a good number of Aboriginal peoples had been subjected as children and young adults to the missionary and government-run schools. After more than one hundred years of schooling and efforts by missionaries to assimilate through education and language training, individuals inevitably began to emerge who could read and write relatively well in the languages and texts of the colonizers, and increasingly the use and knowledge of Aboriginal languages was on the decline. Book publishing with an Aboriginal audience in mind had also begun to change in character. Increasingly, Aboriginal languages were used less and less in published books as missionary and government printers focused their attentions on eliminating Aboriginal languages in favor of English and French. The libraries that began to emerge in the later part of the nineteenth and early twentieth centuries were developed at a critical time in the history of First Peoples and non-Aboriginal relationships—when Aboriginal languages and cultures were seriously threatened and perhaps on the verge of succumbing to the dominant colonial influence. Libraries, under these circumstances, emerged as educational tools for cultural and political purposes. From a government and missionary perspective, libraries and books could be used clearly as instruments of social control and cultural assimilation. But for some Aboriginal people, books and libraries also emerged to suit their interests as subtle tools of resisting colonial threats and for political and social gain. Having been schooled in a Western tradition, where alphabetic writing and literacy were the preferred means of communication, some Aboriginal people recognized the strategic values of mastering Western understandings of literacy and employing the printed word for their own purposes.

"An Indian National Library": The Indian Affairs departmental library and the efforts of Charles A. Cooke, 1893-1926

On 1 March 1893, a young Mohawk originally from Kanesatake, named Charles Angus Cooke, was hired as a clerk within the Records Branch of the Indian Affairs department with the responsibility of classifying documents and acting as a translator and interpreter for the Iroquois dialects.[45] In late December of that same year, Duncan Campbell

Scott, then the Chief Accountant at Indian Affairs, announced that he had "commenced the organization of a library in connection with [the] Dept."[46] The department's hiring of Cooke and the establishment of a departmental library in the same year is not merely coincidence. Cooke's involvement with the Department included efforts to organize a library, manage its records, and effectively collect works relating to First Peoples in Canada for the research uses of departmental employees. While the Department in general was around this time recognizing the benefits of effectively collecting and organising its records,[47] Cooke's efforts stand out as an attempt to bring the knowledge and ideas of Aboriginal peoples into the educational and policy realm of Indian Affairs. His efforts also illustrate an instance of Aboriginal articulation and integration of the Western form of information and knowledge preservation. Through his initiatives, Cooke intended to build an "Indian National Library" that would be built encompassing both the knowledge and interests of the Department of Indian Affairs and First Peoples.

In January 1904, almost ten years after his hiring, Cooke wrote to the Honourable Clifford Sifton, Minister of the Interior, suggesting that the Indian Affairs department should properly organize its collection of books, accept contributions from Aboriginal peoples, and provide free and open circulation of its materials to members of the Department and status Indians. In his position as a records clerk, Cooke had the responsibility of interpreting, translating, and classifying documents in the Department's possession that were in the Iroquoian dialects. Additionally, he was supplementing his duties as a clerk in compiling a history of Aboriginal cultures and languages, and he thought Indian Affairs ought to be collecting literature and building archives relating to and originating from Aboriginal peoples. Cooke's highly progressive suggestions included:

> 1. An Indian National Library of literature ... might be established.
> 2. That such a library be established and maintained under the control of the Department of Indian Affairs, at Ottawa, owing to the peculiar parental relationship which the Department holds with the Indians, it would be a fitting custodian of such a Library.
> 3. A fund might be established out of which the books, etc, could be purchased–probably five hundred dollars would be ample to make a good start. It would of course be for those interested to consider and suggest the best means of raising the amount necessary, whether by individual sub-

scription, pro rate charged on Indian funds, or by some
other means.
4. That a portion of the Library might be made circulating
especially where possible to reach accredited Indians
through the Agents.[48]

Cooke's initiatives in gathering support for the cause of his Indian National Library were most impressive. Recognizing that a great deal of
knowledge and records were "in the possession of bands scattered
throughout the Dominion, and others ... published in book form, issued
in small editions, and having a limited circulation, and so are gradually
lost to succeeding generations," Cooke went to great efforts to write to
rare book dealers, missionaries, and members of band councils across
the country, asking for suggestions and their support of his project. For
his efforts, he collected no less than twelve letters of support from band
representatives, and numerous other positive responses from missionaries, Indian Agents, book dealers, and other interested parties, including
the glowing support of John Mawson, a Naturalist with the Geological
Survey of Canada, who observed: "It has always been a great matter of
surprise to me that no safe repository for the preservation of our native
Indian records should exist in Canada, and the only point in your circu-
lar which I do not entirely agree with is the use of the word 'might' in
the several clauses."[49] Josiah Hill, writing from the Ohsweken Council
House at Six Nations, notes: "I have consulted two or three Chiefs upon
the subject ... and they all seem to think that it would be a benefit to the
Indians if such establishment could be carried out conveniently, and I
quite agree with them."[50] Also from the Six Nations Reserve, Chief J.
W. M. Elliott adds, "I have spoken to some of our most intelligent and
influential Chiefs about the project of starting an Indian Library in connection with the Department of Indian Affairs and like my self they are
in favour of it."[51]

As this range of support would indicate, Cooke's vision was
clearly understood outside of the Department of Indian Affairs to be of
great historical, social, and political value.[52] However, Sifton transferred the matter of an Indian National Library to the responsibility of
Duncan Campbell Scott, the Department's accountant at the time, who
effectively dismissed the most progressive of Cooke's suggestions
within a month before the clerk could even effectively build his case.
Scott responded with favorable comments relating to Mr. Cooke, describing him as "an intelligent young Mohawk who takes great interest
in matters affecting his race, and his influence I am sure is always

Charles Angus Cooke (Thawennensere, or Da-ha-wen-nen-se-re) (1870-1958)
in 1952, at the age of 82 (Photograph courtesy of The American Philosophical
Society).

exerted for good," but unfavorably dismissed Cooke's ideas regarding
his vision of an Indian National Library: "There is certainly an idea at
the bottom of this scheme of his which is worth considering, but ... it
has no great practical utility in its present form. There are two features
which should not be adopted as part of an official scheme; I do not
think the Indians ought to contribute, and I do not think the library
should be circulating."[53] As was the case with an overwhelming number
of crucially important decisions made by Scott during his tenure, the
matter was refused on the grounds of its potential cost.[54] Although Scott
undoubtedly presumed he was working in the best interests of First
Peoples, his predominant fiscal concerns give an impression of a general lack of concern relating to the livelihood and aspirations of Aboriginal peoples, resulting in, as was the case in Cooke's proposal, ample
opportunity lost. Cooke's Indian National Library might have made a
significant contribution towards fostering relations between the department and Aboriginal peoples, and provided a priceless contribution to
future scholars and researchers, had it not been shrugged off at such an
early date.[55]

Nonetheless, Cooke's suggestions had considerable influence on Scott, resulting in the formation of a workable departmental library. From the time that the Department's collection of books and journals was first envisioned in 1893, until 1904, the library stood as a small collection of ethnographic reports and similar publications (many being American in origin) collected mostly by D. C. Scott and later, Frank Pedley, for the use of select Department employees. The collection was not organized in any useful way, nor was there a librarian or other individual charged with its care and maintenance.[56] When Cooke expressed his ideas about the library in 1904, Scott was quick to dismiss his suggestions relating to Aboriginal contributions to and uses of the collection: "I think Mr. Cook [sic] will find that the existing records of the Indian tribes in Canada are meagre and not of much importance." Scott, however, was prompted by Cooke's suggestions to turn what had amounted to an unorganized collection of books and journals into an organized library under the supervision of a librarian:

> I think we should have a library in the Department which would contain books dealing with the early history of the country in which the Indians played such an important part; works of value relating to ethnology, folk-lore, dictionaries, vocabularies, and books in native languages, etc. It would not cost very much to gradually amass a serviceable set of works upon all these subjects.... I may say that the Parliamentary Library is not very well equipped in this special section.
>
> I must point out the difficulty of properly administering the library. All the books now in the Department should be collected and kept together; they should be under the custody of some competent person and should be kept under lock and key and be subject to ordinary library regulations. I would be glad to take the supervision of any purchases ... and Mr. Stewart, the Assistant Secretary, should be librarian as he has a working knowledge of the literature in these subjects. Hardly a month passes in which I do not see in some collector's catalogue one or more books of interest at moderate prices which we should have in our Department.[57]

However, while Cooke suggested that a yearly budget of $500 would be the minimal amount of funding needed to organize and build the collection, Scott directed that $200 a year be allotted to the library.

Scott, obviously recognizing the merit in Cooke's suggestions relating to collecting and organising works of historical value, also or-

dered that Department records scheduled for transfer to the Dominion
Archives should be copied and kept for future reference within the Department:

> We have in the Department a number of valuable old re-
> cords which should be of great service which we are now
> directed to hand over to the Dominion Archivist. The con-
> tents of these should be thoroughly sifted and copies made
> of the most interesting. We should also have copies of all
> the documents and letters referring directly to Indian sub-
> jects which may now be in the Archives. These should be
> copied from time to time at small expense upon uniform
> paper, bound, and indexed so that in short time, if the mat-
> ter were properly carried out, we could have a complete
> basis for a history of the Indians of North America under
> British Rule.... I think if we give careful attention to a li-
> brary of Indian literature and a repository for copies of all
> Indian archives, we shall be doing a useful and necessary
> work.[58]

Scott's insistence and belief, however, that the records and reflections
of Aboriginal peoples themselves were not valuable or worthy of con-
sideration was unfortunate. Succumbing to the common Western belief
that history does not exist unless it is written (and for that matter, by
individuals of European descent), Scott effectively killed Cooke's suggestion that First Peoples' own understandings of their histories and
visions of the future be included in the Department's library. In striking
out Cooke's progressive suggestion, Scott closed the Department to the
inclusion of Aboriginal histories and ideas, overlooking and dismissing
what could very well have been an invaluable undertaking that may
have had the potential to produce positive effects on the future relationship and lines of communication between Indian Affairs and Aboriginal
peoples.[59]

Although his ideas were not considered to be of great vision or
value in the eyes of Scott and the decision makers at Indian Affairs at
the time, Cooke continued to work subtly, every now and then gathering materials for the library, and attempting to do good in the interests
of First Peoples as an employee working within the department. By August of 1904, Cooke suggested that all photographs taken for inclusion
in the Department's annual reports be included and cataloged in the
library, noting that "A collection of this kind would, in years to come,
prove very interesting and useful."[60] Less than a year after Cooke's initiatives and Scott's decision to establish a proper library, the collection

was still not properly cataloged or organized in such a way so as to be readily accessible. Cooke thus issued a memorandum in November, commenting that although a number of books had been collected for the library, Department personnel desiring to use the collection were still waiting to do so because the uncataloged and unorganized collection was inaccessible and scattered throughout the Department: "I beg leave to suggest that some one be now designated ... as Librarian. The books should be catalogued, and those which are now in the Secretary's Rooms should be placed with those recently acquired."[61] Access issues to the collection for Department employees working under Scott and Pedley were clearly frustrating. Not only was Scott's vision of a library one of a collection "kept under lock and key," but materials were apparently dispersed throughout the Department and apparently only available to select officials. Cooke's interests in building a workable and accessible departmental library appear to be rooted in a desire to provide the tools for Department employees, beyond the Deputy Superintendent General and the accountant, to access information and make educated decisions and to encourage consultation and exchange ideas with Aboriginal peoples whose knowledge may have provided unique insight and vision to the department.

Without outside Aboriginal involvement, the library developed instead as one might expect throughout the next twenty-five years. The vast majority of all publications ordered for the collection were chosen by Duncan Campbell Scott, and the library contained no surprises.[62] Titles ordered following 1904 were largely representative of non-Aboriginal interpretations of Aboriginal histories, cultures, and languages, and a seemingly disproportionate number of titles had little or nothing at all to do specifically with First Peoples–*Canadian men and women of the time* (1906), *Catalogue of Canadian plants* (1916), and *Birds of Canada* (1926) serve as examples of works of a more general interest, widely available in seemingly less specialized collections. In a 1918 letter to the Associate Director of Public Information, Scott describes the library as follows: "Our catalogue is a card catalogue, and I regret, therefore, that there is no copy available ... our library consists in the main of volumes dealing with the history of the native tribes of North America, including many Ethnological and Anthropological works. We have also a number of volumes treating with the general history of the country, particularly the earlier periods in which the Indians of Canada played a prominent part."[63] The library remained quite small throughout Scott's tenure with the Department, and operated on the slimmest of budgets. B. Parker is given as the librarian in 1924, with a collection size of 1,189–all for reference purposes. Parker reportedly received no salary as librarian, and was thus charged with the care of the library in addition to other, seemingly more important duties. Further, the librarian reports no receipts and no expenditures in connection with the library in that year (the only year for which such a report is available).[64] Clearly Cooke's grand vision of an Indian National Library failed to develop during his time of employment with the Department. Instead, a rather small collection emerged that was only available to employees of the Department headquarters in Ottawa. Although it contained many books relating to Aboriginal peoples, the library also included a number of titles that would have been included in a much more generalized collection. Budgetary concerns dominated any selection of materials that did take place, and the collection was under the guardianship of only a part-time and unpaid librarian at best. In 1938, twelve years following the retirement of Charles A. Cooke and his efforts in lobbying on behalf of a departmental library, the collection was considered to be of even lesser value, much as it had existed before 1904: "I would state that there is no organisation in connection with the library in the Indian Affairs Branch. It is not a circulating library but rather a private collection of books for the use of the Branch. There is no librarian in charge."[65]

Although his proposed Indian National Library failed to emerge, Cooke's initiatives as an employee of Indian Affairs were characterized by a consistent lobbying in the interests of First Peoples, and an apparent expectation and hope that the relationship between Indian Affairs and Aboriginal peoples could be one rooted in cooperation, equality, and fair consultation. Upon his hiring in March of 1893, Cooke (Da-ha-wen-nen-se-re or Thawennensere), was one of the first Aboriginal employees of the Dominion government's Indian Affairs department.[66] He would remain in their service within the Records Branch, first as a temporary clerk, until his retirement in 1926, by which time he had attained the title of Principal Clerk. During his tenure as an employee of the Department of Indian Affairs, Cooke was a key figure not only in the establishment of the Department's library, but also in compiling a "Comparative and Synoptical Indian Dictionary" for the Department, publishing a newspaper in the Mohawk language, and in recruiting First Peoples from reserves throughout Ontario and Quebec to enlist for service in the First World War–he was, in fact, one of the few commissioned Aboriginal officers of the 114th Battalion. Following his retirement from the civil service, Cooke acted as a lecturer and recitalist from 1926 to 1934, touring Canada and the United States, reciting Iroquois and Huron lore, songs, and dances. When he was in his eighties, Cooke joined the National Museum of Canada, working with Marcel Rioux and Marius Barbeau in 1949 and 1951 in surveying and completing a grammatical study of Mohawk, Cayuga, Onondaga, and Tuscarora. And in 1950, Cooke assisted the film director Allan Wargon in making a film representation of the life and religious activities of the Handsome-Lake (Cayuga and Onondaga) group of Five Nations in Ontario, which resulted in *La Grande Maison*, or the *Longhouse people*, released by the National Film Board of Canada in 1951.[67]

Cooke's ideas in establishing an Indian National Library through the Department of Indian Affairs were rooted in his earlier initiatives within the Department in compiling a "Comparative and Synoptical Indian Dictionary" and in his efforts to compile, edit, and publish a newspaper in the Mohawk language. Each of these initiatives was Cooke's own, which he presented to officials within the Department and gathered moderate support. In May of 1899, Cooke solicited the department for funding in researching and compiling a comparative dictionary of Aboriginal languages, which he described as "embracing as many as possible of all the spoken Indian languages of today throughout Canada & U. S., and will be particularly invaluable with interests of philology & ethnology."[68] This massive undertaking was one that Cooke would continue to work on throughout his career and well into his retirement, culminating in 1950 in an extensive manuscript on Iroquois personal names. This manuscript, sponsored in part by the National Museum of Canada, contained more than 6,000 names taken down in missionary spelling with phonetic renderings and tape recordings made by Cooke, and is today housed in the library of the American Philosophical Society and the library of the Canadian Museum of Civilization.[69]

In October 1900, Cooke would also take the initiative to compile and edit a newspaper in the Mohawk language, which he entitled, *Onkweonwe* (Mohawk for "Aboriginal peoples"). The department appears to have had no involvement in the project except to have provided a publisher, but Cooke took advantage of his position within Indian Affairs to correspond widely with Mohawk Chiefs throughout Ontario, Quebec, and the United States, asking for their support, to encourage subscribers, and elicit Aboriginal involvement and contributions to the paper. Cooke originally envisioned the paper to be published every two weeks, and:

> to contain as a rule general news of the day, local Indian
> news, information helpful to Indians in agriculture, trading,

> hunting, household, education as re: information bureau, a
> vocabulary in Indian and English and any other miscella-
> neous matter that would help and enlighten the Indians.
> Religious controversy and personal (ill) remarks to be
> strictly avoided. A page may be devoted to in English deal-
> ing exclusively with Indian matter. There will be no adver-
> tisements in it.[70]

The subscription price was set at twenty-five cents a year for "Indians
who are able to pay, and free to the unable" and fifty cents a year for
"white subscribers." The first issue of *Onkweonwe* was published 25
October 1900, but almost immediately afterwards Cooke ran into considerable difficulties in publishing additional issues. Only five days following the publication of the first issue, Cooke appeared frustrated in
his efforts to gather sufficient Aboriginal contributions, as is illustrated
in the following exchange with a Mohawk Chief stateside:

> Will you *not fail* [original emphasis] to send me lots of
> news around American Indians by next Saturday for my
> next issue of the paper. I was disappointed last time in not
> having heard from you. Now will you not fail to send me.
> Send me in English or Indian, never mind if it is poor. I'll
> fix it when it comes. Hoping you have nearly got rid of all
> the papers I sent you. Will expect to hear from you by
> Monday and no later.[71]

Failing to gather enough interest and contributions to publish again
within two weeks, Cooke on the 29th of November in a letter asking for
financial donations described the paper as fortnightly, and although he
then claimed to have "400 subscribers ... [?] throughout Canada and
Ontario and in the state of New York,"[72] it is unclear how many further
issues of *Onkweonwe* were published. Although short-lived, the paper
constituted one of the very earliest attempts in Canada at publishing a
serial publication in an Aboriginal language, and constituted the first
newspaper in Canada compiled and edited solely by an Aboriginal person.[73]
    As in his efforts to establish an Indian National Library, in
Onkweonwe, and in his lifelong efforts to compile a comparative vocabulary of the Iroquoian languages, it is clear to see Cooke trying to balance his position within the Department of Indian Affairs as a "civilized
Indian" with his Mohawk identity. Cooke's proposed Indian National
Library, the short-lived newspaper, *Onkweonwe* and his "Comparative
and Synoptical Indian Dictionary" illustrate Cooke's articulation,

ONKWEONWE

Aterientarajera naah ne Kasatstensera.

VOL. I. OTTAWA, CANADA, OCTOBER 25, 1900. NO. 1

The front page of Charles A. Cooke's Mohawk language newspaper, *Onkweonwe*, vol. 1, no. 1, published in Ottawa by F. X. Lemieux, 25 October, 1900. *Onkweonwe* was the first newspaper in Canada compiled, edited, and published solely by an Aboriginal person.

integration, and efforts in employing Western modes of information and communication, being literacy in the printed word. Each of Cooke's initiatives, whether successful or not, were clear attempts at redefining the largely Western technology of the printed word for the social, cultural, and political benefit of Aboriginal peoples without compromising Aboriginal cultural interests and beliefs. In his library, newspaper, and dictionary projects, Cooke showed a sincere interest in protecting, strengthening, and promoting Aboriginal languages (particularly Iroquoian), histories, and cultural practices, and his efforts appear to have been motivated by a desire to create an environment within which Aboriginal peoples could have some say in the affairs of the Department. At the same time, Cooke framed these efforts within contexts that the colonial Indian Affairs department could understand and justify as potentially worthy projects (although all parties involved were not always completely sold on his proposals). In each case, Cooke attempted to sell his ideas on the basis that they were designed to "help and enlighten Indians" in colonial and assimilative interests, but each was also articulated in a way so as to help maintain the languages, histories, and practices of the First Peoples. The mandate of *Onkweonwe*, for example, was to provide insight into "agriculture, trading, hunting, household, education" and other information–a clear mix of Indian Affairs' interests, and the interests of First Peoples themselves. Often frustrated by a lack of interest or initiative on behalf of the Department, Cooke was similarly frustrated by a lack of Aboriginal interest in his proposals. The failure of *Onkweonwe* provides an obvious example, as do the observations of a colleague, the distinguished ethnographer and anthropologist Marius Barbeau,[74] who noted in 1951: "To [Cooke's] regret he found out that the Indians themselves, instead of being interested in their own language and names, would give him scant encouragement. Suspicious, they did not respond whole-heartedly to his questions."[75]

Cooke clearly lived between two cultures–on the one hand he complied with the stated colonial Canadian agenda, being a "civilized" Indian. On the other hand, his efforts to protect and strengthen Iroquoian languages and promote Aboriginal involvement in the larger Canadian society on equal terms positioned Cooke at once as committed to two cultures, between clashing world views and multiple ideologies. In Cooke's later efforts to enlist Aboriginal peoples for service in the First World War, he made the following observation regarding his status as an Aboriginal person working for Indian Affairs:

> I wish to add that the reception given me on the different
> Reserves, all due no doubt to my nationality, and connec-
> tions with the Department, have been most cordial, and that
> my visits have done much to reconvince the Indians that
> our Government is willing to recognise its wards by hon-
> ouring them in having one in its service.[76]

While he was often frustrated by both the Indian Affairs department and
by Aboriginal peoples themselves, each for demonstrating at times a
lack of interest and initiative, the insightful efforts of Charles A. Cooke
were important in that they provided at least some semblance of Aboriginal agency at work within the Department and attempted to employ
Western ideas of literacy and the book in ways meant to benefit First
Peoples.

Chippewas of Sarnia Reserve, 1901: a proposal for a free circulating library

In January 1901, Joshua Adams, the Dominion Government Indian
Lands Agent at Sarnia, Ontario, and a former mayor of the city, made a
request of the department of Indian Affairs that a library be established
on the Chippewas of Sarnia Reserve:

> Some of the Councillors and Indians of the Sarnia Reserve
> have spoken to me and expressed a desire to have a free
> circulating library established on the Reserve for the mental
> improvement of the young men and women of the Reserve
> and as a means of inducing them to spend their nights and
> spare time in reading at their homes.[77]

Adams had been an active observer of the Aamjiwnaang for several
years, and was willing to act as a sponsor to the community's proposed
library.[78] It is significant to note that although the library was proposed
by members of the Aamjiwnaang community, Adams was asked to
write to the secretary of the department on their behalf, skirting the presumed authority and position of the community Indian Agent who
would have normally been responsible for acting on such proposals.

In his letter to the Department, Adams notes that individual community members "have very few books" and that the influence of a library and reading materials would presumably act as deterrents to morally inappropriate behavior. Reasons cited for the establishment of a
library at the Sarnia Reserve are, in fact, not unlike the intentions cited

by non-Aboriginal nineteenth century library pioneers and moral reformers. Libraries and their carefully selected collections, particularly
in Upper Canada and Ontario, were commonly built upon the premises
of morally reforming the lower, working, and immigrant classes under
the guise of education. Adams' words were precisely that a library
would act as "a stimulus to mental and moral improvement [of the
young men and women of the Reserve] and help to keep them from ill
habits and wasting their time about town to no good purpose."[79]
Whether these are the words of Adams himself, or if they are sentiments passed on from members of the Aamjiwnaang community, is
unclear. But Adams' background in politics would seem to indicate that
these are ideas held firmly by the former mayor and councillor. His tenure as mayor of Sarnia was marked by policies that resulted in the hiring of a town marshal to patrol the streets of the city after dark in the
hopes of protecting respectable people and females who had the occasion to be out after hours from the disorderly conduct of young ruffians,
and to clear the streets of stray dogs by giving police the authority fo
shoot unmuzzled canines running at large.[80] A library to deter young
Indians "from ill habits and wasting their time about town to no good
purpose" falls directly in line with Adams' efforts to clean up the streets
of the city of Sarnia during his mayorship.

        Members of the Aamjiwnaang community may have also shared
these sentiments, as the community had, at the time, a seventy year history of Methodist missionary influence, and Adams himself was reportedly a staunch Methodist. The Methodist world view emphasized that
members of the church follow the denomination's perceived destiny of
supplying and shaping the spiritual and moral characteristics of community life. Methodism was first introduced into the Aamjiwnaang community in 1829, when the Ojibwe missionary Peter Jones first visited
the St. Clair River region. Jones was not immediately successful in con-
vincing Chief Wawanosh to persuade members of his community to
convert to Methodism, but the missionary labored in the area for three
years. During his tenure, Jones introduced alphabetic translations of
biblical literature in the Ojibwe (Chippewa) language to members of the
Aamjiwnaang community in his efforts to convert the people to
Methodism. Jones' efforts constituted the community's first introduction to the Western printed word, and by 1832, Jones' successor,
Thomas Turner, had established a Methodist church in the community
and a school under the Methodist's authority. From 1832 forward there
has existed either a Methodist or Anglican church in the community.

In 1834, Reverend James Evans arrived in the St. Clair River region. Evans would expand greatly on the printed word tradition first introduced by Jones five years earlier, continuing to translate and publish biblical works in the Ojibwe (Chippewa) language. Acting as missionary to the community for four years, it was among the Aamjiwnaang that Evans first began his work of translating and printing biblical literature. This work would lead to his syllabic translations among the Cree of Norway House some years later, and it was in Sarnia that Evans secured the help of Peter Jacobs and Henry Steinhauer, Ojibwe (Chippewa) translators and assistants, who would prove invaluable in his later work. Undoubtedly Jacobs and Steinhauer did not receive due credit, helping Evans to earn his reputation as the "inventor" of Cree syllabics.[81] A Methodist influence, including the belief that literature should be written and distributed in the interests of uplifting the spiritual and moral practices of a community, was thus well established in the Chippewas of Sarnia community in 1901. Undoubtedly some members of the Aamjiwnaang community would have shared Adams' beliefs that the library should work to deter the young from wandering the streets of the city at night, while also working to educate.

Adams' letter to the Superintendent of Indian Affairs was unfortunately passed back into the hands of the Sarnia Indian Agent, Adam English, who then promptly refused the request for a free circulating library, citing his belief that there would be problems with managing the collection, encouraging the return of books, and finding an interest in reading from members of the community. English notes, however, that the issue of establishing a library had been raised at least once before: "Mr. Adams idea is not a new one, this matter has been thought over for a considerable time...."[82] Although it is not clear when, or by whom, the matter had been previously raised, it is clear that members of the community had been thinking along the lines of establishing a library and encouraging the young of the Reserve to read in the Western tradition for some time. Considering the community's Methodist history and the indelible influence left by Reverends Jones and Evans, it is no surprise that members of the community would desire further reading materials. The Reserve's very close proximity to the city of Sarnia was also of influence–the public high schools which the Ojibwe (Chippewa) attended after a primary education on the Reserve[83] contained libraries and books. Further, the city of Sarnia had a Mechanics' institute since the late 1830s, and a free public library was opened in the city less than one year before Adams' request that a free lending library be established on the Reserve in January 1901.[84] Adams and some members of the Aamjiwnaang community expected that those services available to the residents of Sarnia should also be available to the Aboriginal inhabitants of the Reserve.

If English expected that the Aamjiwnaang would peruse and make use of a library collection in a similar manner as their non-Aboriginal neighbors in the city, seemingly the Indian Agent would have denied their request for a library on the grounds that a public library already existed in Sarnia. However, English's reasons for declining the idea make no mention of the nearby public library. His reasons, which he had presumably used before to reject an earlier library proposal, were twofold: "I ...[?] could never see a way wherein ..[?] it could be managed satisfactorily as I think it would be impossible to have the books brought in after they have been given out"; and "I think too that it will be a difficult matter to interest the Indians very much in reading."[85]

English's reasons are curious. Given the long history of exposure to the Western book form within the community, and the fact the request for a library is made by some of the people themselves, an interest in reading, although perhaps not widespread, was certainly evident among the Aamjiwnaang. Further, Adams paints a picture of the proposed library as "a stimulus to mental and moral improvement," reasons that would seemingly have been in line with the Department of Indian Affairs' philosophies and ideologies regarding assimilating Aboriginal populations. The Agent's concerns in managing the collection are equally curious given that Adams clearly notes:

> A suitable place could be had for it in the Council House or Basement and the expense would be but trifling ... the Indian School Teacher or Secretary of the Band could be the Distributor without salary ... it would probably be unnecessary or not advisable to have a large equipment of books ... and no special grant of money from the Trust Funds [are] needed to establish it ... and subsequently the Indian Council might probably recommend a grant for its more efficient work.[86]

Members of the Aamjiwnaang community and Adams had certainly made a strong case for establishing a free lending library on the Reserve, keeping costs to a minimum for the Department and framing the library within the popular contexts of moral and mental improvement of the youth. This was language that the Indian Agent and the Department would have understood, thus implying that English's mind was already made up on the matter. If the issue of a free lending library had been raised before, and had "been thought over for a considerable time," as English stated, then the Indian Agent's excuses were probably well practiced.

English must have suspected that a free lending library for the Aamjiwnaang community would not work in the best interests of the colonial and assimilating policies of the Department of Indian Affairs. If the Aamjiwnaang were to establish and manage their own library, selecting those materials that best suited their political, social, and cultural interests, and in the meantime setting an example for other Reserve communities, then the Department's intentions of assimilating the Aboriginal population in the Western image could risk being undermined. The Aamjiwnaang, in proposing a library, were likely thinking in terms of their own best interests. In other words, English had reason to fear that the library collection was envisioned as a means of supporting, maintaining, and preserving Ojibwe (Chippewa) history, culture, and language. Further, a library could assist the people in becoming self-sustaining and being better prepared in disputes with the Department of Indian Affairs and with the non-Aboriginal population that was increasingly encroaching upon the Aamjiwnaang's land.

A desire to oversee and shape the reading interests of the Aamjiwnaang community appear instead to be English's primary concern: "I am going to try a plan of supplying the Indians with papers and magazines of different kinds which I will distribute from my office ... and I will see if it will have the effect of cultivating a taste for reading and if it has that effect we will see later on ... [?] what we can do in the way of establishing a library."[87] Perhaps because the idea for a free circulating library had emerged from within the community–from some of the Ojibwe (Chippewa) themselves–English is concerned with the nature of materials the library might include. If some interest in reading and in articulating the Western printed word for their own purposes was not already present, it would have been unlikely that the community would make such a request. The Indian Agent's refusal to support the idea of a free lending library was instead supplanted by a rather different method of disseminating the printed word–one where he could hand-pick and distribute print materials to members of the community himself. English's concerns reflected a departmental attitude that would more clearly emerge a few years later. Indian Affairs authorities were beginning to envision libraries as tools that they could, in effect, control as censors, manipulating the self-motivated interests of First Peoples in reading, learning, and communicating via the printed word.

Only three years later, in correspondence with Charles A. Cooke regarding the establishment of Cooke's proposed Indian National Library at the Department of Indian Affairs, Francis W. Jacobs, an Ojibwe (Chippewa) from the Sarnia region would observe: "I was very much struck with the scheme you proposed. I have for some years past been thinking of something of the kind should be established. I think it would be of great benefit both to our desandants as well as to the Indians of today ... So you can imagine how heartily I would enter into the scheme you proposed and any thing I can do to advance its cause I will be most happy to do so."[88] Obviously English was right–the Aamjiwnaang were indeed envisioning a library collection to work in their own benefit. Reading and writing, as introduced and taught by the missionaries for assimilative purposes, had come to be articulated and integrated into Aamjiwnaang ideology as having the potential to work in the best interests of Aboriginal peoples. Books and library collections were by the first quarter of the twentieth century envisioned and articulated by some Aboriginal peoples as integrative tools to resist assimilation and support their own political, social, and cultural interests. Some time later, Indian Affairs would also take an interest in libraries. The Department's vision, however, was not of libraries under Aboriginal control, but of collections selected by department officials meant to supplement the assimilative and "civilizing" roles of the schools.

The "Lady Wood Library" and the Mi'kmaq of Lennox Island, 1910-11

With the exception of school libraries, collections of books and reading materials for the use of First Peoples in Canada were not widespread in the first quarter of the twentieth century. Despite the fact that there was some Aboriginal support and initiative to establish such institutions, authorities at the Department of Indian Affairs held ultimate control over the establishment of libraries. While the missions had, for the most part, been responsible for the formal education and schooling of First Peoples through the nineteenth century, Aboriginal initiatives in establishing libraries, such as those by Charles A. Cooke and the Aamjiwnaang, demonstrate that some First Peoples saw ample room to make use of and manage such institutions. Aboriginal efforts in attempting to establish libraries and collections of books in a Western tradition of historical preservation and communication emerge within the early part of the twentieth century, at a time when the propagation of the English and French languages and Western forms of schooling in the interests of assimilation have begun to take a toll on traditional forms of Aboriginal knowledge, languages, and understandings of history. However, the establishment of libraries for Aboriginal use had first to be approved and supported by the Department of Indian Affairs if such projects were to take root successfully. As was demonstrated in the efforts of Charles A. Cooke and the Aamjiwnaang, financial reasons and a belief that First People had little interest in books or any significant knowledge to share or preserve were cited by the Department as deterrents to such initiatives. Clearly, if Aboriginal peoples were to be successful in establishing their own libraries, they could not count on the support of the Indian Affairs department. Band funds, also under the control of Indian Affairs, were also off limits, meaning that philanthropy was the only alternative available in establishing such collections.

The earliest successful establishment of a "library" outside of a residential, day or industrial school within an Aboriginal community in Canada appears to be that of the Lady Wood Library in late 1910 within the Mi'kmaq community of Lennox Island, Prince Edward Island. This community library and meeting place was established with funds willed to the Lennox Island community by Lady Augusta Wood, a daughter of former Lieutenant Governor of the colony, Edmund Fanning. In March 1911, the Catholic priest of Lennox Island, Reverend J. A. McDonald, reported a fondness for reading among members of the community and described the library as follows: "The Hall or Lady Wood Library is a place where they can meet and give concerts ... There is a catechism prayer book and History in their own language. They also have a newspaper printed once a month...."[89] One month later, John (Jean) O. Arsenault, the Indian Superintendent for Prince Edward Island, reported to Indian Affairs, that:

> During the past year a very fine structure was erected on the reserve of Lennox Island to serve as a public hall, and known as the 'Lady Wood Library.' ... The building is 50 x 25 feet with trussed roof, giving a beautiful arched ceiling finished in natural wood. The walls are finished with plaster, and the building has a good stage and a flag-pole. It is furnished with hardwood chairs, and has been supplied with stove, lamps, oil, and fuel. About $1,000 was expended on the building apart from the furniture...and it is hoped that when it is stocked with books, it will be a centre of culture and refinement, as well as a place where they can meet for social intercourse.[90]

Located at the heart of the community, the Lady Wood Library was built in the general vicinity of other public buildings, including the church, the school, and the store.[91]

Although it was not immediately furnished with books, it was a remarkable and historic feat that the Mi'kmaq of Lennox Island were able, at least in part, to fulfill the vision of a community library. To their advantage, the community had the benefit of sidestepping the Indian Affairs department, having sufficient funding for the construction and furnishing of the building through the estate of Lady Wood. Having died in England in 1872, Lady Louisa Augusta Wood in her will bequest a sufficient sum of money from the sale of her lands on Prince Edward Island "for the benefit of the Micmac Indians of Prince Edward Island."[92] Monies from the estate took nearly forty years to trickle down to the Mi'kmaq, but they eventually were used, in addition to such cultural pursuits as the library, for the advancement of agriculture, industry, and in the relief of the sick and aged members of the community.

The Lady Wood Library was not only the first such institution of its kind within an Aboriginal community in Canada, it was also unique and forward-looking in its mandate and structure. From its inception, it was envisioned by the community and Arsenault as both a library and public hall for the sharing of knowledge through a multitude of resources. Less than a year after its founding, the Indian Superintendent would report that, "One of the aged Indian women has opened a class for the purpose of instructing the young girls in the art of making moccasins and bead-work. During the past winter the young Indians have given a couple of concerts...."[93] The Lady Wood Library was not established to strictly house a collection of books. It was founded, presumably by members of the community, with the understanding that traditional methods of Mi'kmaq knowledge transfer, teaching methods, storytelling, and literacies could also be nurtured and shared within its walls.[94] In this way, the library and public hall was founded on the principles of uniquely mixing and sharing traditional Mi'kmaq ways of knowing and learning with Western book learning and reading and writing.[95]

In addition to the benefits of the ability to circumvent the Department of Indian Affairs provided to the community through the estate of Lady Wood,[96] the Mi'kmaq of Lennox Island's unique relationship with the Catholic missionaries to the region provided an environment whereby the community could more easily integrate with the non-Aboriginal population and articulate Western practices. Like other Mi'kmaq communities in eastern Canada, the Mi'kmaq of Lennox Island had, in 1910-11, a long history of cooperation and friendly relations with missionaries representing the Catholic faith. As John Joe Sark explains, "The Micmac did not have a problem with Christianity because they felt that it was much the same as what they already believed in."[97] The Mi'kmaq were the first Aboriginal peoples in Canada to adopt Christianity, combining the Catholic faith with their own traditional beliefs. In adopting Catholicism and Christianity, thus fostering friendly and cooperative relations with non-Aboriginal missionaries, settlers, and government officials, the Mi'kmaq were in a rather unique position to then negotiate, articulate, and adopt other aspects of Western culture. This integrated relationship had the effect of giving the Mi'kmaq some advantage in negotiating for increased control and decision-making powers in their own affairs (for example, the Lady Wood Library, which appears to have been a community initiative), even though they, like all other First Peoples in Canada, were limited and controlled in large part by the Indian Act and the Indian Affairs department.

In the case of the Lennox Island band, an ability to make and influence some decisions regarding their own affairs was further bolstered by the additional leverage provided to the community through the Lady Wood fund, the results of which are demonstrated in the construction of the Lady Wood Library in late 1910. Further evidence that the Mi'kmaq of Lennox Island were exercising some control over the development of their community in this period can be seen in the hiring of John J. Sark as the local school teacher in 1910. Sark was educated within the community and at St. Dunstan's College in Charlottetown, earning a teaching degree, and was the son of a Chief of the Lennox Island band. Soon after his hiring, the Indian Superintendent for Prince Edward Island reported that "all the children of school age are enrolled, and those who attend regularly are doing well ... the children are very obedient and seem to love their teacher." Further, "The Indians on the reserve are all civilized and the majority can read and write, and with very few exceptions show an interest in the education of their children." Additionally, the public school inspector for the province reported the following regarding Mr. Sark: "I was very favourably impressed with Mr. Sark's method of teaching and his manner in the school-room. He is very energetic, commands respect of this pupils and seeks to improve them."[98] Although as an Aboriginal teacher John Sark was by no means unique (others, although few, had taught in the schools as early as 1830), the Department was particularly hesitant to hire Aboriginal teaching staff during the tenure that he taught at Lennox Island.[99] Sark's influence among the community was considerable (the public school today is named in his honor) and he would continue teaching within the community until his death in 1945.

The Mi'kmaq were, of course, also well equipped culturally to integrate and articulate the Western traditions of reading, writing, and books. The existence of a hieroglyphic reading and writing tradition among the Mi'kmaq, first noted by the Catholic missionaries LeClercq and Maillard in the seventeenth and eighteenth centuries, helped to facilitate a close relationship and understanding of the Catholic faith, and closely resembled Western notions of the book and literacy. The Mi'kmaq were perhaps in a better position than many other Aboriginal groups to embrace and integrate similar Western notions of reading and writing, resulting in what missionaries and Indian Agents would later describe as a "fondness for reading," and the eventual establishment of the Lady Wood Library, for instance.

"Books prescribed by the department": school libraries, 1911-1916

Although the Lady Wood Library at Lennox Island would be the only successfully established public library in an Aboriginal community for several decades, the establishment and growth of school libraries would continue through the first part of the nineteenth century, constituting the only library-related efforts on behalf of the Department of Indian Affairs and the missions. The involvement or inclusion, if any, of Aboriginal peoples in the establishment and building of these collections is uncertain, but likely minimal. Detailed lists of school library materials were not required or made by the schools until after 1930, leaving the content and mandate of the school libraries before this date largely speculative. However, there is nothing to suggest that the school libraries served any other purpose than to supplement the ideological and educative concerns of the residential, day, and industrial schools from the perspectives of the Department and missions.

In the same period that the Mi'kmaq of Lennox Island were building a library in their image and for their own purposes, a number of schools run by the missions and Indian Affairs department also established libraries. Following 1911, a number of schools in Ontario would report library collections as new additions to the educative and civilizing process. These included the Rama Agency and Cape Croker school in 1911;[100] and James Oliver, teacher at the day school at the Christian Island Reserve would report, "Reading from the Bible and the books prescribed by the department is an essential element in the daily round of work," also adding that he hoped the Department would help the school in funding the establishment of a library.[101] By 1915, the Moraviantown Agency reported a library had been recently installed in one of its schools, with "books suitable for children"; and the Saugeen Agency reported new libraries at the Saugeen, Scotch Settlement, and French Bay schools, as had the No. 8 day school at Port Elgin.[102] The last acknowledgment of school libraries of any sort would appear in the Department's *Annual report* for 1916, being the following announcement from the Cape Croker Agency: "All the schools in this agency are built of stone. They have individual desks and libraries."[103] No further announcements regarding libraries of any sorts would appear in the annual reports again until the 1950s.

That no other discussion regarding libraries or collections of reading materials in the schools or in Aboriginal communities would be made by the Department for much of the next thirty-five years points to the relative unimportance placed on such institutions by Indian Affairs. Further, the brief mentions of reading materials and libraries in the reports up until 1916 also points to a reluctance on behalf of the Department to take much initiative in sponsoring these endeavors. Although Indian Affairs was reportedly taking greater interest and initiative in the affairs of Aboriginal education through the early part of the twentieth century, tools such as libraries were still largely left to the responsibility of the missions and individual philanthropists. The Department was quick to suggest the establishment of libraries, and regularly issued suggestions as to the kind of reading materials that should be present in the schools, but the missions and individual schools were still largely responsible for acquiring these items on their own. As a result, relatively few schools would establish libraries, in large part due to the financial constraints that were placed on them. The schools through this period were still largely preoccupied with the job of assimilating and educating Aboriginal children in the skills of tradesmen, housewives, and domestic workers. While education for non-Aboriginal children through the early part of the nineteenth century was beginning to take strides towards a more diverse and literary approach to teaching and learning, the Indian schools were still largely struggling under their original mandates.

As a result, the collections of books and libraries that the Indian schools did acquire were scant and poor in quality. Further, it would appear that few, if any, were developed at the initiative of Aboriginal peoples and failed to suit their cultural and community wants and needs. The philosophy of education practiced in the schools by the missions and Indian Affairs was also envisioned dramatically differently by most First Peoples. Some Aboriginal peoples, for example, interpreted the agreements and treaties they had signed and agreed to as incurring certain fiduciary obligations with respect to education.[104] Thus, many First Peoples understood there to be a kind of trust relationship involved in the operation of the schools. This meant that First Peoples, in some cases, sought a Western education as a means of adapting and integrating Western ways to their own cultures while on the other hand, the missions and government envisioned education as a means of assimilation. Of course, the missions and government largely maintained control over Aboriginal education throughout the early part of the twentieth century, so it was in their vision that education prevailed and was practiced. Collections of books and libraries in the schools then were an extension of the missions' and government vision. And any initiatives to establish libraries outside of the school setting in Aboriginal communities that might have suited the educational needs envisioned by First Peoples were discouraged and failed to emerge, with the unique exception of the Lady Wood Library at Lennox Island.

Notes

1. For more on Indian Affairs, see E. Brian Titley, *A Narrow vision: Duncan Campbell Scott and the administration of Indian Affairs in Canada* (Vancouver: University of British Columbia Press, 1986).

2. Wilson 67, 71; Appeals to "civilize" Indians figured prominently in the original declarations of intent at several important universities in North America, including King's College and Victoria College (both predecessors to the University of Toronto), Harvard University, and Dartmouth College. None followed through with their intent. For additional discussion, see: Anthony J. Hall 117.

3. Peter F. McNally, "Libraries in Canada: a précis," *Feliciter* 48.2 (2002): 75-77. For other histories outlining the development of libraries in Canada see for instance: Lorne Bruce, *Free books for all: the public library movement in Ontario, 1850-1930* (Toronto: Dundurn Press, 1994); Violet L. Coughlin, *Larger units of public library service in Canada: with particular reference to the provinces of Prince Edward Island, Nova Scotia, and New Brunswick* (Metuchen: Scarecrow Press, 1968); Peter F. McNally, ed., *Readings in Canadian library history* (Ottawa: Canadian Library Association, 1986); John A. Wiseman, *Temples of democracy: a history of public library development in Ontario, 1880-1920*, PhD. thesis, Loughborough University of Technology, 1989.

4. See: Harvey J. Graff, *The Literacy myth: cultural integration and social structure in the nineteenth century* (1979; New Brunswick NJ: Transaction Publishers, 1991); and Susan E. Houston and Alison Prentice, *Schooling and scholars in nineteenth century Ontario* (Toronto: University of Toronto Press, 1988).

5. Bruce Curtis, "'Littery merrit', 'Useful knowledge' and the organization of township libraries in Canada West, 1840-1860," *Ontario History* LXXVIII.4 (1986): 285.

6. Curtis, 287.

7. Graff, xxv-xxvi.

8. See also: Lorne Bruce, *Free books for all: the public library movement in Ontario, 1850-1930* (Toronto: Dundurn Press, 1994).

9. Graff, 290-291.

10. J. Donald Wilson, "'No Blanket to be worn in school': the education of Indians in nineteenth century Ontario," *Indian Education in Canada: volume 1: the legacy*, Jean Barman et. al., eds. (Vancouver: University of British Columbia Press, 1986), 66-67.

11. Dominion of Canada, *Annual report of the Department of Indian Affairs for the year ended 31ˢᵗ December 1884* (Ottawa: 1885), 155.

12. Dominion of Canada, *Annual report of the Department of Indian Affairs for the year ended 30ᵗʰ June 1893* (Ottawa: 1893), 187; *Annual report 1898*, 290.

13. *Annual report 1896* , 330.

14. *Annual report 1896,* 351.

15. J. R. Miller, *Shingwauk's vision: a history of Native residential schools* (Toronto: University of Toronto, 1996), 160.

16. Isobel McFadden, *Living by bells: a narrative of five schools in British Columbia, 1874-1970* (Toronto?: Committee on Education for Mission and Stewardship, United Church of Canada, 1971), 9.

17. *Annual report 1896,* 349-350.

18. *Annual report 1898*, 312.

19. *Annual report 1897*, 258-259; *Annual report 1898,* 297.

20. *Annual report 1897,* 230; *Annual report 1898*, 349.

21. *Annual report 1898,* 256, 258; *Annual report 1899,* 356.

22. *Annual report 1900,* 318, 338; *Annual report 1901,* 304; *Annual report 1902,* 194; *Annual report 1903,* 437, 468.

23. *Annual report 1903*, 417.

24. *Annual report 1910*, 459, 472.

25. See: Jean Barman, Yvonne Hébert, and Don McCaskill, eds. *Indian education in Canada: volume 1, the legacy*, Nakoda Institute occasional paper no. 2 (1986; Vancouver: University of British Columbia Press, 1992); J. R. Miller, *Shingwauk's vision: a history of Native residential schools* (Toronto: University of Toronto Press, 1996); John S. Milloy, *"A National crime": the Canadian government and the residential school system, 1879 to 1986*, Manitoba studies in Native history XI (Winnipeg: University of Manitoba Press, 1999).

26. *Annual Report 1898,* 256, 258.

27. William Jones, *The Jubilee memorial of the Religious Tract Society: containing a record of its origins, proceedings, and results. A. D. 1799 to 1849* (London: Religious Tract Society, 1850), 578.

28. *Mohawk ideals, Victorian values: Oronhyatekha M. D.*, museum exhibit, Royal Ontario Museum [Toronto] March-August 2002; Ray Conlogue, "Burning Sky, blazing trail: a new exhibit captures the forgotten vision and passion of Oronhyatekha, Canada's first native doctor," *Globe and Mail* [Toronto] 18 March 2002, Ontario ed.: R1, R7.

29. F. Barlow Cumberland, *Catalogue and notes of the Oronhyatekha Historical Collection* (Toronto: The Supreme Court, International Order of Foresters, 1904), 3.

30. D. F. McKenzie, "The Sociology of a text: orality, literacy, and print in early New Zealand," *The Book history reader*, ed. David Finkelstein and Alistair McCleery (New York: Routledge, 2002), 189-215.

31. "Report of the Committee on Aborigines," *Parliamentary Papers* 7 (1836): 47-48.

32. Dan Kennedy, *Recollections of an Assiniboine Chief*, ed. James R. Stevens (Toronto: McClelland and Stewart, 1972), 54-55.

33. Mike Mountain Horse, *My People the Bloods*, ed. Hugh A. Dempsey (Calgary: Glenbow-Alberta Institute & Blood Tribal Council, 1979), 15.

34. "Christianity in the Longhouse: The Educational problems of the Confederacy about 1810," *The Valley of the Six Nations: a collection of documents on the Indian lands of the Grand River*, Charles M. Johnston, ed. (Toronto: The Champlain Society for the Government of Ontario; University of Toronto Press, 1964), 245.

35. Qtd. in Winona L. Stevenson, "'Our man in the field': the status and role of a CMS Native catechist in Rupert's Land," *Journal of the Canadian Church Historical Society* xxxiii.1 (1991): 67-68.

36. Note Luther Standing Bear's comments, for instance: "Countless leaves in countless books have robbed a people of both history and memory" in Luther Standing Bear, *Land of the Spotted Eagle* (1933; Lincoln: University of Nebraska Press, 1978), 28; and contemporary Aboriginal storyteller Louise Erdrich's descriptions of Aboriginal versus Western ways of knowing as demonstrated in the characters of Eli and Nector in "The World's greatest fishermen," *Love medicine*, New and expanded version (1984; New York: HarperCollins, 1993), 19.

37. "Educational problems of the Confederacy," *Valley of the Six Nations*, 245.

38. There are numerous studies documenting the history of Indian education in Canada–see for example: Jean Barman, Yvonne Hébert, and Don McCaskill, eds., *Indian education in Canada, volume 1: the legacy* (Vancouver: UBC Press, 1986); Canada. Royal Commission on Aboriginal Peoples, *Looking forward, looking back*, Volume 1 of the Report of the Royal Commission on Aboriginal Peoples (Ottawa: Canada Communications Group, 1996); J. R. Miller, *Shingwauk's vision: a history of Native residential schools* (Toronto: University of Toronto Press, 1996); and John S. Milloy, *"A National crime": the Canadian government and the residential school system, 1879-1986* (Winnipeg: University

of Manitoba Press, 1999).

39. George Copway's [Kahgegagahbowh] published works include: *The Traditional history and characteristic sketches of the Ojibway nation* (London: Charles Gilpin, 1850); *Recollections of a forest life; or, the life and travels of Kah-ge-ga-gah-bowh, or George Copway.* 2nd edition (London: Charles Gilpin, 1851); and *Running sketches of men and places, in England, France, Germany, Belgium, and Scotland* (New York: J. C. Riker, 1851). Copway also wrote for the *Saturday Evening Post.*

40. Peter Jacobs' [Pahtahsega] published work includes: *Journal of the Reverend Peter Jacobs, Indian Wesleyan missionary, from Rice Lake to the Hudson's Bay Territory, and returning, commencing May, 1852* (New York: Published by the author, 1858).

41. Peter Jones' [Kahkewaquonaby] published works include: *Life and journals of Kah-ke-wa-quo-na-by (Rev. Peter Jones), Wesleyan Missionary* (Toronto: Published by Anson Green, at the Wesleyan Printing Establishment, 1860); *History of the Ojebway Indians: with especial reference to their conversion to Christianity* (London: A. W. Bennett, 1861). Jones also published numerous articles, sermons, and speeches.

42. Hilary E. Wyss, *Writing Indians: literacy, Christianity and Native community in early America* (Amherst: University of Massachusetts Press, 2000), 5.

43. George Copway, *Life, history, and travels of Kah-ge-ga-gah-bowh* (Philadelphia: James Harmstead, 1847), 20.

44. Peter Jones, *History of the Ojebway Indians: with especial reference to their conversion to Christianity* (London: A. W. Bennett, 1861), 71.

45. Charles A. Cooke was one of the first Aboriginal persons to be hired by the Indian Affairs department in an era notorious for excluding First People's contributions; NAC RG 10, Volume 2675, File 135480, Reel C-11261, Headquarters - Ottawa - Personnel file on extra clerks working for the Department of Indian Affairs, 1893-1897; and Marius Barbeau, "Charles A. Cooke, Mohawk scholar," *Proceedings of the American Philosophical Society* 96.4 (1952): 424-426.

46. NAC RG 10, Volume 2740, File 145131, Reel C-11273, Extract from Dept. letter of Dec. 26, 1893, to W. J. McGee, Esq., Ethnologist in charge, Bureau of Ethnology, Washington.

47. G. M. Matheson, the Registrar for Indian Affairs and Head Clerk, Records Branch between 1888 and 1936, and other departmental personnel were for instance during the late nineteenth and early twentieth centuries working towards creating a series of subject indexes to provide subject access to records relating to Indian Affairs (both those in the department custody and elsewhere). It does not appear, however, that Matheson had anything to do with the establishment and organizing of the Indian Affairs departmental library.

48. NAC RG 10, Volume 3081, File 270000-2 pt. 2A, Letter to the Hon. Clifford Sifton, from Charles A. Cooke, January 1904.

49. NAC RG 10, Volume 3081, File 270000-2 pt. 2A, Letter to Charles A. Cooke, from John Mawson, Naturalist, Geological Survey of Canada, 21 March 1904.

50. NAC RG 10, Volume 3081, File 270000-2 pt. 2A, Letter to Charles A. Cooke, from Josiah Hill, Ohsweken Council House, 22 February 1904.

51. NAC RG 10, Volume 3081, File 270000-2 pt. 2A, Letter to Charles A. Cooke, from Chief J. W. M. Elliott, Six Nations Reserve, 29 February 1904.

52. In the correspondence included in NAC RG 10, Volume 3081, File 270000-2 pt. 2A, there are at least fifteen letters in glowing support of Cooke's idea to establish an Indian National Library. A number of letters are in very poor condition, and are thus unreadable. All those included, however, appear to express positive support. Cooke himself extracts from twelve of these in a letter to Frank Pedley, Deputy Superintendent General.

53. NAC RG 10, Volume 3081, File 270000-1, Reel C-11321, Letter to the Hon. Clifford Sifton, Minister of the Interior, from Duncan Campbell Scott, Ottawa, 29 January 1904.

54. See: Titley passim.

55. Interestingly enough, the Royal Commission on Aboriginal Peoples recommended in 1996 that a "National Aboriginal Documentation Centre" be established to "research, collect, preserve, and disseminate information related to residential schools, relocations, and other aspects of Aboriginal historical experience." See recommendation 3.5.36, *Gathering strength: volume 3 of the Report of the Royal Commission on Aboriginal Peoples* (Ottawa: Canada Communications Group, 1996), 538-539. Cooke's proposed Indian National Library would appear in some ways to have been more than ninety years ahead of its time.

56. NAC RG 10, Volume 2740, File 145131, Reel C-11273, Ottawa, Ontario – Correspondence regarding the establishment of a library in the Department of Indian Affairs (orders, accounts, clippings), 1893-1904.

57. NAC RG 10, Volume 3081, File 270000-1, Reel C-11321, Letter to the Hon. Clifford Sifton, Minister of the Interior, from Duncan Campbell Scott, Ottawa, 29 January 1904. Scott's reference to the Parliamentary Library is important since there was no National Library of Canada in 1904. Until the establishment of the National Library of Canada in 1953, the Parliamentary Library provided national library functions in Canada.

58. Letter to Hon. Clifford Sifton, from Duncan Campbell Scott, 29 January 1904.

59. However, the opposite might also be said given the contemporary shaky relationships between museums and many Aboriginal communities, for example.

60. NAC RG 10, Volume 3081, File 270000-1 pt. 1, Reel 11321, Letter to The Deputy Superintendent General of Indian Affairs, from Charles A. Cooke, 29 August 1904.

61. NAC RG 10, Volume 3081, File 270000-1 pt. 1, Reel C-11321, Memorandum to the Deputy Superintendent General of Indian Affairs, from Charles A. Cooke, 10 November 1904.

62. See those records contained within: NAC RG 10, Volume 3081, File 270000-1 pt. 1, Reel-C-11321.

63. NAC RG 10, Volume 3081, File 270000-1 pt. 1, Reel C-11321, Letter to F. Grierson, for the Associate Director of Public Information, from Duncan Campbell Scott, 14 November 1918.

64. NAC RG 10, Volume 3081, File 270000-1 pt. 1, Reel C-11321, Report filed for the Dominion Bureau of Statistics, Library Statistics, 1923.

65. NAC RG 10, Volume 3081, File 270000-1 pt. 1, Reel C-11321, T. H. L. MacInnes, Secretary of Indian Affairs, to R. R. Coates, Dominion Statistician, Dominion Bureau of Statistics, 4 April 1938.

66. Charles A. Cooke was unique in the fact that as an Aboriginal employee of the department, although largely unsuccessful, he took efforts to influence the ideologies of Indian Affairs' dealings with First Peoples. Douglas Leighton has noted that Indian Affairs recruited a number of Aboriginal employees in the nineteenth century, most as interpreters, clerks, and timber rangers. However, while many were employed and relied upon within the department, few Aboriginal peoples were in the position to influence the formulation of policy. See: Douglas Leighton, "The Compact Tory as bureaucrat: Samuel Peters Jarvis and the Indian Department, 1837-1845," *Ontario History* LXXIII.1 (1981): 42; and James Douglas Leighton, *The Development of Federal Indian policy in Canada, 1840-1890*, Doctoral dissertation, University of Western Ontario, 1975, 66-67.

67. Charles A. Cooke (1870-1958) was born Thawennensere or Da-ha-wen-nen-se-re, at Oka, Quebec on 22 March 1870, to Adonhgnundagwen (later Angus Cooke) and Thiweza (Katrine). He attended the Methodist Mission school at Oka and worked with his father on the family farm until the family moved in 1881 to the Muskoka area of Ontario. It was here that Angus Cooke was engaged by the Methodist Missionary Society to preach at the Gibson Reserve. Charles was sent to the Mount Elgin residential school at Muncey, Ontario among children of Algonkin decent, but failing to learn proper English, he later attended a public school at Gravenhurst, Ontario. Prior to working for the department of Indian Affairs, Cooke was employed by the Methodist Missionary Society as a teacher on the Gibson Reserve, and worked for the Georgian Bay Lumber Company as a clerk. Upon his graduation from high school, Cooke intended to study medicine at McGill University, but was instead persuaded to take a position with the department by the federal member of Parliament for his district, Colonel O'Brien, a friend of his father. For further biographical details, see: Barbeau, 424-426.

Charles A. Cooke's publications include: *A-de-rih-wa-nie-ton on-kwe-on-we neh-ha: a message to the Iroquois Indians*, translated by Charles A. Cooke (Toronto: Baha'i Publishing Committee, 19??); *Iroquois personal names*, unpublished manuscript and on recorded tape, edited by Marius Barbeau, (Ottawa: National Museum of Canada, 1950); "Iroquois personal names–their classification," *Proceedings of the American Philosophical Society* 96.4 (1952): 427-438; and *Onkweonwe* 1.1 (25 October 1900), edited by Charles A. Cooke (Ottawa: F. X. Lemieux, 1900).

68. NAC RG 10, Volume 2974, File 209860, St-François Agency –
Correspondence regarding the *Comparative Indian Vocabulary*, Charles A. Cooke
(List of words frequently used by Indians).

69. For more information on Cooke's work in compiling the vocabulary, see:
Barbeau, 424-425; and Cooke, "Iroquois personal names," *Proceedings*, 427-438.
Cooke's manuscript and tape recordings are today held in the American
Philosophical Society Library's American Indian Manuscripts collection, in
Philadelphia, PA, and in the Library and Archives of the Canadian Museum of
Civilization in Gatineau, Quebec.

70. NAC RG 10, Volume 1307, Reel C-13907, Records concerning an Indian
newspaper edited by Charles Cooke.

71. NAC RG 10, Volume 1307, Reel C-13907, Letter from Charles Cooke
dated 30 October 1900.

72. NAC RG 10, Volume 1307, Reel C-13907, Letter from Charles Cooke
dated 29 November 1900.

73. To get a sense of the range of serial publications in Aboriginal languages
in Canada and the United States, see: James P. Danky, ed. *Native American
periodicals and newspapers 1828-1982: bibliography, publishing record and
holdings*, compiled by Maureen E. Hady (Westport CT: Greenwood Press, 1984).

74. Marius Barbeau, 1883-1969, was arguably the most prominent
anthropologist in Canadian history. A member of the Anthropological Division of
the Geological Survey of Canada between 1911 and 1948, his anthropological,
folklorist, and ethnomusicological work was tremendously influential at both
academic and political levels. Charles A. Cooke acted as one of Barbeau's
informants between 1911 and 1914 in his anthropological study of the Huron-
Wyandot in Ontario, Quebec and Oklahoma. And Cooke later worked with
Barbeau in the late 1940s and early 1950s in his assessment of Iroquoian
languages. Barbeau's biographer, Laurence Nowry, describes Cooke as "an
indispensable go-between who skillfully wended a path through Six Nations
politics and sensitivities ..." whose perspective and scholarly work "was unique
and probably indispensable for [the] successful completion of Barbeau's Iroquois
work" (350-351). Cooke's relationship with Barbeau was complicated by the fact
that the anthropologist concluded that the Huron had been assimilated into white
society, and that the Huron nation effectively no longer existed. The Indian
Affairs department and the Canadian state readily agreed with these conclusions,
citing Barbeau's research in disestablishing a Huron reserve and forcibly
enfranchising its population, abolishing their Indian status.
For more on Barbeau, see in particular: Laurence Nowry, *Marius Barbeau, man
of mana: a biography* (Toronto: NC Press, 1995); and Andrew Nurse, "'But now
things have changed': Marius Barbeau and the politics of Amerindian identity,"
Ethnohistory 48.3 (2001): 433-472.

75. Barbeau, 424.

76. NAC RG 10, Volume 6765, File 452-7, War 1914-1918 – Recruitment
by Charles A. Cooke among the Indians of St. Regis, Caughnawaga, and Oka,
1916-1917.

77. NAC RG10, Volume 3027, File 230,000, Reel C-11313, Joshua Adams to the Secretary of the Department of Indian Affairs, 12 January 1901.

78. Joshua Adams (1825-1906), a relative of the United States President, John Adams, was educated as a lawyer and active in the public affairs of the city and district of Sarnia. Serving as a school trustee and town councillor following his arrival in Sarnia in 1855, Adams was most notably the mayor of the city between 1862 and 1865. In 1899 he was appointed by the Dominion Government Indian Lands Agent at Sarnia, a post he held until his death on 23 December 1906. See : J. H. Beers & Co., *Commemorative biographical record of the County of Lambton, Ontario: containing biographical sketches of prominent and representative citizens and many of the early settled families* (Toronto: The Hill Binding Company, 1906), 384-385; "Death of Joshua Adams," *Sarnia Observer* [weekly edition] 28 December 1906; and "Joshua Adams first city mayor to be thrown out by the voters," *Sarnia Observer* 26 August 1995: 13.

79. Joshua Adams to the Secretary of the Department of Indian Affairs, 12 January 1901.

80. *Sarnia Observer* 26 August 1995: 13.

81. For further history on the Chippewas of Sarnia Reserve, see: Chippewas of Sarnia First Nation, *Aamjiwnaang First Nation* (Sarnia: Chippewas of Sarnia First Nation, 2001?); Mrs. B. C. Farrand, *Indians at Sarnia* (1889; Brights Grove ON: George L. Smith, 1975); Nicholas Plain, *The History of Chippewas of Sarnia and the history of Sarnia Reserve* (Sarnia?: the Author, 1950); Terry Plain, *"Aabiish-Enjibaayin": Chippewas of Sarnia oral history project* (Sarnia: Chippewas of Sarnia First Nation, 1994); and Leslie K. Smith and George L. Smith, *Historical references to Sarnia Indian Reserve* (Brights Grove ON: George Smith, 1976).

82. NAC RG 10, Volume 3027, File 230,000, Reel C-11313, Adam English to the Secretary of the Department of Indian Affairs, 23 January 1901.

83. Chippewas of Sarnia First Nation, *Aamjiwnaang First Nation* (Sarnia; Chippewas of Sarnia First Nation, 2001?).

84. Glen C. Phillips, *Sarnia: a picture history of the Imperial City* (Sarnia: Iron Gate Publishing, 1990), 12.

85. Adam English to the Secretary of the Department of Indian Affairs, 23 January 1901.

86. Joshua Adams to the Secretary of the Department of Indian Affairs, 12 January 1901.

87. Adam English to the Secretary of the Department of Indian Affairs, 23 January 1901.

88. NAC RG 10, Volume 3081, File 270,000-2 pt. 2A, Reel C-11321, Letter from Francis W. Jacobs, Sarnia, to Charles A. Cooke, 11 March 1904.

89. Great Britain. Oxford University. Rhodes House Library. British & Foreign Anti-Slavery Society and Aborigines Protection Society fonds, MG 40-Q 31 [located at the NAC on microfilm reels A-1647 to A-1650], Correspondence - Rev. John A. McDonald to Mr. Travers Buxton, 21 March 1911.

90. *Annual Report 1911*, 78.

91. For further description of the Lennox Island Reserve, in and around the time of the establishment of the Lady Wood Library, see M. Olga McKenna, *Micmac by choice: Elsie Sark–an island legend* (Halifax: Formac Publishing, 1990).

92. MG 40-Q 31, Bequest of Lennox Island, P. E. I., 6 July 1887.

93. *Annual report 1911,* 78.

94. The records are not entirely clear as to who was responsible for the founding of the Lady Wood Library. However, Superintendent Arsenault's description of the building made in his report to the Department in 1911 and additional correspondence by Reverend John A. McDonald indicate that Indian Affairs certainly was not responsible. McDonald's letters to persons involved with the Lady Wood estate in England seem to indicate that the initiative and planning of the library came from within the Lennox Island community, although it is difficult to say so with absolute certainty.

95. The Lady Wood Library still serves these purposes today. Now known as the Lennox Island Community Access Centre, it is a place where members of the community can participate in upgrading classes and basic computer and Internet training six days of the week, and free access to computers and the Internet is provided. Additionally, the Centre also houses a science camp every summer for children ages six through thirteen and a small collection of reading materials. The Lennox Island Community Access Centre is coordinated by Emily Bernard: (902) 831-3438.

96. Until approximately January of 1911, the title of the Lady Wood Estate was held by Trustees of the Aborigines Protection Society in England, and administered by a committee of management in Prince Edward Island. In early 1911 the title was transferred to "His Majesty the King, as represented by the Superintendent General of Indian Affairs in trust for the Indians of Prince Edwards Island." The building of the Lady Wood Library in late 1910 appears to have been the last activity administered by the trust before its transfer to Indian Affairs. See: Great Britain. Oxford University. Rhodes House Library. British & Foreign Anti-Slavery Society and Aborigines Protection Society fonds, MG 40-Q 31 [located at the NAC on microfilm reels A-1647 to A-1650], Correspondence - J. D. McLean, to Aborigines Protection Society, 26 January 1911.

97. John Joe Sark, *Micmac legends of Prince Edward Island* (Lennox Island: Lennox Island Band Council & Ragweed Press, 1988), 17.

98. *Annual report 1911,* 301.

99. Milloy, 176-177.

100. *Annual report 1911*, 316, 324.

101. *Annual report 1911,* 596, 598.

102. *Annual report 1914* pt. II, 136, 139; *Annual report 1915* pt. II, 142.

103. *Annual report 1916* pt. II, 136.

104. See: Jean L. Manore, "A Vision of trust: the legal, moral and spiritual foundations of Shingwauk Hall," *Native Studies Review* 9.2 (1993-94): 1-21; and J. R. Miller, *Shingwauk's vision: a history of Native residential schools* (Toronto: University of Toronto Press, 1996).

4

1930 through 1960

Community development, philanthropy, and educational neglect: Aboriginal and non-Aboriginal literary perspectives

> It seems a pity that a book or books, containing subjects of
> interest, or information, to the Indian youths were not
> provided for the use of Indian schools.[1]

Libraries in a neglected and underfunded education system

The first quarter of the twentieth century saw a movement towards the discussion and establishment of libraries for First Peoples in Canada, particularly within the day, residential, and industrial schools administered by the missions and the Department of Indian Affairs. In most cases, however, little development actually took place. With the exception of the Lady Wood Library at Lennox Island, it would appear that no library collections were established in any communities outside of the schools. The mandate and philosophy behind the establishment of the Lady Wood Library, in combining the notions of Western print culture with a community hall and meeting place where traditional knowledge could also be shared, was likewise unique. Although little documentary evidence of the nature of their collections exists, it can be said with near certainty that those libraries that were established within the Indian schools were chronically underfunded and heavily weighted towards a curriculum entirely unsuited to the educational needs and interests of Aboriginal children. Discussions surrounding libraries and the purchasing of books for the schools that take place within the Department after 1930 are better documented and support these assertions, but unfortunately do not indicate that much improvement was made until well into the 1950s.

John S. Milloy, historian of Aboriginal education, has discussed the neglectful state of teaching and learning that was present in the schools up until the mid-1940s, demonstrating that the Indian education system was generally ineffective in producing well-educated students.[2] He notes that by the end of the second World War, the system had failed to meet its goals of producing a well-educated, resocialized generation of children who could be assimilated into non-Aboriginal communities. This failure had occurred in large part due to the poor and neglected education to which most Aboriginal children were subjected. Inadequate funding, a lack of supervision on the operation of schools, and a general lack of insight or vision on behalf of the Department had been the main reasons for this poor education, resulting in a situation where every element of the school curricula and the system's administration was saturated with problems. In part, this had originated from the rapid and uncontrolled growth of the school system driven by the churches and missions through the latter part of the nineteenth century, which meant that by the early 1900s, the system had been pushed beyond the means of its financial resources. But additionally, the Department under Duncan Campbell Scott, and later R. A. Hoey, failed to exercise or demonstrate any significant insight or action into the improved operation and output of the schools. The Indian educational system essentially drifted without any application of corrective measures to solve rather obvious problems until well into the 1940s, with actual improvement not arising until after 1970.[3]

The quality of learning at the schools was generally poor at both vocational and "literary" levels. In the interests of assimilation, the Department dictated a curriculum of agricultural training to be exercised at most schools, despite their location and what the local job prospects might be following graduation. On a "literary" level, meaning the arts of reading, writing, and arithmetic, students were even more poorly taught. At best, most students acquired little more than a basic literacy education.[4] Furthermore, children were more likely to be busy most of the day doing routine chores and working to maintain the school and its grounds than being subjected to a classroom curriculum. In 1930, it was reported that three quarters of all Aboriginal pupils in Canada were in the grades one through three, and only three in every one hundred advanced beyond grade six. In comparison, the general average at non-Aboriginal public schools in all the provinces in 1930 indicated that well over half were beyond grade three, with a third studying at levels above grade six.[5] In 1946, a survey of Ontario Indian day schools revealed that 63 percent of students in grades three through eight were reading in English at an accuracy rate determined to be low or very low.[6] These statistics are particularly telling, given that it was the provincial curricula to which the Department of Indian Affairs consistently compared the curricula of the Indian schools. The "literary" part of the Indian curricula was almost entirely modeled after their provincial counterparts, meaning that Aboriginal children were expected to learn and be inspired by reading materials and textbooks that were designed for better educated non-Aboriginal children who attended better financed schools and came from dramatically different cultural and linguistic backgrounds. Few Department officials questioned the appropriateness of curricula that were designed for non-Aboriginal children, and the schools continued to teach them for several decades. Very little or nothing in the Indian school curricula reflected anything of Aboriginal cultures and histories. Furthermore, the financial constraints held over the schools meant that few could afford to hire effective or even qualified teachers who might have been inspired or motivated enough to work creatively with the inappropriate tools at hand. And the hiring of Aboriginal teachers, like John J. Sark at Lennox Island, was extremely rare and generally not preferred by the Department.[7]

On occasion, however, there were signs of educational success within the schools. The general effects of a Western education, although not well suited culturally to Aboriginal children, and rarely taught effectively, were indelible for some students. Exposure to books and Western literacy, although minimal in most schools, had the eventual effect of producing the occasional student that excelled within the classroom and after graduation. At the Red Deer Industrial Institute, for instance, a school which had established a library in 1908, students were said to have written essays of such quality that "some of them were published in the local newspaper and might have brought credit to many white pupils."[8] Frederick H. Paget, a departmental accountant and regular critic of the schools, noted in 1908 that graduates of the Battleford Industrial School were all generally improved citizens as a result of their education, and were "meeting with a fair success" following graduation. One of these students, Louis Laronde, had gone on to graduate from the University of Manitoba with high honors to become a missionary.[9] The Battleford Industrial School had been the first school in the country to establish successfully a library for its students in 1893.

Nevertheless, the overwhelming consensus of opinion generally indicated that the schools were underfunded, weighting their time more heavily on manual labor than a literary education, taught by exceedingly poor teachers, and expected to teach a curriculum that was entirely unsuitable for the cultural and linguistic backgrounds of most Aboriginal children. Except in the cases of the Red Deer Industrial Institute and the Battleford Industrial School, library collections under these circumstances in the schools during the first part of the twentieth century appear to have been of little value in nurturing the interests of students. Lists of books in the day school libraries, and correspondence within the Department regarding the acquisition of "supplementary reading books" for the schools between 1931 and 1943, serve to better illustrate the nature of these library collections, their intended purposes, and their minimal value to students.

Day school libraries and supplementary reading books, 1931-1943

Some forty years following the first discussions surrounding the establishment of libraries in Indian schools, the Department of Indian Affairs began compiling lists of books it deemed worthy to be used by students for "supplementary reading" purposes, and which could be included in the school library collections. Although the Department had been responsible for the purchasing and distribution of "stationery and books" to the schools since at least 1917[10] (before which time the school's themselves had been mostly responsible for purchasing and acquiring reading materials for their libraries), it did not make any significant efforts in selecting or evaluating materials for use outside of the prescribed classroom curricula. The lists which the Department began compiling in 1931 were for materials suitable for "supplementary reading," meaning printed materials other than the readers and textbooks intended for use in the classroom, that were to be collected for inclusion in the school libraries.

This marked a rather sudden change in the nature of how the Department viewed books and libraries as part of the education experience. Previously, libraries and books for use outside of the classroom experience were little more than an afterthought at best, but following 1931, they began to take on a marked importance. Such a dramatic change was likely influenced in part by the fact that the Department underwent a major restructuring in 1932 following the retirement of Superintendent Duncan Campbell Scott. Scott's successor, Dr. Harold W. McGill, signified a new era within Indian Affairs, one characterized by an emerging concern with the outcomes of the education provided at the

Indian schools, and a noticeable emphasis in fostering community development. This resulted in a considerable degree of discussion within the Department concerning library books, particularly by Philip Phelan, Chief of the Training Division, who began to compile lists of works deemed suitable to act as supplementary reading materials in the schools.

Philip Phelan and George Dill, a teacher at Little Current on Manitoulin Island, Ontario, began compiling lists of supplementary reading materials for the Indian schools across the country in 1932. The Department had been in the habit of supplying the schools with textbooks for classroom instruction for a number of years. These textbooks were for the most part the same textbooks that were supplied to non-Aboriginal public and separate schools by the provinces. The lists of supplementary materials compiled by Phelan and Dill in the 1930s would continue to follow this trend, consisting of book titles derived from similar provincial lists, the education catalogs of mainstream publishing houses, and recommended titles from such organizations as the American Library Association and the American-based National Council of Mothers.[11]

The make-up of these lists did not appear in any way to have considered the educational needs and interests of Aboriginal children, or that theirs might have differed from the needs and interests of non-Aboriginal children in the mainstream provincially-run schools. In fact, the concerns of Dill and Phelan in compiling these lists of titles were not in researching and grading the literature themselves. Their concern was with where they might obtain lists of materials that had already been graded and recommended, and at what cost to the Department. The only indication that the educational needs of Aboriginal children might demand different titles comes in Dill's observation that some of the prepared lists were "poorly graded," and that to compensate he planned to "turn my children loose on them, watch them carefully and listen to their comments. With this information in hand, I shall revise the list's grading. In the case of any book which they do not appear to like, and which I think they should, I shall enlist the aid of other teachers and so on until I am satisfied."[12] Dill's critique that the lists are "poorly graded" reflects, on one hand, the dismal quality of education that most Aboriginal children were subjected to, but also highlights the fact that books designed for educating and stimulating non-Aboriginal children might not be the same titles or preferred method of learning suitable for students in the Indian schools. This insight, however, appears to have been lost in the actions of Phelan and Dill, who instead assumed the grading to be the problem–not the books themselves. Further, Dill's insistence that any book not liked by his students would then be scrutinized by other teachers, "until I am satisfied," implies in the end that his opinion and, if necessary, the opinions of other teachers, were all that truly mattered in the selection of supplementary reading materials–not the students.

The far from sophisticated methods of Phelan and Dill in compiling the supplementary book lists, and their apparently minimal concerns for the educational wants and needs of the children of the Indian schools, reflected the departmental view that the education of Aboriginal children should closely resemble the education of children in the mainstream, provincially-run schools. Further, ordering titles that were already included on the provincial lists meant that the Department could obtain a great number of titles in the most cost-efficient means. Publishing houses would be sure to have a large stock of titles that were known to be in demand from the provincial school authorities, and Indian Affairs could benefit from the cost reductions of large publishing runs.[13] The actions of Phelan and Dill also reflect an admission of sorts that the "literary" part of the education of Aboriginal children had up until that point been very poor. In compiling lists of supplementary reading materials, the Department was acknowledging that the reading and Western literacy skills of the students in the Indian schools were not meeting the standards set by the provincial education authorities, the students of which Aboriginal children were expected one day to fully integrate with.

Given that the Indian schools' mandates were essentially geared towards integrating and assimilating Aboriginal children into the wider Canadian population, it is of little surprise to discover that the books the Department was collecting to include in the school libraries were no different than those materials found in the libraries of non-Aboriginal schools. Titles, such as C. C. Goldring's, *We are Canadian citizens*, the Blackie's *Bible stories* series and *A Work book in British history* published by J. M. Dent and Sons, are typical of the general nature of the supplementary lists, as are fictional works like *Robinson Crusoe, Aesop's fables* and *Children of the pioneers*.[14] All of these titles were commonly purchased and stocked by non-Aboriginal school libraries throughout the country, and reflected little or nothing of the North American First Peoples' experience. Titles included that did address an Aboriginal experience or presence, like *War trail of Big Bear, Men of the North, Three little Indians*, and the *Red man's wonder book*, were under almost any circumstances poor, inappropriate, and mostly fictional stories written by non-Aboriginals that would have done little to instill a sense of cultural awareness or pride in students at the Indian schools. Efforts to include unique works that might appeal to or encourage students at the Indian schools, such as that of British Columbia Indian Inspector, Captain Gerald H. Barry, to publish a book of legends compiled by Aboriginal students near Vancouver, were rare and unfruitful.[15] Requests made to the Department by individual schools and teachers who requested to purchase materials on their own that they deemed more appropriate were likewise refused. The Supervising Principal at the Roman Catholic Indian Day School at Caughnawaga, Sister Mary Cleophas, made one such request to the Department in June of 1938, only to be refused by Phelan on the grounds that "I regret that it is not possible to authorize you to buy books, but we are required by Act of Parliament to purchase all books through the Government Stationery Office."[16] Given the financial constraints felt by many of the schools and missions, few could afford to go out of their way to purchase reading materials on their own account behind the back of the Department, but it is entirely possible that a few teachers did bypass Indian Affairs.

Library collections, like most other aspects of the Indian education experience, were clearly deemed by the Department to act as tools in the process of integrating and assimilating Aboriginal children into the wider population. Libraries of materials selected largely from provincial curricula, from the Department's point of view, were assumed to promote the highly coveted Western practices of literacy, embodying preferred notions of citizenship, family, morality, and capitalism. The collections, however, were instead highly ineffective in fostering these ideals. Most students at the Indian schools failed to engage with the books chosen by the Department. This was in part because they were generally poorly taught and spent little time engaging in literary pursuits, but also because the library collections were largely built on the ideological foundations of the Department and placed in the hands of uninspired teachers. Most books were therefore of little cultural interest or value to Aboriginal students. These works failed to raise much interest in reading or learning in general because they did not speak to Aboriginal experience.

It was not until 1942 that the Department at last recognized that the library and reading materials they had been recommending for more than ten years were ineffective. Based on long experience, the Synod of the Diocese of Qu'Appelle in June of that year passed the following resolution:

> Whereas the curriculum for the Course of Study in Indian Schools is at present expected to be the same as in the Public Schools of the Province: Be it resolved that the Indian Department be asked to consider the revision and adjustment

of the Course of Study to the effect that it may be made more
suitable to the needs and preparation for after school life of
our Indian children.[17]

By 1942, the Department under R. A. Hoey, who was then the Superintendent of Welfare and Training, was beginning to take steps to formally
recognize that the education provided at the Indian schools across the
country was generally ineffective in meeting its goals, and was attempting
to take action in correcting this long-overlooked situation. Hoey replied to
the Synod explaining, "At the present time we are endeavouring to revise
the curriculum for Indian schools so as to make it more practical for Indian
children."[18] The tenure of Duncan Campbell Scott, and for several years
following his retirement, had been marked by an educational system that
remained largely unchanged and without any corrective measures taken to
address obvious problems. These included notably poor teachers, poor
teacher salaries, a system of learning that undermined both classroom and
skills training, and the uninspired selection of text books and reading
materials that worked to inhibit learning rather than foster knowledge.
Although Hoey, Phelan, and other senior staff would appear to be more
receptive to the problems facing the Indian education system through the
1930s, as John Milloy has noted, "they moved no more quickly to reform
them, and realistically, to the extent that some were caused by funding
problems, they had no greater resources at their disposal to attend to them
than had ever been the case."[19]

In his letter of response to the Synod of Qu'Appelle in the spring of
1942, R. A. Hoey finally acknowledged that reform of the education
policies of the Department could no longer be avoided. In the fall of 1944,
he would go on to remark that, "The time has come for the Churches and
the Government to undertake a very careful survey of our whole Indian
education setup."[20] However, the speed at which this required reform
would take place was painfully slow. In Hoey's own words, "You will
understand, of course, that it will require a considerable period of time to
effect this necessary improvement."[21] A considerable period of time
indeed. The nature of the Indian school libraries, although at least
surveyed in 1943, would be not be changed in any significant way until
after 1960.

Hoey appeared to be true to his word that reform was necessary when
he requested that a Departmental survey be conducted of all library
materials in the Indian day schools in 1943:

> The Department desires to gradually build up a library in

every school. In order to do so effectively it is necessary to have a list of books at present in the library of each school. When compiling your record of books list them according to grade, giving the title, author, publishing company and also the number of copies. The above refers to library books, supplementary readers, but not to authorized text books.[22]

This survey of the existing day school libraries in 1943 offers a first glimpse into the collections that had been built and maintained by various teachers and school officials through the previous fifty years. Considering that the day schools up until the 1940s had been the least well funded of the three types of schools endorsed by the Department, it is unfortunate that no similar surveys of the early residential and industrial school libraries were conducted. In the mid-1940s, most day schools in the country were quite small. Following the model of non-Aboriginal rural school houses, most consisted of only one room, some had functional basements, and the majority had insufficient natural light and were generally unequipped with electricity.[23] Beginning in the early 1940s, the Department began to take steps to improve the conditions and equipment at the Indian day schools. It is in this light that Hoey conducted his survey of the day school libraries, and from the responses he received, improvement in this area was much welcomed and sorely needed.

The survey was conducted between April and June of 1943, at which time there were 253 day schools across the country. Of these, slightly over half, 140, were reported to have some kind of school library. These libraries varied widely in size, with the largest reported to house 143 books, and the smallest only one item (which technically does not constitute a library, but gives some indication as to the conditions that some schools faced). The national average, in terms of collection size, amounted to approximately 72 books (see Table 1 for more detailed statistics from the survey). Provincially (excluding Alberta, where the only reporting day school in the province had a library), New Brunswick boasted the highest percentage of schools with libraries, at 90 percent; Manitoban school libraries on average housed the largest collections, reportedly at 123 books; while Ontario schools, on average, had the smallest collections, at 36 books. The Ontario day school libraries also fluctuated the most in size. The Moraviantown day school on the Thames River,[24] for instance, maintained the largest collection in the country at 143 items, while on the other hand, the Buzwah day school at the east end of Manitoulin Island reported a library with only one item.

In the midst of forwarding to Hoey their statistics on the existence

Table 4.1. Day school libraries in 1943[25]

Region	Total schools	Libraries	Smallest	Largest	Average size
CAN	253	140	1	143	71.9
PEI	1	0	–	–	–
YK	2	0	–	–	–
ON	79	46	1	143	36.4
SK	26	12	45	58	52.3
AB	1	1	69	69	69
PQ	24	11	59	141	71.9
BC	52	28	6	97	74
NS	11	9	71	114	104.6
NB	10	9	99	113	105.6
NWT	4	2	117	118	117.5
MB	42	22	115	140	123.3

and/or size of their school collections, many teachers and school officials took the liberty to explain to the Superintendent the existing state of their libraries, and their feelings in general towards this new departmental initiative. Again and again the teachers, principals and Indian Agents writing to Hoey complained that their existing collection was either too small, in terrible disrepair, collected on their own initiative (thus contra-dicting Departmental policy regarding the purchasing of books), or made up of inappropriate donations from local philanthropists. Many wrote that their school had no library at all, and almost all who responded welcomed warmly the initiative to establish and improve the day school libraries. Take for instance the comments of Mary B. Ross, a teacher at Walpole Island, who remarked, "I have made a survey of our libraries here and the books are really in a bad state of repair. Some I could not find the fly leaf for the publisher's name. I debated whether they were worth reporting–but merely say our library was nil save for those sent us last year. However, my conscience dictated I send in the list; here it is."[26] Mr. McDonald, teacher at the Red Pheasant Day School in Saskatchewan noted, "As you see there are very few [library books] and we would very much appreciate any books which the department may be able to send."[27] The Principal at the Restigouche Day School in Quebec explained, "I am unable to do so [report on the school library], as we have not a supplementary reader at our disposal. All we have on hand are the authorised text books."[28] Janet McCaig, teacher at the day school at Shawanaga, Ontario, was one of the rare teachers that admitted to building a library on her own initiative: "During the past six years which I have taught at Shawanaga Indian Day School I have collected one hundred and fifty discarded library books from Parry Sound Library."[29] Others would note that their existing collections mostly consisted of donations. The teacher at the Oka village school remarked, "There are many books donated by church societies which are really for older people, so I did not include many of them in my grade VII list," also explaining "You will note that the books for Beginners and Junior grades are very few. Most of my students are in the lower grades...."[30] Ethel George, a teacher (who was likely an Aboriginal person) at the No. 2 Day School on Walpole Island, noted that the books at that school were largely inappropriate, having been "donated by the I. O. D. E. [Imperial Order Daughters of the Empire] of Wallaceburg, but in general are too Difficult for the pupils in this school."[31]

The responses to Hoey's survey of day school libraries unanimously applauded the idea of establishing new libraries and upgrading old ones. And it was very clear that existing collections in the schools were mostly haphazardly organized, almost entirely unsuitable or in desperate disrepair. Other teachers took this opportunity to make suggestions to Hoey on what role they felt the new libraries should take, and what items they felt best suited their children. A teacher at the West Bay Indian Day School in Excelsior, Ontario would note, "[I] have found that the children in the school are more interested in the 'Read and Do' books than in straight story books. However, any books which would increase their knowledge of English would be much appreciated."[32] Many teachers, in fact, would note their desire to have books that could assist their efforts in teaching their students the English language. And even more noted that their students did not much like reading, instead preferring books with a heavy visual element. For example, the teacher at the Scotch Settlement School would remark, "I find that the children of this school read very little. They prefer pictures.... Large print simple stories. These children can read but the story has to be very simple for them to get any meaning from them. Personally I think no books greater than grade V should be sent to the schools in this agency. A few nursery rhyme books with pictures and a number of national Geographics [sic] (second hand) are very advisable."[33]

Some of this evidence suggests that many Aboriginal students read books quite differently than their mostly non-Aboriginal teachers expected. Rather than demonstrating the conventional traits of Western literacy, Aboriginal children's preferences for the visual, rather than textual, elements of books suggests a unique form of literacy in and of itself, a kind of reading without words. Several teachers intuitively seemed to have understood that alternative literacies needed to be addressed in the teaching of Aboriginal students, but interpreted these not as skills, but merely as signs of a pre-literate stage. Other teachers incorrectly interpreted Aboriginal children's preferences for picture books as demonstrating a lack of mental capacity to read and learn at the same level as non-Aboriginal children, failing to consider that differences in cultural ways of knowing and poor education may have also been factors. While some teachers recognized the value of expanding upon visual literacies and reading and writing without words, the primary concerns of the Department and most teachers in the day schools was not to foster these ways of learning and knowing, but was instead to find success in promoting and drilling a Western literacy in the English language. Library collections, by extension, were in most cases interpreted by the Department and teachers for these same purposes.

If Hoey showed some initiative in surveying the day school libraries in 1943, it does not appear as though he followed up with much significant funding and support in the immediate years that followed. The funding difficulties that faced the Department in the realm of education were particularly evident throughout the 1930s and into the 1940s. Despite Hoey's 1943 survey of libraries which clearly indicated that improvement was necessary, no significant or immediate increase in attention to libraries or books emerged. Only in 1948, three years following the second World War, would more monies became available to buy books. Between 1917 and 1960, the Department spent a minimum of 0.7% (in 1918) of their entire education budget on "Stationery and books," and a maximum of

2.8% (in 1948, 1952, 1954, and 1957), rarely fluctuating any great amount from year to year. On average, the Department was spending 2.0% of their education budget on the purchasing of stationery and books for all of the schools across the country.[34] These included text books, supplementary reading and library materials, and general writing materials such as paper, scribblers, envelopes, pens, pencils, and so on. That much improvement within the day school libraries emerged before 1960 is difficult to pinpoint. Certainly an awareness that improvement was desperately needed was fostered, but without significant increases in its budget relating to books and libraries, it is doubtful that many improvements were ever undertaken by the Department of Indian Affairs.

"Admittedly an experiment": Traveling libraries in Ontario and British Columbia, 1939-1945

School libraries aside, and with the request of the Chippewas of Sarnia having been declined at the turn of the century, the Lady Wood Library at Lennox Island would remain the only publicly accessible library within an Aboriginal community for nearly fifty years. In lieu of a Departmental interest or initiative in establishing public libraries on the Reserves, a few communities in Ontario and British Columbia began approaching the issue of community accessible libraries from a different angle, beginning in 1939. In February of that year, the Indian Agent of the Rice and Mud Lake Agency near Peterborough, Ontario, V. M. Eastwood wrote to R. A. Hoey requesting that the Travelling Library Service offered by the Public Library Branch of the Ontario Department of Education be made available to the school and the Reserve of Mud Lake:

> I think that this service would be of considerable help and enjoyment to members of the Band as a whole and the cost very slight. For some years past I have endeavoured to build up a small library from donations of books and discarded books from the Peterborough Public Library, which Mr. Dela Fosse, the Librarian, has been kind enough to give me. This has, in the past, been kept up by the principal of the school and although limited in scope, I find they have been very much enjoyed by the members of the Band.... If you approve of taking advantage of this service, I would also like to take the matter up with Mr. John Loukes, teacher for the Alnwick Band, with the idea of providing the same service there.[35]

Traveling libraries were first introduced in British Columbia, Quebec, and Ontario shortly before the turn of the century, and similar initiatives were also organized and operated by the universities of Alberta, Dalhousie, Manitoba, and McGill, and by provincial authorities in Saskatchewan and Ontario. The objectives of these services were to supplement the available collections of small public libraries, as well as serving organized clubs, institutes, and schools in rural and urban communities where public library service was not available. In Ontario, for instance, the Travelling Libraries Service was known to serve a diverse group, including railway, mining and lumber camps, and forest rangers.[36] These services by 1939 were mostly provided through the provincial government authorities in conjunction with the province's public library legislation. In most cases, books were shipped to communities in cases of forty to fifty volumes, or alternatively by bookmobile (literally a library on wheels), and were to be made available without charge to the entire community.

If any charge was associated with a traveling library, it was usually in the form of carriage or shipment charges, and in the case of the Mud Lake Agency request, the cost would not have been more than two or three dollars for shipment from Toronto. However, despite the small price tag and Hoey's supposed concerns with improving education to Aboriginal peoples through the 1930s and 1940s, the Mud Lake request to take part in the Ontario Travelling Library Service was flatly denied by the Department. In Hoey's own words, "I feel that in the case of Indian schools it would be preferable to add some books each year to the library in the school and this would make a good selection of books available. The Department is prepared to supply a reasonable number of library books to the Mud Lake school each year."[37] Hoey completely ignored addressing the issue of providing library service to the community outside of the school environment, eliminating a clear opportunity for community development and ensuring that the Department would maintain sole control over the education of the members of the Mud Lake Band.

Five years later, another request regarding traveling libraries was made, this time by F. Earl Anfield, Indian Agent at Bella Coola, British Columbia. Anfield's request, however, was noticeably different in one important way–he proposed that the Department be responsible for "the establishment of two or three small traveling libraries, say of 50 books each, for the use of these larger coast villages. It will admittedly be an experiment."[38] The Indian Agent went on to justify the case for traveling libraries by explaining, "The reading material of most villages consists almost entirely of the type of magazines found on the coast steamer newstands, generally speaking a far from appetizing type of reading material for Indians." Clearly the nineteenth-century notions of literary merit, useful knowledge, and moral improvement were alive and well in some circles well into the twentieth century. This was particularly so, it seems, when one considers the education of Aboriginal peoples who, for lack of any other interesting or inspiring books, chose "reading material that is both salacious and definitely dangerous."[39] In Anfield's mind, "a well chosen travelling library" could deter the young members of the coastal villages from reading such morally inappropriate material, and instill in them a sense of reading for useful knowledge, rather than pleasure.

Anfield claimed that the idea of improving the available reading material was not his alone, but had been inspired by the queries of a number of young people, "and in Bella Coola where a young people's group is now functioning regularly, it was the subject of a motion last evening."[40] As had been the case in Sarnia some forty-three years earlier, and more than thirty years previously at Lennox Island, libraries were envisioned by some Aboriginal peoples as beneficial to their education and rightful place within the Dominion. The Department and the missions had consistently failed to provide enough adequate resources for reading materials and were predominantly concerned with encouraging Aboriginal children to read the same materials as their non-Aboriginal counterparts (and when it came to salacious reading materials, they were evidently successful). Ignoring repeated requests for culturally appropriate reading materials by First Peoples and non-Aboriginals alike, the Department had neglected to pick up on the opportunity to truly inspire Western literacy within the communities for more than forty years.

Hoey's initial response to Anfield's request for a traveling library service is very similar to his rejection of the Mud Lake proposal some five years previous. Once again the Superintendent confused the traveling library proposal to be an extension of the existing day school libraries, and informed Anfield that although the Department was "deeply interested," there were no funds available for the establishment of such libraries.[41] Refusing to let Hoey's apparent confusion stand in the way of the proposal, Anfield responded:

> My inquiry regarding the provision of travelling libraries had no reference to the small school libraries now at certain Indian Day Schools. I was interested in books for adults and I had in mind the establishment of a two hundred book library at the Agency itself. This would be broken down into four fifty-

book libraries which would be circulated in our larger
villages.... I am convinced that unless something of this nature
is undertaken our Indians will come to the conclusion that the
white man's literary tastes run largely to the present pulp type
of magazine which is really the only form of reading material
to which he at present has access.[42]

An increasing desire and motivation to read appears to have been evident
in many coastal Aboriginal communities, but the people faced dismally
inappropriate collections maintained by the day schools and were unable
to purchase books due to insufficient resources on the Reserves. Anfield
heard the plea of the people at Bella Coola, Bella Bella, and Kitamaat, and
was adamant in his repeated requests to the Department that improvement
in reading material was necessary. Remarkably, however, his strong case
for the Department taking an initiative in establishing and funding a
traveling libraries service in the province went unanswered. Despite the
rhetoric after 1943 that community development would be a funding
priority for the Department, Hoey's only understanding of libraries would
continue to be limited to initiatives exclusively within the day schools.
Presumably this was in part due to insufficient funding available to Indian
Affairs, but more importantly because the Department could maintain a
degree of power over the selection and purchasing of books if libraries
were contained within the schools. Encouragement of libraries outside of
the schools was thus effectively nullified.

It would take one more request, this time from the Indian Agent of the
Rama Agency in Ontario, in September of 1944, for the Department finally
to get the message that the day school libraries were simply ineffective and
insufficient to meet the reading and education demands of Aboriginal
communities. A teacher within the Rama Agency, a Mr. Hayward, made
a request almost identical to that of Mr. Eastwood's at Mud Lake more
than five years earlier, suggesting that the school at Rama be allowed to
make use of the Ontario Department of Education's Travelling Library
Service. Hayward was particularly keen to obtain slides and films through
the service.[43] Cautious of the Department's war-time funding, Hoey
hesitantly agreed to the proposal:

> In view of the critical times in which we are living you can
> readily appreciate that we are not at all anxious to assume
> additional obligations, particularly at a school such as Rama
> where the attendance has been wholly unsatisfactory. How-
> ever, it has occurred to me that the use of this library and
> these slides by the teachers in charge might result in an

awakened interest in the school on the part of the parents. In
any event it might be undertaken as an experiment....[44]

In approving the Rama proposal, the Department had finally approved the
use of traveling libraries on the Reserves. However, it did so under the
premise that a traveling library be used to supplement the existing
collections at the Rama Day School. There is no indication that the
Department encouraged the use of such libraries outside of school
contexts, and it is difficult to gauge the extent to which the Travelling
Libraries Service was made available to adult members of the communities. In Ontario in particular, the mandate of the Travelling Libraries
Service was to provide a collection of books "without charge to the entire
community and not only to members of an association, club or church."[45]
But in 1956 W. A. Roedde, of the Thunder Bay District Library Co-
Operative in the north western part of the province, would report visiting
the Pic River Reserve only to provide reading materials to a small group
of university educated teachers.[46] Despite repeated pleas throughout the
country to extend library services to all Aboriginal community members,
adults and children alike, the Department of Indian Affairs effectively
stalled all initiatives, limiting the extent of libraries to the day schools.
Only in the apparently isolated instance of philanthropic support at Lennox
Island was a community successful in establishing its own library. Most
communities did not have the financial means to hire their own teachers,
let alone have the resources to establish something like a library.

Abiding by the Missionary Society: the literary efforts of Edward Ahenakew, 1923-1961

Reverend Canon Edward Ahenakew, D.D. (1885-1961) was not a
well-known writer in his lifetime, but his literary accomplishments and
aspirations are significant. Born into a Christian Cree family at the Sandy
Lake reserve in Saskatchewan, Ahenakew was schooled on the reserve at
the Atahkakohp Day School and later Emmanuel College Boarding School
in Prince Albert,[47] Wycliffe College in Toronto, and the Anglican
Theological School at the University of Saskatchewan in Saskatoon before
his ordination as an Anglican priest in 1912. Reverend Ahenakew later
attended medical school at the University of Alberta where he was a
member of the University of Alberta Literary Club.[48]

Ahenakew became rather well-known as a writer after his death in

1961 when Ruth Buck edited his handwritten manuscripts of Cree stories and published a collection of these as *Voices of the Plains Cree* with McClelland and Stewart in 1973. One half of the collection are stories which Ahenakew recorded on paper after interviewing Chief Thunderchild, and the second half of the collection is a fictional story called "Old Keyam" written by Ahenakew himself. These stories are now considered historical documents and capture something of the Cree ethos and way of thinking, according to Cree scholar Stan Cuthand, but were never published or widely shared during Ahenakew's lifetime.[49]

Reverend Ahenakew's literary aspirations began as early as 1903, when at the age of eighteen he began producing a handwritten newsletter in Cree syllabics while teaching at the John Smith's Day School. The newsletter was short-lived however, as Ahenakew only taught at the school for one year before continuing his own studies in Toronto. Twenty years later, while recuperating on Thunderchild's reserve from a severe illness brought on by the stresses of medical school, Ahenakew began recording in writing the oral stories of Chief Thunderchild, and wrote "Old Keyam." While at medical school in Edmonton, Ahenakew had become friends with Professor Paul Wallace through the University of Alberta Literary Club.[50] Wallace was a professor of English at Lebanon Valley College in Pennsylvania, and during Ahenakew's convalescence on Thunderchild's reserve the two corresponded extensively about Ahenakew's aspirations to publish "Old Keyam" and to write "as things appear to the Indian himself."[51] Ahenakew even hoped that his stories, if published, might provide him with a small income through royalties. The majority of his writing was based on the old stories told to him by Chief Thunderchild, and Ahenakew was successful in publishing twenty-six of these as "Cree Trickster tales" in 1929 in the *Journal of American Folklore*.[52] The remainder of the stories, including "Old Keyam," would remain unpublished until after his death.[53]

Ahenakew recovered his health within the year and resumed his position with the Anglican Diocese of Saskatchewan. From this point forward, until his death, Ahenakew wrote exclusively from the perspective of an Anglican priest, abiding in the tradition of the Missionary Society. In February 1925, he began self-publishing the *Cree Monthly Guide*, a newsletter which he used to promote Christianity among the Cree. The newsletter was written in both Cree syllabics and the Roman alphabet, with editorials and articles on spiritual matters, and lessons in catechism. There were no Cree stories included in the newsletter, and Stan Cuthand recalls that there was little, if any, evidence of a Cree perspective in the writing.[54]

The Missionary Society was sponsoring the paper and providing some funds for its publication, and it appeared that Ahenakew did not wish to test the limits of the Church's generosity.

Ahenakew's writings in the *Cree Monthly Guide* stand in contrast to the stories that he recorded from Chief Thunderchild. In life he vigorously promoted the Anglican faith, but in death Ahenakew was largely remembered and praised for his Cree story, "Old Keyam," and for recording Cree cultural beliefs. Ahenakew, like other Aboriginal peoples who chose writing and publishing as a means of sharing his message to a wider Canadian audience, understood that in order to be heard and taken seriously it was necessary to adopt or conform to the "civilised" standard. Peter Jones and George Copway understood this necessity, and chose the Methodist church as a vehicle to communicate with non-Aboriginal audiences. Similarly, Charles Cooke and Dr. Oronhyatekha sought bureaucratic and professional status to make their marks. Ahenakew's own introduction in the *Voices of the Plains Cree* offers some insight: "The time has come in the life of my race when that which has been like a sealed book to the masses of our Canadian compatriots... should be known.... We have our own view of the life that has been imposed upon us, and these pages are written that others may glimpse what we feel and experience."[55] In an article Ahenakew wrote in the early 1950s about the Little Pine Day School, he expresses his optimism about the role and necessity of education for the First Peoples of Saskatchewan.[56] An initial reading suggests that Ahenakew is merely towing the line of his non-Aboriginal Church of England superiors, citing the need to "civilize" the Indians, but Ahenakew's active involvement in organizations like the League of Indians suggests his motives were deeper. In his introduction to "Old Keyam," Ahenakew encourages his Aboriginal readers, and points out to non-Aboriginal readers that as contemporary First Peoples, "we must face the challenge of our day, not as white men, but as good Indians."[57]

Events in Ahenakew's life point to a desire and demonstrate the difficulty of balancing the cultures. Ahenakew served for a brief period as the vice-president of the League of Indians for western Canada, an Aboriginal organization which lobbied the federal government to allow Indians to vote without losing their status and to allow them greater control over band properties and funds.[58] The Department of Indian Affairs and Bishop Walter Burd forced Ahenakew to discontinue his work with the League, however, insisting that a churchman should not meddle in the affairs of the state. Ahenakew's resignation from the League troubled his conscience greatly.[59]

The Native Brotherhood of British Columbia and *The Native Voice*, 1946

Despite the inadequacies of the Indian schools, there were instances where First Peoples were able to draw something out of their schooling, combine Western skills with traditional approaches to literacy and communication, and articulate some means to effectively employ Western understandings of the printed word. A good number of First Peoples in British Columbia, for instance, were successful in rising above the neglectful Western education supplied for them by the Department. The Native Indian Brotherhood of British Columbia in December of 1946 published the first issue of their official organ, *The Native Voice*, a newspaper that would eventually be issued widely throughout the province and abroad twice a month. The Native Brotherhood of British Columbia (NBBC) was first organized in 1931 by Alfred Adams of Masset, a Tsimshian lay minister within the Anglican Church. Adams modeled the British Columbian Brotherhood after the Alaska Native Brotherhood that had been established some years earlier. The internal structure of the NBBC was modeled after that of a labor union, but at its founding meeting in 1931, the organization clearly proposed a mandate that aimed to improve Aboriginal schooling and to promote the increased recognition of Aboriginal rights in the province. The Brotherhood's interests were, and have been for more than six decades, that of British Columbian and Canadian Aboriginal issues, including education, health benefits, and economic pursuits, particularly those of Aboriginal commercial fishers, for whom the NBBC served as an official bargaining agent.[60]

Adams characterized the NBBC's vision as follows: "We will knock on the doors, and we will knock on the doors, and we will knock on the doors of Government and one day, our children will walk through."[61] Some influential historians and anthropologists have labeled the NBBC as an organization demonstrating the degree to which Aboriginal peoples in British Columbia had become acculturated to the dominant Western society, largely because of the Brotherhood's resemblance to and cooperation with the non-Aboriginal-based United Fishermen and Allied Workers Union, and its ties to Protestantism.[62] But as Paul Tennant and others have noted, the Brotherhood and its supporters have held strong in their belief in Aboriginal title, opposing assimilation and favoring maintenance of an Aboriginal identity.[63] The NBBC in this light was envisioned as an adaptive mechanism to the outside pressures being imposed on Aboriginal communities and workers, particularly in the fishing industry, by non-Aboriginal workers and governments. In the interests of speaking to Western society on terms it could understand, the Brotherhood closely resembled non-Aboriginal organizations and methods of protest. Similarly, Alfred Adams and other leaders of the NBBC's close associations with Protestantism were rooted in an interest to maintain Aboriginal identity, rather than give it up. As Tennant has remarked, "Of critical importance in establishing and maintaining the strong linkage between Indian political action and Protestantism on the coast [the original organizing communities behind the NBBC were coastal] was the continuation of the potlatch, in only slightly disguised form, within Protestant religious ceremonies."[64]

The Brotherhood's official newspaper, *The Native Voice*, was envisioned in the words of the Brotherhood's President in 1946 as "a voice that will work for the advancement of our own common native welfare.... Through the *Native Voice* we will blend the whole of our problems into a common meeting ground for the discussion of whatever action that is necessary to benefit the well-being of all natives in B.C."[65] Well-written and consisting of articles composed by newspaper staff and contributors from throughout the country, the paper was in 1946 the culmination of a vision that had first emerged several years earlier. But in the editor's own words: "The trials and troubles of breaking into the ranks of journalism for Native people had not been fully appreciated; nor did we anticipate the responsibilities that would be heaped upon your organization when the start was made."[66] These difficulties prompted the NBBC to seek the assistance of Maisie Hurley, the non-Aboriginal wife of Tom Hurley, a well-known lawyer who had represented First Peoples in the province in a number of cases, and who often provided legal advice to the Brotherhood's leaders. Maisie Hurley was, in fact, the only non-Aboriginal person to ever be prominently associated with the NBBC or *The Native Voice*, but her involvement in the establishment of the paper would draw further criticisms from those who saw the Brotherhood as evidence of Aboriginal acculturation.[67]

The paper was clearly an outlet of Aboriginal protest and resistance to the increasing domination and interests of non-Aboriginal society in the second quarter of the twentieth century, particularly on social welfare and labor fronts. The publication of *The Native Voice* as early as 1946 was a unique and remarkable achievement. Following its establishment, a nationwide movement of periodical publication by Aboriginal groups and organizations began to emerge, which coincided with a growing political expression and a desire for Indian control of Indian affairs among First Peoples in Canada. These publications were distributed widely, drawing communities together in political causes, as well as assisting in the reassertion of Aboriginal languages and knowledge.[68]

The Brotherhood's motivations in establishing a widely distributed and accessible newspaper at this relatively early date were undoubtedly influenced by its leaders' close ties to Protestantism. Protestant missionaries were remarkably effective in employing the printed word among Aboriginal populations throughout the country, leaving an indelible effect. In the case of the First Peoples of British Columbia, Protestantism was uniquely articulated and embraced in particular by the coastal groups, many of whom were visited in the nineteenth century by Reverend William Duncan and were subsequently converted. Duncan's efforts amounted to the establishment of the Aboriginal Protestant settlement of Metlakatla in 1862, an isolated community which Duncan envisioned as ideal in bringing First Peoples together and facilitating the indoctrination of Western and Christian values. At Metlakatla, Duncan mobilized and expanded economic development in trades and industry, such as blacksmithing, weaving, brick making, and other manufacturing pursuits, as well as a community operated and marketed sawmill and salmon cannery. Playing a significant role in the culture of the community was also the existence of missionary operated schools, including a Sunday school.[69] The Protestants' use of Sunday schools was widespread, and such schools made wide use of books and the printed word in spreading their message. A good number of Sunday schools also had libraries. *The Native Voice*, when it emerged in 1946, although decidedly undenominational, was a highly successful, articulated and adaptive product of a Protestant-influenced education in Western understandings of literacy. The newspaper achieved its goals in offering a public voice for bringing attention to Aboriginal issues, and its publication brought the Brotherhood increased membership, particularly on the coast.

The degree to which Aboriginal peoples in British Columbia, both Protestant and Catholic, had successfully articulated and integrated Western modes of communication would be further illustrated by the establishment of a community library at Fort St. James some ten years later by the Indian Homemakers' Club of the Nak'azdli Reserve.

Day school libraries in the 1950s: endeavors to improve

It is in the 1950s that the environment for library development in Aboriginal communities began to change noticeably, leaving room for the unprecedented development that would take place following 1960. Developments in the 1950s would continue to be marked by the stalling of the Department of Indian Affairs, but also by very significant and mostly successful efforts on behalf of philanthropists and Aboriginal women. Aboriginal library developments that took place in this decade were marked by an unprecedented degree of diversity and relative success, resulting in a publicly accessible special collection devoted to community health and Aboriginal women's interests and the first instance of a provincial initiative that would finally awaken Indian Affairs to the information needs and wants of at least one Aboriginal community, paving the way for a number of similar initiatives in the decades that followed.

By 1953, the Department of Indian Affairs was again showing some interest in the libraries of the day and residential schools after nearly a ten year absence of any substantial discussion. In that year, the Department reported that "Approximately 500 individual items of text books, supplementary reading, library books, and other miscellaneous supplies [were] distributed annually by the Queen's Printer on requisition from the Education Service."[70] Unfortunately the breakdown between text books, supplementary reading materials, library books, and miscellaneous supplies is not provided by the Department, but it is noted that "An endeavour is being made to improve the use of supplementary and library books." A full ten years following the completion of Superintendent Hoey's survey of day school library materials and the first Departmentally compiled lists of supplementary reading materials, Aboriginal children in the Indian schools were reportedly still not making wide use of the collections or taking an active interest in reading the books provided by the Department. Indian Affairs at this time was still in the business of reviewing and selecting books from lists compiled by the provincial departments of education, for the most part because to do so was cheaper than employing their own officials and, more importantly, because the Department's policy regarding Indian education had not changed. Departmental policy in the 1950s was much the same as it had been some ten years earlier, which was to educate Aboriginal children to enter the mainstream of Canadian life and integrate them into the culture of their non-Aboriginal fellow citizens. The only noticeable improvement that the Department had made in the preceding decade was to arrange with the provincial authorities, in some provinces, for the schools to be included in their traveling libraries circuits, and the creation of a small film library maintained by the Education Service Branch.[71] The extension of provincial traveling library services in some provinces to Aboriginal communities was an indication that the Department was beginning to recognize the potential value of such services to their educative cause. However, as the efforts of Angus McGill Mowat in Ontario would demonstrate a few years later, the extension of these services was, in fact, very minimal. According to the Department's own annual reporting of expenditures, the total funds spent from year to year on books and school supplies, as a percentage of the Department's total expenditure through the 1950s, continued to hover around the two percent mark. Although the Department rhetoric was one of increased attention being paid to text books, supplementary reading, and library books,[72] improvement was generally slow in coming and dependent from year to year on the total funds available to the Department for education.

There is at least some indication, however, that the nature of these books and library materials was perhaps beginning to change. The notable mention of the film, *No Longer Vanishing* (National Film Board of Canada, 1955), in the *Report of the Indian Affairs Branch* in 1956, indicates a possible shift in the Department's ideological approach to Indian education. This film, reported to have been given "wide distribution" throughout the Indian school system, and "favourably received by both Indians and non-Indians,"[73] was unique in its content because it featured Aboriginal support and direction, notably that of James Sewid, a Kwakiutl Chieftain. Sewid's involvement in the film amounted to a depiction of his significant efforts to maintain and revive Kwakiutl traditions while at the same time working to improve his people's living standards through Western economic institutions. The film was unique for its time in providing a positive example of an Aboriginal person successfully articulating Western practices and integrating these with traditional ways of living and knowing.[74] The inclusion of this film on the Department's lists of approved library materials is also significant because it signaled the first instance where Indian Affairs began including materials that were at least in part produced by and for Aboriginal peoples, and were not necessarily lifted directly from a provincial school curriculum.

The Fort St. James Indian Homemakers' Club library, 1954

In 1954, the Fort St. James Indian Homemakers' Club, (which would later join the provincial intertribal organization, the Indian Homemakers' Association of British Columbia), established a library for its members and for neighboring families on the Nak'azdli Reserve.[75] This would constitute only the second known publicly accessible library in an Aboriginal community in the country outside of the Indian schools, and, most notably, this collection was created and meant to serve an Aboriginal women's audience whose interests were rooted in homemaking, childcare, and health issues. One of many similar clubs that existed in Aboriginal communities throughout the country, the Fort St. James Indian Homemakers' Club was founded in 1942 for the purpose of providing learning programs for Aboriginal women in such projects as "knitting, dressmaking, fruit preserving, the canning of vegetables, and lectures on health, sanitation, and child care."[76] Sharing a similar vision and mandate, but from a female perspective, to the Native Brotherhood of British Columbia, which had established its own newspaper in 1946, the most remarkable trait associated with the Indian Homemakers' clubs was that although the movement was promoted by Indian Affairs, by the Department's own admission they were organized "with little departmental assistance or supervision"[77] and were present in communities across the country.

The women's interests were firmly rooted in improving community welfare conditions, and by the nature of the programs they provided were also deeply rooted in balancing traditional skills with the Western skills taught in the Indian schools.[78] The Fort St. James Club's formation of a library in 1954 was thus a physical embodiment of a Western institution meant to assist the women in the duties they had been formerly involved with for more than fifteen years–mainly the dissemination of information to the community, and educating women in ways to preserve, strengthen, and develop their communities. As had been the case with the library established at Lennox Island in 1910-11 and their provincial brothers' establishment of a newspaper in 1946, the Aboriginal women involved in the Homemakers' Club in 1954 were successful in articulating and integrating a Western institution in such a way so as to have it serve traditional Aboriginal knowledge and social concerns. The Homemakers' Club library, like the Brotherhood's newspaper in *The Native Voice*, was established in the interests of providing a collective resource which could assist the organization in its community and provincial goals. In this way, the Homemakers' Club library was interpreted by both the Department of Indian Affairs and the Carrier people of the Fort St. James region as an encouraging sign of community development, although probably for very different reasons.

The Carrier people that lived in and around Fort St. James in 1954 had long exercised a pictographic writing tradition. In 1885 they were introduced to a syllabic form of writing by the Catholic missionary, Father Adrien-Gabriel Morice. Father Morice adapted a Carrier form of syllabic from writing systems used for other Athabaskan languages in the north west, which in turn had been derived from the Cree syllabary attributed to Reverend James Evans. Although related to these other systems, Carrier syllabics were sufficiently different in detail, and knowledge of one system did not enable one to read any of the others. Morice is said to have taught the syllabics only a few times, but as with the Cree, use of the syllabic system spread rapidly from one person to another and soon became widely used in the north central part of British Columbia. The first known document in syllabics was reportedly a lengthy message written on the wall of the Richfield jail, near Barkerville, British Columbia, created within a few months of the system's first introduction into the region.[79] A considerable number of printed materials were published in Carrier syllabics, including two editions of a Roman Catholic prayer book, a reading primer, and twenty-four issues of a bimonthly newspaper between 1891 and 1894 compiled by Father Morice.

Use of the syllabics among the Carrier people was also widespread. Headstones were inscribed in the writing system, and correspondence, diaries, business accounts, and messages blazed into trees also point to a mass literacy in the syllabics. However, beginning in 1920, when the Necoslie Day School was built on the Reserve and non-Aboriginal families began to permanently settle at Fort St. James, use of the syllabic system began to dramatically decline. Use of the Carrier language was largely forbidden in the school, except for prayer and singing hymns. And in 1938, a third edition of Morice's prayer book was published, this time in the Roman alphabet, effectively eliminating the use of the syllabic system within the school. William J. Poser has noted also that many Carrier people learned the syllabics from older relatives in the winter and on the trapline. When children began spending most or all of their year at school, they largely did not go out on the trapline, no longer having the same opportunities to foster a literacy in the Carrier syllabics.[80]

Thus, in 1954 when the Indian Homemakers' Club established a library for their members and local families, it was following in a long tradition of literacy among the Carrier people. Pictographic writing traditions, which had been employed by the people for generations, led to the quick adoption of a syllabic form of writing in the late nineteenth century, and by the mid-twentieth century at least one generation had been fully exposed to Western literacy in the Roman alphabet.[81]

The efforts of Honoré Jaxon, former secretary to Louis Riel

For two days in mid-December of 1951, human interest stories about a ninety-year-old, self-described "champion of the Indians" ran in New York's two major daily newspapers. The *New York Times* reported:

> Maj. Honore Joseph Jaxon, 90-year-old champion of the Indians and a man whose individualistic habits of living have caused him a wigwam full of trouble, found himself once more out on the street yesterday. With him on the sidewalk on East Thirty-fourth Street, near Third Avenue were his possessions—a couple of truckloads of 'historical documents' heaped high and awaiting official inspection to determine exactly how historical they are.[82]

The pile of documents, which consisted of books and papers that Jaxon had been collecting for more than forty years, was said to be at least thirty-five feet long, ten feet across, and six feet high. Within a month, Jaxon passed away, and the whole of his massive collection was either sold or destroyed. Jaxon had estimated the documents to number approximately eight thousand items, with a value of more than $100,000. The tale of the Major's truckloads of historical documents is of significant interest because Jaxon intended for these materials to be one day removed to a 288-acre plot of land that he owned in Saskatchewan, where he planned to establish a library for the Aboriginal population there. He believed that the First Peoples of Saskatchewan, in particular the Duck Lake community with whom he had close ties, could use this library to educate themselves, and "they'd get a better deal in this generation than they had in the past."[83] Jaxon held the belief that "an interesting and instructive and useful library constitutes, as Thomas Carlyle said, the best of all universities."[84] The life story of Honoré Jaxon is a dramatic tale that has been well told, but is worth a brief re-telling.[85] The man and his massive personal collection of books and papers with which he intended to build a library for the First Peoples of Saskatchewan served to highlight, yet again, another case of opportunity-lost in the historical relationship of Aboriginal peoples, print culture, and the establishment of libraries.

Jaxon, born William Henry Jackson in Toronto to a staunchly Methodist and reasonably well-off family around 1861, was raised in Wingham, Ontario, and was well educated, attending a model school and the University of Toronto. His academic career was cut short, however, when his family relocated to Prince Albert, Saskatchewan, to take up farming. At Prince Albert, Jackson dabbled in local farming politics, publishing a small editorial sheet called *The Voice of the People*, and with other farmers formed the Settler's Union. The organized union was almost exclusively made up local farmers who attacked the federal government's land regulations, and shared a great dislike for the politics of the Conservative regime under John A. Macdonald. In 1884, Jackson approached the local French Métis for their cooperation in opposing Macdonald, which coincided with the Métis' decision to bring Louis Riel back to Canada to lead the protest in the district. The Settler's Union and the Métis Committee maintained separate identities, but Jackson maintained a close link between the two bodies, becoming baptized into the Roman Catholic Church with the name, Henri Jaxon, to further his influence with the Métis. Jaxon admired the Métis' "passion for freedom,"[86] becoming Riel's secretary and loyal supporter long after Riel lost the support of the settlers. He was brought to trial on charges of treason-felony in July of 1885 after the Métis Rebellion was crushed, acquitted on grounds of insanity, and committed to a mental institution but soon escaped. Resurfacing in Chicago, Jaxon denounced his Anglo-Canadian roots following the execution of Riel, and began identifying himself as a Métis. His Chicago years were characterized by Jaxon further voicing his concerns relating to the treatment of workers and Aboriginal peoples, and he became prominently active as a labor organiser. Within the Chicago Federation of Labor, Jaxon acted as an editorial writer for the organization's newspaper, *The Union Labor Advocate*, expressing his dislike for all that resembled the status quo, and in the 1890s he converted yet again, this time to the Baha'i faith, which emphasized simple living and service to alleviate human suffering. Jaxon returned to Canada in 1907, launching himself as a lecturer through western Canada, and running in the federal election of 1908 for the constituency of Prince Albert. Aiding his campaign was Jaxon's publication of *Fair Play and Free Play*, an irregular newspaper which he provided free of charge on the condition that readers sent a monetary donation to the Aboriginal community at Duck Lake, Saskatchewan. Disillusioned with old injustices, Jaxon returned to Chicago a year later, and in the 1920s relocated to New York where he became attracted to anarchist-thought and began collecting and storing books and papers with which he intended to build his library for the people of Duck Lake.[87]

Jaxon's views and actions towards Aboriginal peoples and workers have been characterized by historians as being ahead of their time.[88] In his lifetime he was widely labeled by the mainstream as an eccentric and most of his initiatives were thus thwarted or largely ignored. The Canadian government and mainstream population largely viewed the Métis Rebellion under Riel as the illegitimate action of an uncivilized group of madmen, but Jaxon would continue to voice the message of Aboriginal rights for the rest of his life–several decades before most of the Canadian population would come around to seeing the Métis' claims as legitimate. He also understood that poor education was a significant inhibitor to the success of Aboriginal claims. Jaxon's collecting habits for his proposed library were motivated in the interests of providing an opportunity for First People in Saskatchewan to engage with the non-Aboriginal population through the Western understood medium of the printed word. The loss of Jaxon's books and papers was a tremendous loss, and the indifference shown by the mainstream authorities towards his efforts were unfortunately not uncommon during Jaxon's lifetime. Indeed, Jaxon's efforts were remarkably forward-looking and unique, but were tragically wasted. In the decade following his death, however, the political and ideological environment surrounding education and Aboriginal peoples in Canada began to change rather dramatically. By the end of the decade the federal government had finally come around to seeing Aboriginal libraries as worthy of support. This change, however, would come after decades of lobbying by the likes of Jaxon and Aboriginal peoples, and was finally spurred by a prominent and respected member of the Ontario civil service.

Angus McGill Mowat's public library for Aboriginal peoples at Moose Factory, 1958-59[89]

In the last two years of his tenure as the Ontario Director of Provincial Library Services, and for five years following his retirement, long-time public servant, Angus McGill Mowat (1892-1977) worked tirelessly for library development in Aboriginal communities in Ontario. Mowat's career is well documented by Stephen Foster Cummings, who notes that beginning in 1958, Mowat "brought virtually all aspects of thirty-six years' experience to bear on a single problem: developing public library service to Ontario natives on reservations [sic]."[90] Mowat's efforts ceased when, at age 73, he found the job of lobbying for Aboriginal libraries too taxing, but not before his efforts resulted in the establishment of a fully-formed public library for the Cree and Ojibwe of Moose Factory, and the expansion of traveling library services to the Aboriginal communities at Moose Factory, Shoal Lake, Whitefish Bay, Alnick, Curve Lake, Gibson, Golden Lake, Mississauga, Muncey, Parry Island, Rice Lake, Tyendinega, and the Indian Folk School at Craigleith, Ontario. In addition, Mowat also paved the way for Aboriginal representation on the Northwestern Regional Library Cooperative board in June of 1958–the first such representation in Ontario and Canada. With the efforts of the former Director, the Ontario provincial government and the federal Department of Indian Affairs would for the first time acknowledge some financial responsibility in developing library services for First Peoples.[91] In the decades that followed, library development in Aboriginal communities began to take firm root across the country in large part because of Mowat's successes. His battles for Aboriginal library development, however, were not readily or easily won. Mowat's sternness with the right politicians of the day, his sincerity and persistence in working with members of Aboriginal communities, and the credibility of his position won him battles that might otherwise not have been fought for another decade.

The library at Moose Factory was first established in the community hall, owned by the Department of Indian Affairs, in the spring of 1958. With its inception and subsequent support from both provincial and federal authorities, the Angus Mowat Moose Factory Library, as it would later be named, was the first formally recognized public library in an Aboriginal community in Canada. Although it was certainly not the first, it was formally recognized and recorded in history as such because it was the first library in an Aboriginal community to receive financial and political support and recognition from government authorities. As a branch of education, public library legislation was the responsibility of the provincial government. With Aboriginal peoples falling under the legislative authority of the federal government, including their education, library development in the area was also understood as a federal responsibility. However, the federal government had consistently failed to offer much initiative or financial backing in developing libraries outside of the Indian schools, leaving the responsibility solely in the hands of Aboriginal peoples and philanthropists. Mowat struggled with these legislatively imposed complications, and worked carefully to gather support on both the provincial and federal end. His efforts might have been wasted, however, were it not for his tenacity.

Mowat had to negotiate delicately with the Department of Indian Affairs. Early responses from the Department Superintendent, R. F. Davey, questioned Mowat's intentions, and firmly noted that there were already three educational institutes at Moose Factory: the Moose Factory Hospital School; the Moose Fort Anglican Residential School; and the Moose Factory Island Day School. Davey would go on to say that he was "sure that the adults and the school children will welcome your library service,"[92] but was careful to inquire as to the costs involved. Mowat assured Davey that there would be no cost to Indian Affairs, but hinted at the matter of physical accommodation, and stressed the point that his intentions were to establish a library for Aboriginal use: "while I certainly have the white people of both Moosonee and Moose Factory in mind when talking about library service, my hopes are directed even more strongly towards the Cree people ... I have a dream and it isn't precisely a daydream either, of the day when book service will be available to both peoples on equal terms."[93] In a private letter to Ethel Brant Monture,[94] Mowat stressed more forcibly his intentions for the library: "The Crees predominate but there are a lot of whites as well. I'll make that my excuse, although the books, particularly the children's books, are going to be damn well biased in the direction of the Crees. I am a biased man."[95] At hearing there would be little or no cost to Indian Affairs, Davey pledged his support of Mowat's development plans. But the Ontario civil servant would have to twist some arms on the provincial end, and Davey would later express some hesitation regarding the matter of physical space, as neither level of government was enthusiastic about picking up the costs involved. Mowat would have to go to no other than the Premier of Ontario, Leslie M. Frost, to gain some provincial support, and that only after Mowat obtained additional assurances from Indian Affairs. Eventually the matter would be solved in part through Mowat's persistence, but also through the fact that he would retire as the Provincial Director of Public Libraries in 1959 and continued to take up the matter of Aboriginal libraries, mostly at his own cost (he would receive only five hundred dollars a year for traveling expenses from Indian Affairs), following his retirement from other provincial library duties. In this way, Mowat acted in part as a philanthropist, but one with a considerable knowledge and widespread connections within the library and government worlds.

The Cree and Ojibwe people of Moose Factory had, in 1958, a long history with the printed word. The syllabic writing and reading tradition that Reverend James Evans adopted in the 1840s had been in widespread use through the region for generations. Although use of the syllabary declined in the twentieth century, the Cree and Ojibwe of the region were well versed in Western notions of literacy by the late 1950s. However, there is nothing to suggest that Mowat was aware of the region's long history with the written word. It appears as though his motivations for establishing a library for the First Peoples of Moose Factory were solely rooted in his own personal interests in Aboriginal peoples,[96] and in his close involvement with the Northwestern Regional Library Cooperative which had been created in 1957. Predecessors of the Northwestern Cooperative, including the Thunder Bay District Library Co-Operative, had provided bookmobile library services to rural communities in the region for years, including to teachers at the Pic River Reserve. Mowat toured this vast region of the province in early 1958, helping to identify people willing to serve on the new regional cooperative board, and in doing so he visited the community of Moosonee. Moose Factory, which lies on an island in the Moose River, was a short canoe ride away from Moosonee. While in the immediate region Mowat paid a visit to Moose Factory, and it was then he noticed the glaring differences between the availability of reading materials for Aboriginal children schooled on the island compared to the mostly non-Aboriginal children who were schooled in the town of Moosonee. It was from this one visit that Mowat took on the task of single-handedly establishing the Moose Factory library.

Although Mowat's approach to developing a public library at Moose Factory can be viewed as slightly paternalistic, if not romantic, he appeared to understand that, even if he was initiating the project, the matter of an Aboriginal library should be something that in the end would be under the control of Aboriginal peoples. Admitting that he did not know anyone from Moose Factory, nor had he ever met any of the community members, on one of his earliest trips to the community he insisted on staying with a local family. He explains his motivations to Ethel Brant Monture:

> I had never met the Crees before and did not want to stay at the tourist lodge. It is the kind of place that spoils my disposition, catering to white 'hunters' from Toronto and Detroit with too much money, far too much whisky and no wisp of understanding in their hands at all. So I took my diffidence in my hands and asked if a family of the People would take me in, and they would—after looking me over with great care—and after a time, when they had decided that I must be a bit queer but at least wasn't trying to do anything to them or get anything from them—harmless and innocent—they first set me to drawing the daily forty gallons of water through three feet

> of ice, then made me a temporary member of the family, and
> it all came out the kind of warm, merry, happy kind of visit
> that a man never can forget.[97]

Mowat inherently understood the complications of being perceived by the community as coming from "away," and took great pains to alleviate any notions that he was working merely in his own best interests, or with the thought of forcibly introducing another ineffective government tool of education. Inevitably he hoped the library at Moose Factory could serve as a tool for the Cree and Ojibwe, working in the community's favor–but not without the community's approval. In a letter to Fred Greene, Chief of the Shoal Lake Band, he explains: "Integration may be, and in many cases I have seen, is a good thing. But *only* where your People want it that way. To try to force integration is, to me, little short of criminal folly."[98] Upon getting the project up and running, Mowat promptly withdrew from the affairs of the Moose Factory library, leaving it in the capable hands of Nellie Faries, who would continue as librarian until 1964. Ms. Faries was the wife of Gilbert Faries, and a member of the Cree family with whom Mowat had stayed on a number of trips to Moose Factory and struck up a close friendship.

After the establishment of the Moose Factory library, Mowat continued in his endeavors to develop libraries for other Aboriginal communities in Ontario. In a 1961 letter to John P. Robarts, then the provincial Minister of Education, Mowat outlined his plans, and his belief in how the provincial authorities should play a part: "Because the Provincial Library Service is responsible for promoting libraries for the people of Ontario and because (a truth not generally understood) Indians are people, I offered my services upon retirement, and without salary, to further promote library service among Ontario Indians as I had long been promoting it among Ontario Whites."[99] Robarts, however, was initially unimpressed, but following a campaign of letter writing to the Department of Indian Affairs and Premier Frost, Mowat received some support, eventually working to expand the Travelling Libraries Service to a number of Reserves throughout Ontario. While at times he seemed to be fighting an uphill battle, Mowat nevertheless through persistence obtained the attention of Indian Affairs and the Ontario government. His efforts in achieving financial support from both levels of government, minimal though it was, had the effect of setting a precedent of sorts, resulting in the matter of Aboriginal libraries taking on an increased presence in the affairs of Indian education throughout the country in the decades that would follow.[100]

Notes

1. NAC RG 10, Volume 8452, File 773/23-5-004, Reel C-13802, Letter from J. Markle, 10 February 1914.

2. John S. Milloy, *"A National crime": the Canadian government and the residential school system, 1879 to 1986* (Winnipeg: University of Manitoba Press, 1999), 157-186.

3. Milloy, 157-186.

4. Jean Barman, Yvonne Hébert, and Don McCaskill, "The Legacy of the past: an overview," *Indian education in Canada, volume 1: the legacy* (Vancouver: University of British Columbia Press, 1986), 9.

5. Barman et al., 9.

6. Elgie E. M. Joblin, *The Education of the Indians of western Ontario* (Toronto: Ontario College of Education, 1947), 72.

7. Milloy, 157-186.

8. Qtd. in Milloy, 165.

9. Qtd. in Milloy, 165.

10. It is difficult to determine the exact date that the Department began purchasing books on behalf of the schools, although as early as 1911 we see teachers at the Indian schools remarking on "books prescribed by the department" (see: *Annual report 1911*, 596). The *Annual report* for the year 1917, however, is the first instance where Indian Affairs reports expenditures on "stationery and books."

11. NAC RG 10, Volume 6032, File 150-41, part 1, Reel C-8149, Letter to Philip Phelan from George Dill, 2 November 1932.

12. NAC RG 10, Volume 6032, File 150-41, part 1, Reel C-8149, Letter to Philip Phelan from George Dill, 29 October 1932.

13. It is interesting to note, however, that although the provincial school authorities regularly updated their reading lists, for cost reasons the Department generally did not. When J. E. Pugh, Indian Agent of the Blood Agency in Alberta, notified Indian Affairs of a new provincial curriculum in November of 1936, Philip Phelan replied: "regarding the text books, you should inform the teachers ... that the Department does not intend to change these at the present time... we are not obliged to use the same text books in Indian schools as in White schools." NAC RG 10, Volume 6032, File 150-41, part 1, Reel C-8149, Letters dated 30 November 1936 and 11 December 1936.

14. For further titles, see Appendix 1; NAC RG 10, Volume 6032, File 150-41, part 1, Reel C-8149, Headquarters – Supplementary reading books for Indian schools, 1931-1942.

15. NAC RG 10, Volume 6032, File 150-41, part 1, Reel C-8149, Letters to Philip Phelan from J. M. Dent & Sons, Ltd., 31 July 1934 and 13 August 1934; Captain Barry's efforts were apparently in vain. A published edition of compiled Aboriginal legends of British Columbia, which he had hoped would be approved by the Department as a junior reader, never emerged. The publishing company to

which Barry proposed the idea, J. M. Dent & Sons out of Vancouver, wrote to Philip Phelan asking his opinion regarding the value of the work, assumingly meaning to ask how probable it would be that the Department would purchase the title if it was published. Although Phelan's response is unavailable, the work was never published, which only leads one to gather that his response was unfavorable.

16. NAC RG 10, Volume 6032, File 150-41, part 1, Reel C-8149, Letter to Sister Cleophas from P. Phelan, 13 June 1932.

17. NAC RG 10, Volume 6032, File 150-41, part 1, Reel C-8149, Resolution passed by the Synod of the Diocese of Qu'Appelle, sent to the Secretary of Indian Affairs, 19 June 1942.

18. NAC RG 10, Volume 6032, File 150-41, part 1, Reel C-8149, Letter to the Right Rev. E. H. Knowles, Bishop of Qu'Appelle, from R. A. Hoey, 23 June 1942.

19. Milloy, 181-182.

20. Qtd. in Milloy, 186.

21. Letter to the Right Rev. E. H. Knowles, Bishop of Qu'Appelle, from R. A. Hoey, 23 June 1942.

22. NAC RG 10, Volume 6035, File 150-83, part 1, Reel C-8150, Memorandum to Principals and Teachers of Indian Day Schools, re: Day School Libraries, from R. A. Hoey, 21 April 1943.

23. Joblin, 44-45.

24. In 1943, the Moraviantown Day School was unique, at least among Ontario schools, as it was still taught by a missionary teacher (at the time a nominee of the United Church of Canada). Indirectly influenced by the wider English-Canadian phenomenon of secularization that swept much of the country through the late nineteenth and early twentieth centuries, and also by an increased degree of control by the Department of Indian Affairs over education in this same period, missionary interests in the education of Indians by the second quarter of the twentieth century had begun to decline dramatically. Further, the Moraviantown community had been among the earliest in the country to be widely exposed to the printed word in the form of missionary translations and text books.

25. For a complete list reporting the size of all day school libraries that responded to the Department's survey, see Appendix 2; NAC RG 10, Volume 6035, File 150-83, part 1, Reel C-8150, Survey of Indian Day School libraries, 1943.

26. NAC RG 10, Volume 6035, File 150-83, part 1, Reel C-8150, Letter to R. A. Hoey, from Mary B. Ross, 26 June 1943.

27. NAC RG 10, Volume 6035, File 150-83, part 1, Reel C-8150, Letter to R. A. Hoey, from G. A. McDonald, 2 June 1943.

28. NAC RG 10, Volume 6035, File 150-83, part 1, Reel C-8150, Letter to the Secretary, Indian Affairs Branch, from the Principal, Restigouche Indian Day School, 10 May 1943.

29. NAC RG 10, Volume 6035, File 150-83, part 1, Reel C-8150, Letter to R. A. Hoey, from Janet McCaig, 14 May 1943. It would appear that Ms. McCaig may have exaggerated the number of books collected from the Parry Sound

Library, or at least did not keep all of the discards for library purposes. While she claims to have collected 150 books, the Department reports the Shawanaga day school as having a library of merely 34 items. It is possible that a good number of books were dispersed among students for their personal use or were found to be in too poor condition for continued use. The discrepancy may also indicate potential inaccuracies in the survey which may have stemmed from misunderstandings between the Department and teachers regarding the definition of library books or poor statistical methods. Unfortunately, there is no way of testing the accuracy of the numbers reported by the survey against those provided by Ms. McCaig, or to know the reasons for such discrepancy.

30. NAC RG 10, Volume 6035, File 150-83, part 1, Reel C-8150, Letter to R. A. Hoey, from D. K. Diabo, 20 May 1943.

31. NAC RG 10, Volume 6035, File 150-83, part 1, Reel C-8150, Letter to R. A. Hoey, from Ethel E. George, 17 May 1943.

32. NAC RG 10, Volume 6035, File 150-83, part 1, Reel C-8150, Letter to P. Phelan, from Mary Whelan, 20 April 1943.

33. NAC RG 10, Volume 6035, File 150-83, part 1, Reel C-8150, Letter to R. A. Hoey, from J. Swibb, 13 May 1943.

34. Statistics derived and compiled by the author from the yearly reporting of expenditures included in the Department of Indian Affairs' *Annual reports* between 1917 and 1960.

35. NAC RG 10, Volume 3251, File 600,533, Reel C-11349, Letter to the Secretary of the Indian Affairs Branch, from V. M. Eastwood, 10 February 1939.

36. Archives of Ontario, RG 2-42, Department of Education select subject files, 1902-1905.

37. NAC RG 10, Volume 3251, File 600,533, Reel C-11349, Letter to V. M. Eastwood, from R. A. Hoey, 14 February 1939.

38. NAC RG 10, Volume 3251, File 600,533, Reel C-11349, Letter to Major D. M. MacKay, British Columbia Indian Commissioner, from F. Earl Anfield, 24 February 1944.

39. Letter to Major D. M. MacKay, British Columbia Indian Commissioner, from F. Earl Anfield, 24 February 1944.

40. Letter to Major D. M. MacKay, British Columbia Indian Commissioner, from F. Earl Anfield, 24 February 1944.

41. NAC RG 10, Volume 3251, File 600,533, Reel C-11349, Letter to Major D. M. MacKay, Indian Commissioner for British Columbia, from R. A. Hoey, 15 March 1944.

42. NAC RG 10, Volume 3251, File 600,533, Reel C-11349, Letter to Major D. M. MacKay, Indian Commissioner for BC, from F. Earl Anfield, 6 April 1944.

43. NAC RG 10, Volume 3251, File 600,533, Reel C-11349, Letter to the Indian Affairs Branch, from H. J. Featherston, 14 September 1944.

44. NAC RG 10, Volume 3251, File 600,533, Reel C-11349, Letter to H. J. Featherston, from R. A. Hoey, 18 September 1944.

45. NAC RG 10, Volume 3251, File 600,533, Reel C-11349, Department of Education, Ontario, Public Libraries Branch, Traveling Libraries Service [1939].

46. W. A. Roedde, "I Drive a bookmobile: the story of the Thunder Bay District Library Co-Operative, Fort William, Ontario," *CLA Bulletin* 13.1 (1956): 6-7.

47. The Emmanuel College Boarding School was established in the early 1880s by the Bishop of Saskatchewan, John McLean, on behalf of the Church Missionary Society of the Church of England to train Cree, Blackfoot, and Ojibwe as teachers and missionaries to work among their own people. See: Frank A. Peake, "Church Missionary Society: policy and personnel in Rupertsland," *Journal of the Canadian Church Historical Society* 30.2 (1988): 70.

48. Stan Cuthand, "Intoduction to the 1995 edition," *Voices of the Plains Cree*, by Edward Ahenakew, edited by Ruth M. Buck (Regina: Canadian Plains Research Center, 1995), x-xi, xiii.

49. Cuthand, xii.

50. Professor Wallace's papers and correspondence are today housed in the manuscript collection of the American Philosophical Society Library in Philadelphia, Pennsylvania.

51. Qtd. in Cuthand xiii.

52. Edward Ahenakew, "Cree Trickster tales," *Journal of American Folklore* 42 (1929); Three of the stories were later reprinted in Carlyle King, ed., *Saskatchewan harvest: a golden jubilee selection of song and story* (Toronto: McClelland and Stewart, 1955).

53. During his lifetime Ahenakew was successful in updating the Cree-English part of *A Dictionary of the Cree Language* with Archdeacon R. Faries (Toronto: General Synod of the Church of England in Canada, 1938). He also translated some works into Cree syllabics for the Society for Promoting Christian Knowledge, including: A. Leigh, *Cree New Testament stories*, translated by Edward Ahenakew (London: Society for Promoting Christian Knowledge, 1936); and Caroline M. Duncan Jones, *Everybody's prayer*, translated by Edward Ahenakew (London: Society for Promoting Christian Knowledge, 1933?).

54. Cuthand, xvii.

55. Edward Ahenakew, *Voices of the Plains Cree*, edited by Ruth M. Buck (Regina: Canadian Plains Research Center, 1995), 9.

56. Edward Ahenakew, "Little Pine: an Indian day school," edited by Ruth Matheson Buck, *Saskatchewan History* XVIII.2 (1965): 55-62.

57. Edward Ahenakew, "Introduction to Old Keyam," *Voices of the Plains Cree*, edited by Ruth M. Buck (Regina: Canadian Plains Research Center, 1995), 51.

58. For more on the League of Indians, see: Olive Patricia Dickason, *Canada's First Nations: a history of founding peoples from earliest times* (Toronto: McClelland and Stewart, 1994), 328; Peter Kulchyski, "A Considerable unrest: F.O. Loft and the League of Indians," *Native Studies Review* 4.1-2 (1988): 95-113.

59. Cuthand, xviii.

60. Paul Tennant, *Aboriginal people and politics: the Indian land question in British Columbia, 1849-1989* (Vancouver: University of British Columbia Press, 1990), 116.

61. Alfred Adams, qtd. in Chris Cook, "Communications link between our communities," *The Native Voice* [*Courier-Islander*, Campbell River] 6 October 2001: B2.

62. See for instance: Philip Drucker, *The Native Brotherhoods: modern intertribal organizations on the northwest coast*, Smithsonian Institution. Bureau of American Ethnology. Bulletin 168 (Washington: United States Printing Office, 1958); H. B. Hawthorn, C. S. Belshaw, and S. M. Jamieson, *The Indians of British Columbia: a study of contemporary social adjustment* (Toronto and Vancouver: University of Toronto Press and the University of British Columbia, 1960); Forrest E. LaViolette, *The Struggle for survival: Indian cultures and the Protestant ethic in British Columbia* (Toronto: University of Toronto Press, 1961).

63. See: Tennant 116-117; and James Nwannukwu Kerri, "Studying voluntary associations as adaptive mechanisms: a review of anthropological perspectives," *Current Anthropology* 17.1 (1976): 31-32. Further discussion of the Native Brotherhood of British Columbia can also be found in Alicja Muszynski, *Cheap wage labor: race and gender in the fisheries of British Columbia* (Montreal and Kingston: McGill-Queen's University Press, 1996); and Jacqueline P. O'Donnell, *The Native Brotherhood of British Columbia 1931-1950: a new phase in Native political organization*, M. A. thesis, University of British Columbia, 1985.

64. Tennant, 77.

65. Chief William D. Scow, "President's message," *The Native Voice* 1.1 (1946): 1.

66. Jack Beynon, "Publication dates," *The Native Voice*, 1.1 (1946): 4.

67. Tennant, 119; See also: Cyril S. Belshaw, "The Struggle for survival: Indian cultures and the Protestant ethic in British Columbia, by Forrest E. LaViolette," rev. of *The Struggle for Survival* by Forrest E. LaViolette, *Ethnohistory* 8 (1961): 302-303.

68. Aboriginal print media emerged largely out of western Canada in the late 1960s, and flourished through the 1970s, with the establishment of a number of small, politically motivated publications. The *Saskatchewan Indian*, for example, had a readership of more than 30,000 in 1971. Financial insecurity, however, meant that much of the periodical publishing by Aboriginal organizations through the early 1970s was short-lived. As a means of assistance to existing publications, and to support the establishment of new ones, the federal government weighed in with the Native Communications Program in 1973 (which was eliminated in 1990, having a devastating effect on Aboriginal print media). For more on Aboriginal newspapers, see: Valerie Alia, *Un/covering the North: news, media, and Aboriginal people* (Vancouver: UBC Press, 1999); Shannon Avison and Michael Meadows, "Speaking and hearing: Aboriginal newspapers and the public sphere in Canada and Australia," *Canadian Journal of Communication* 25 (2000): 347-

66; James P. Danky and Maureen E. Hady, *Native American periodicals and newspapers 1828-1982: bibliography, publishing record, and holdings* (Westport CT: Greenwood Press, 1984); Jöel Demay, "Clarifying ambiguities: the rapidly changing life of the Canadian Aboriginal print media," *Canadian Journal of Native Studies* XI.1 (1991): 95-112; Enn Raudsepp, "Emergent media: the Native press in Canada," *Canadian Journal of Communication* 11.2 (1985): 193-209.

69. Eugene Stock, *Metlakahtla and the North Pacific mission of the Church Missionary Society* (London: Church Missionary House, 1880), 69; Henry S. Wellcome, *The Story of Metlakahtla* (London and New York: American News Company, 1887), 89.

70. Canada. Department of Citizenship and Immigration, *Report of the Indian Affairs Branch for the fiscal year ended March 31, 1953* (Ottawa: Queen's Printer, 1953), 61.

71. *Report of the Indian Affairs Branch, 1954*, 60. The day schools by the mid-1950s had also been improved structurally. Many were expanded to include more than one classroom, and the majority had been equipped with electricity or been altered so as to improve their access to natural lighting.

72. Take for example the following statement made in the Department's Annual report for 1953: "An endeavour is being made to improve the use of supplementary reading and library books. To this end, approximately 600 titles were reviewed in compiling the library lists for the fiscal year under review" (page 61). Such rhetoric was repeated from year to year between 1953 and 1959, and was always framed as an improvement.

73. *Report of the Indian Affairs Branch, 1956*, 45.

74. For more on James Sewid, see: James Sewid and James P. Spradley, *Guests never leave hungry: the autobiography of James Sewid, a Kwakiutl Indian* (New Haven: Yale University Press, 1969).

75. *Report of the Indian Affairs Branch, 1954*, 68.

76. Canada. Department of Mines and Resources, *Report of Indian Affairs Branch for the fiscal year ended March 31, 1940* (Ottawa, 1940), 187; Indian Homemakers' Clubs first originated in Saskatchewan in 1937, and spread to Manitoba, Ontario, Quebec, Nova Scotia, New Brunswick, and British Columbia by the early 1940s. They were assisted by the Department of Indian Affairs only in the provision of supplies such as sewing machines, piece goods, wool, thread, and other materials for newly organized clubs. See: Canada. Department of Citizenship and Immigration. Indian Affairs Branch, *Constitution and regulations for Indian Homemakers' Clubs* (Ottawa: King's Printer, 1951).

77. *Report of Indian Affairs Branch for 1943*, 151.

78. The Indian Homemakers' Association of British Columbia, for example, which enveloped the Fort St. James Indian Homemakers' Club in 1960, is still in existence today and is extremely active within the province. Their contemporary mandate has changed only slightly, embodying many of the principles first set out in the early Homemakers' clubs. These are to "assist women and their children, on and off reserve in British Columbia, in the struggle for the restoration of Aboriginal and women's rights. The Association provides information to reserve

and urban First Nations women about issues that affect these women and their families. In turn, it presents these concerns to government and the general public ... struggling to achieve social justice, to obtain economic independence, to preserve the integrity of the family, and to live in harmony with nature." For more, see: "Indian Homemakers' Association of B. C.," *BC Institute Against Family Violence Newsletter* (Summer 1994) http://www.bcifv.org. The Indian Homemakers' Association of B. C. also produced a periodical between 1969 and 1983 entitled, *Indian voice* (Vancouver: Canadian Indian Voice Society).

79. William J. Poser, *The Carrier syllabics*, Yinka Dene Language Institute Technical Report #1 (Vanderhoof BC: Yinka Dene Language Institute, 2000), 1.

80. Poser, 1-2.

81. Unfortunately no catalog or listing of materials is available for the Indian Homemakers' Club library, so there is no way of knowing for certain if the collection included any works in Carrier syllabics.

82. "Major Jaxon, who's used to it by now, finds himself, at 90, thrown out again," *New York Times* [New York] 13 December 1951: 50.

83. Honore Jaxon, qtd. in Donald B. Smith, "Right dream, wrong time," *The Globe and Mail* [Toronto] 15 December 2001: F6.

84. Jaxon, qtd. in Smith, "Right dream, wrong time," F6.

85. For more on Honore Joseph Jaxon (William Henry Jackson), see: Sandra Estlin Bingaman, "The Trials of the 'White Rebels', 1885," *Saskatchewan history* XXV.1 (1972): 41-54; W. J. C. Cherwinski, "Honoré Joseph Jaxon, agitator, disturber, producer of plans to make men think and chronic objector...," *Canadian Historical Review* XLVI.2 (1965): 122-133; Louis Blake Duff, *Amazing story of the Winghamite secretary of Louis Riel*, Western Ontario history nuggets no. 22 (London ON: Lawson Memorial Library, University of Western Ontario, 1955); Gregory S. Kealey and Bryan D. Palmer, *Dreaming of what might be: the Knights of Labour in Ontario, 1880-1900* (1982; Toronto: New Hogtown Press, 1987), 19-20; Steven Sapolsky, "The Making of Honore Jaxon," *Haymarket scrapbook*, ed. Dave Roediger and Franklin Rosemont (Chicago: Charles H. Kerr Publishing, 1986), 103-105; Donald B. Smith, "Honore Joseph Jaxon: a man who lived for others," *Saskatchewan history* 34.3 (1981): 81-101; Donald B. Smith, "William Henry Jackson: Riel's secretary," *The Beaver* (Spring 1981): 10-19; and Donald B. Smith, "Right dream, wrong time," *The Globe and Mail* [Toronto] 15 December 2001: F6.

86. Jaxon, qtd. in Smith, "Right dream, wrong time," F6.

87. Cherwinski, 122-133; Duff, passim; Smith, "Right dream, wrong time," F6.

88. Cherwinski, 133; Smith, "Right dream, wrong time," F6.

89. At around the same time Angus McGill Mowat was working to expand Traveling Library services to Reserve communities in Ontario and establishing a public library at Moose Factory, the Alert Bay Public Library and Museum opened on Cormorant Island, British Columbia. Envisioned in 1958, and opened in February 1959, the library and museum at Alert Bay was designed to meet the needs of the Cormorant Island community, which included the village of Alert

Bay, the Namgis First Nation, and the Whe-la-la-u Area Council. Half of the population of the island was, and is, Aboriginal. The library and museum has also housed the community archives, and the museum, library, and archives have all been run as one organization. The Alert Bay Public Library and Museum's relationship with the Namgis First Nation, however, has not been one based on full cooperation, although members of the First Nation have long made use of the library, museum, and archives along with non-Aboriginal residents of the island. For more on this institution, see: Ernie Ingles and Heather Ganshorn, "Alert Bay Public Library and Museum," *Feliciter* 48.4 (2002): 192-194. The Library and Museum's website is located at: http://www.alertbay.com/library.

90. Stephen Foster Cummings, *Angus McGill Mowat and the development of Ontario public libraries, 1920-1960*, PhD dissertation, University of Western Ontario, 1986, 312; See also: Stephen Cummings, "On the compass of Angus Mowat: books, boats, soldiers, and Indians," *Readings in Canadian library history*, ed. Peter F. McNally (Ottawa: Canadian Library Association: 1986), 245-258.

91. Note: The late 1950s marks the beginning of an era of increased federal-provincial cooperation in matters of education and welfare, which in part explains the extension of provincial traveling library services to Reserves, for example.

92. R. F. Davey, qtd. in Cummings, *Angus McGill Mowat,* 317.

93. Angus McGill Mowat, qtd. in Cummings, *Angus McGill Mowat,* 318-319.

94. Ethel Brant Monture (1894-1977) was born at Six Nations. Her publications include: Harvey Chalmers and Ethel Brant Monture, *Joseph Brant: Mohawk* (East Lansing: Michigan State University Press, 1955); Irma Coucill and Ethel Brant Monture, *Indian hall of fame* (Brantford ON: Woodland Indian Cultural Educational Centre, 1967); and Ethel Brant Monture, *Famous Indians: Brant, Crowfoot, Oronhyatekha* (Toronto: Clarke-Irwin, 1960).

95. J. J. Talman Regional Collection, D. B. Weldon Library, UWO, Angus McGill Mowat Collection, File B-132, Letter from Angus McGill Mowat to Ethel Brant Monture, 31 March 1958.

96. The Angus McGill Mowat Collection at the J. J. Talman Regional Collection at the D. B. Weldon Library at the University of Western Ontario includes a great number of newspaper clippings and letters written and collected by Angus Mowat regarding the political and education situations of Aboriginal peoples in Canada. In a letter dated 31 March 1958 written to the Aboriginal lecturer and writer Ethel Brant Monture, Mowat explained, "I feel as if it were my own personal task to try to live down, not only the original evil that we perpetuated in this country, but also a lot of misdirection and even misdirected zeal in our present relations." He was sensitive to the title of "do-gooder" which he thought "almost worse than being mistaken for a condescending stockbroker-tourist from Toronto." Mowat had also adopted some Aboriginal children, whom he raised with his wife some years earlier, and while librarian at Belleville, Ontario, had befriended members of the Tyendinaga community.

97. J. J. Talman Regional Collection, D. B. Weldon Library, UWO, Angus McGill Mowat Collection, File B-132, Letter from Angus McGill Mowat to Ethel Brant Monture, 31 March 1958.

98. J. J. Talman Regional Collection, D. B. Weldon Library, UWO, Angus McGill Mowat Collection, File B-144, Letter from Angus Mowat to Fred Greene, 17 June 1958.

99. J. J. Talman Regional Collection, D. B. Weldon Library, UWO, Angus McGill Mowat Collection, File A-944, Brief submitted to John P. Robarts from Angus Mowat, 6 February 1961.

100. See Edith Adamson's 1969 article outlining Indian Affairs' early efforts in the field of Aboriginal libraries: Edith Adamson, "Public library service to the Indians of Canada," *Canadian Library Journal* 26.1 (1969): 48-53.

Conclusion

Knowledge keepers:
libraries and the printed word

> We put our words on paper for many reasons. First, because the non natives have already written it as they understand it and have not always been correct. Secondly, we have recorded these teachings on paper for our children of today who more and more are reawakening to their culture and heritage. They need this knowledge to find their way back home, back to their people's spiritual way of life.[1]

> First Nations everywhere have begun to understand the role of libraries in maintaining and preserving their identity.[2]

Beginning in the 1960s, successful library initiatives began to take a firm root within Aboriginal communities throughout Canada. In this decade, Mary Donaldson, Provincial Librarian of Saskatchewan, and Frances Whiteway, librarian at the Middlesex County Library in Ontario, made repeated requests to the Department of Indian Affairs asking that local Bands be able to participate in the public library systems of their provinces. In 1962, First Peoples at Walpole Island in Ontario remodeled a former customs house into a library and study center, and stocked it with discards from the Chatham Public Library. In May 1966, the Indian-Eskimo Association held a one day seminar on public library services to Aboriginal communities, and in October of that year the Ontario Federation of Home and School Associations provided used books and ran a one week workshop in Toronto for representatives of Ontario Aboriginal communities. The decade would also see efforts made by David L. Sparvier, reportedly Canada's first Aboriginal professional librarian, to conduct negotiations between the Cowessess, Ochapawace, Sakimay, and Kahkewistahaw Bands of the Crooked Lake area in Saskatchewan, with the Southeastern Saskatchewan Regional Library, resulting in the first formally recognized request on behalf of Indian Bands to the Department of Indian

Affairs for library grants.[3] These efforts in particular, along with the attention obtained by Angus Mowat at the provincial level in the late 1950s, worked finally to get the attention of the federal government of the need for sufficient support and funding for library services in Aboriginal communities.[4] In August of 1966, the Department of Indian Affairs and Northern Development hired Edith Adamson to act as a library consultant in the development of these library services. And by the 1970s, Aboriginal institutions like the Saskatchewan Indian Cultural Centre and the British Columbia Native Indian Teachers Association had begun to establish their own libraries, signifying the growing assertion of Aboriginal control in matters of Indian education and a clear recognition of libraries as Western institutions with potential value as resources for teaching and preserving Aboriginal knowledge.[5]

More than forty years later, most Aboriginal communities have libraries, whether they be part of the provincial public library system, a collection housed by the Band office, or collections maintained to support the activities of schools and community cultural and friendship centers. Few of these, however, are adequately funded or staffed by trained professionals.[6] Library education programs, like the School of Library, Archival, and Information Studies (SLAIS) at the University of British Columbia, have begun to address the unique record keeping and education needs of Aboriginal communities and future Aboriginal librarians and record keepers,[7] nonetheless, many of the issues faced today by First Peoples in establishing and operating libraries are remarkably similar to those frustrations and obstacles faced by earlier generations. At a Vancouver forum on the education and training requirements of Aboriginal librarians and record keepers in November 2000, Lotsee Patterson noted, "There is a misconception by bureaucrats that 'Indians don't want libraries.' On the contrary, people know what they want and they *do* want libraries."[8] This history has shown that First Peoples have played a role in requesting the establishment of libraries in some of their communities for at least the last one hundred years, and have been mostly receptive to Western notions of literacy and the printed word since missionaries first introduced the book as a means of communication early in the colonial relationship with Aboriginal peoples. Furthermore, Aboriginal reasons for embracing libraries and the printed word often have been motivated by a desire to articulate and make use of these Western tools of communication for their own social and political purposes.

Mid-eighteenth century fears by the Roman Catholic missionary, Pierre Maillard, relating to the Mi'kmaq learning to read and write alphabetic script, were clearly well founded. Maillard's assertion, "if they could make use of our alphabet ... they would not hesitate strongly to persuade themselves that they knew much more than those who are intended to instruct them," recognized that First Peoples would embrace and use language and the printed word for their own purposes. While the Roman Catholic approach was generally to limit Aboriginal access to the Bible and the printed word through attempting to maintain strict controls over the content and nature of such literature, Protestant denominations, particularly Methodists, demonstrated a great faith in the power of education and an emphasis on reading the Bible. The Methodist missionary experience in Canada was characterized by a willingness to provide Aboriginal peoples with relatively open access to Western education and, by extension, the printed word. In this light, Aboriginal converts to Methodism, such as Kahkewaquonaby, or Reverend Peter Jones, and Kahgegagahbowh, or George Copway, made use of the English language and Western literacy to draw non-Aboriginal attentions towards the grievances of their people. Likewise, Methodist influences in Aboriginal communities near Moose Factory and Sarnia in Ontario were precursors to early evidence of widespread Aboriginal literacy and an early request for the establishment of a publicly accessible library.

Other Protestant denominations, namely Anglicans, also made wide use of the printed word in their attempts to convert Aboriginal peoples. Their influence, for instance, among coastal First Peoples in British Columbia would play a key role in the eventual establishment of the Native Brotherhood of British Columbia and its widely distributed publication, *The Native Voice*.[9] Even communities that were subjected to a Catholic influence and were intentionally limited by missionaries in their access to alphabetic scripts, like the Mi'kmaq in the east and the Carrier in the central north west, found ways to articulate and adopt Western literacies to suit their own purposes. The Mi'kmaq at Lennox Island and the Carrier at Fort St. James, for instance, with whom Catholic missionaries communicated through hieroglyphic and syllabic characters, were two of the earliest communities in the country to establish their own libraries.

While missionaries were most often responsible for introducing Western ideas of communication and record keeping into Aboriginal communities, and the Department of Indian Affairs was later involved in promoting supplementary reading materials and establishing school libraries, some First Peoples took an active interest in how the printed word and library collections could work in their advantage. Individuals, like Thawennensere, or Charles A. Cooke, who as early as 1904 envisioned and worked towards establishing an "Indian National Library," understood that if Aboriginal peoples were to effectively survive and communicate their histories and cultures within an environment increasingly shaped by non-Aboriginals, they would have to articulate Western modes of communication, including libraries, in uniquely Aboriginal ways. Some of the earliest discussions in relation to libraries found within the records of the Department of Indian Affairs, in fact, were in response to Aboriginal requests.

Although First Peoples often sought libraries and embraced the printed word, Indian Affairs was reluctant to support the establishment of collections outside of the schools. Libraries established with departmental blessing in the schools were for the most part very poor, suffering from few materials suitable for Aboriginal children and chronic underfunding. Most materials included on lists circulated by Indian Affairs of approved supplementary books for inclusion in the school libraries were lifted directly from similar lists produced by the provincial education authorities, and were designed for use in non-Aboriginal schools. This lack of initiative on behalf of Indian Affairs was indicative of the neglectful standard of education provided by the government in conjunction with the missions. But the Department's failure to act on Aboriginal initiatives to build and improve libraries was also an indication that Indian Affairs wished to maintain a certain level of control over the reading materials available to First Peoples, which effectively limited the degree to which the people could educate themselves and articulate Western practices on their own terms. The approach taken towards education by Indian Affairs was primarily motivated by a desire to assimilate First Peoples into the larger non-Aboriginal Canadian fabric, and the Department's use of books and libraries served to support this goal. Future study should seek to determine the extent to which books approved by the Department were actually read and internalized by Aboriginal peoples, and to what extent communities wrote or compiled their own collections that went unnoticed by the Department.

Philanthropy was the only means by which early libraries for widespread community use could be established. The Lady Wood Library at Lennox Island, our one example of such a case, was established with funds over which Indian Affairs at the time had no control. Even Angus Mowat's efforts at Moose Factory, and in expanding provincial services to Reserve communities in Ontario, could be interpreted as philanthropy –the former provincial public servant devoted many years of his retirement to these projects and the only pay or support he received from the federal government was in the form of reimbursed travel expenses. Many of the school libraries relied on donations as well, as did individual Indian Agents in their often lone efforts to inspire and encourage members of their communities to read. The Indian Agent at Mud Lake, for instance, built a small collection made up of discards from the Peterborough Public Library. Similarly, the day school teacher at Parry Island built a library for the school made up of discarded materials from the public library in Parry Sound.[10]

The successful establishment of publicly accessible libraries by Aboriginal peoples before 1960 took place in communities that had long histories of non-Aboriginal relations and integration. In the east, generally positive relations between the Mi'kmaq and Roman Catholic missionaries resulted in a unique mixing of Mi'kmaq and Catholic traditions and beliefs which were communicated widely through Mi'kmaq hieroglyphics. At around the same time as the Lady Wood Library was established at Lennox Island, the community was also among the few in Canada to employ an Aboriginal school teacher. The Lady Wood Library was established with philanthropic funds and provided space for community gatherings and the sharing of knowledge through orality in addition to its small collection of books. In this way, the Lennox Island people were clearly concerned with maintaining traditional ways of communication and learning while also providing opportunity for community members to master Western forms of literacy and communication. At Fort St. James, British Columbia, the Carrier people of the region had a longtime relationship with non-Aboriginal fur traders, and the community was among the earliest in the province to be permanently settled. Roman Catholic missionaries in the region adapted Cree syllabics to the Carrier language and were highly successful in promoting Western understandings of literacy. This early indoctrination of literacy undoubtedly was a factor in the establishment of a library by the Indian Homemakers' Club of Fort St. James in 1954, but the library was also indicative of traditional and modern concerns regarding the health and welfare of the community. At both Lennox Island and Fort St. James, First Peoples' interests in the printed word and in establishing libraries reflected more general concerns shared by many Aboriginal peoples throughout the country, being that of effectively adjusting to the permanent reality of non-Aboriginal peoples while at the same time finding ways to maintain their own histories and knowledge.

Missionaries and Indian Affairs, on the other hand, had envisioned the printed word and libraries as tools of conversion and assimilation. In their efforts to spread Western literacy among Aboriginal peoples, missionaries

168   Conclusion

employed books for the sole purpose of spreading the message of the
Christian faith and introducing the people to the perceived benefits of
"civilized" living. Indian Affairs, in its promotion of supplementary
reading materials and libraries in the Indian schools, was interested in
turning Aboriginal children away from their traditional upbringing and
recreating them in the image of Euro-Canadian children and citizens. Some
First Peoples recognized early the value of adopting these Western means
of communication and record keeping, but did so on their own terms,
articulating these in ways that were of value to their own cultures and
traditions, as tools for maintaining Aboriginal knowledge and history while
simultaneously familiarizing themselves with the colonizers' preferred
means of communication.

   Much discussion regarding the post-1960 establishment of libraries
for First Peoples has been characterized by a concern over a perceived lack
of Aboriginal patronage. If this is the case, it is not because First Peoples
have shown no interest in Western literacy or the printed word. Efforts to
establish libraries and promote Western literacy by First Peoples before
1960 have demonstrated that Aboriginal peoples have had a long interest
in these means of record keeping and communication. Naturally, First
Peoples wanted the printed word and libraries to serve their interests, and
embracing books and libraries was not an outward sign of successful
assimilation to Western culture. Rather, these tools were articulated in
ways to maintain and promote Aboriginal knowledge and cultures in a
world increasingly shaped by non-Aboriginal Canadians.

Notes

1. North American Indian Travelling College, *Traditional teachings*
(Cornwall Island ON: North American Indian Travelling College, 1984), vi.
   2. Lotsee Patterson, "The Work of tribal libraries," Back to the Future: a
forum on the education and training requirements of First Nations record keepers,
First Nations House of Learning, University of British Columbia, 17 November
2000.
   3. Edith Adamson, who in 1966 became the first Library Consultant with the
Department of Indian Affairs and Northern Development, outlined these
developments in her article, "Public library service to the Indians of Canada,"
Canadian Library Journal 26.1 (1969): 48-53.

4. Hugh Shewell has also noted that between 1948 and 1963, the Department of Indian Affairs put much effort into improving methods of providing welfare and on finding ways to encourage the provinces to extend their welfare services to Aboriginal communities. Angus Mowat's efforts in gaining support from the Ontario government in establishing provincial library services in Aboriginal communities can be tied to these efforts. By the late 1950s, the federal policy towards Aboriginal peoples had shifted from "assimilation" to "integration." Shewell notes that integration was less coercive than assimilation, and relied more on ideological persuasion. Integration policies sought to control the behavior of Aboriginal peoples through offering programs and services that diverted their attentions from traditional practices and promised full equality with the larger Canadian population. See, Hugh Shewell, "'Bitterness behind every smiling face': community development and Canada's First Nations, 1954-1968," *Canadian Historical Review* 83.1 (2002): 58-84.

5. Coinciding with these developments, the National Indian Brotherhood of Canada published in 1972, *Indian control of Indian education: policy paper, presented to the Minister of Indian and Northern Development* (Ottawa: National Indian Brotherhood, 1972). Today the work of the Saskatchewan Indian Cultural Centre is complemented and supported by the First Nations University of Canada in Regina (formerly the Saskatchewan Indian Federated College), an Aboriginal-controlled post-secondary institution that has developed a significant library of materials written by, for, and about the First Nations peoples of North, Central, and South America, as well as the Aboriginal peoples of Australia and New Zealand.

6. For discussion on the difficulties faced by contemporary Aboriginal libraries see, for example: Canada. Royal Commission on Aboriginal Peoples, *Report of the Royal Commission on Aboriginal Peoples* (Ottawa: Minister of Supply and Services, 1996); Gordon H. Hills, *Native libraries: cross-cultural conditions in the circumpolar countries* (Lanham MD: Scarecrow Press, 1997); Gene Joseph, *"Library services to First Nations in British Columbia"* (Vancouver: First Nations Interest Group. British Columbia Library Association, 1994) http://web.ucs.ubc.ca/bcla/fnig/gene2.htm ; Mary Land, "Double jeopardy: Native libraries face complex mandate with scarce resources," *Quill and Quire* 61.12 (1995): 14-15; *Proceedings*, Back to the Future: a forum on the education and training requirements of First Nations record keepers, First Nations House of Learning, University of British Columbia, 17 November 2000, http://www.library.ubc.ca/xwi7xwa/fn_lib.htm.

7. For instance, the First Nations Interest Group of the British Columbia Library Association and the First Nations House of Learning at the University of British Columbia co-sponsored, "Back to the Future: a forum on the education and training requirements of First Nations record keepers," on 17 November 2000. There is also the Library and Information Needs of Native People's Interest Group of the Canadian Library Association, a program sponsored by the National Library of Canada in support of Aboriginal librarians, and numerous other initiatives at the federal, provincial, and community levels relating to contemporary library

service issues in Aboriginal communities.

    8. Patterson, "The Work of tribal libraries."

    9. Jacqueline P. O'Donnell has also noted that the formation of the Native Brotherhood of British Columbia in 1931 was affected and influenced by a legacy of traditional social and economic organizations by coastal Aboriginal peoples. Clearly acknowledged hereditary leadership structures within north coast communities provided existing leadership potential and the influence to assume executive positions within modern political organizations. The economic sphere of the commercial fishery provided a common bond and additional structure to the formation of the Brotherhood. These elements coupled with the unique historical experience and grievances of British Columbian First Peoples were key to their producing the first recognized extra-kin Aboriginal political organization in Canada, despite their diverse cultures and composition. See Jacqueline P. O'Donnell, *The Native Brotherhood of British Columbia, 1931-1950: a new phase in Native political organization*, MA Thesis, University of British Columbia, 1985.

    10. Contemporary Aboriginal efforts to establish libraries in Canada are still often reliant on philanthropy. The efforts of young Skawenniio Barnes from the Kahnawake Mohawk Reserve in Québec, and Ontario Lieutenant-Governor, James Bartleman's campaign to acquire books for northern Aboriginal communities are prime examples. Thirteen-year-old Barnes (whose name means "Beautiful Word" in Mohawk) wrote a letter in early 2002 to the Kahnawake band council to ask for a library, and when her plea was ignored, she submitted the letter to the magazine, *CosmoGirl!* Her letter eventually got the attention of the Montreal *Gazette* and quickly Barnes' plea captured the attention of people worldwide. In October 2003 a library was established in Kahnawake made up of donated books from as far away as Australia–all in response to Barnes' plea. (See: Debbie Parkes, "Kahnawake turns a page," Montreal *Gazette* 5 October 2003, A3). Lieutenant-Governor Bartleman (a member of the Mnjikaning First Nation) began in early 2004 to solicit the people of southern Ontario to donate books for Aboriginal communities in northern Ontario. In his travels to the north, Bartleman was appalled by the staggering number of Aboriginal communities that had no books or reading materials. His plea has resulted in the donation of more than a million used books that will be used to fill the empty shelves of northern Aboriginal schools and libraries. (See: Adrian Humphreys, "Viceroy's goal is to fill empty bookshelves," *National Post* 15 January 2004, A8).

Appendix 1

Approved Supplementary Reading Books for Indian Schools, 1931-1938[1]

1.1 List of Special Books in Stock at the Government Stationery Office on 15 September 1931

The Singing Circle (An action song book)	22 copies
Country Life Reader	25 copies

Blackie's "The Lucky Dip" Series   60 copies each

> *A Little Birdie Book*
> *The Lucky Golden Cobbler*
> *Brownie and the Grocer*
> *The Little Tin Tea-set*
> *Three Bad Pups*
> *Three Silver Pennies*
> *The Wizard's Chair*

Blackie's Bible Stories   82 copies each

> *Stories of Jesus*
> *Stories of St. Paul*
> *Old Testament Stories*
> *Stories of Daniel and Elijah*
> *The Child of Bethlehem*
> *Jesus and His Friends*

Blackie's Large Type Concise English Dictionary   76 copies

Blackie's Small School Dictionary   247 copies
The Red Man's Wonder Book – Kennedy   100 copies
Corona Primers   58 copies
Our Little Reader   1000 copies
Gateway Primer   500 copies

1.2 List of Books Forwarded to Mr. Geo Dill from Department, November 7, 1932

Friends – Pennell & Cusack
The Outdoor Primer – Grover
Picture & Story for Little Folk – Sidnell & Gibbon
Little Ones Own Picture Reader
Little Book of Stories & Pictures – Pitcairn
Tom and His Friends – Leddell
Aesop's Fables (Books for Young Readers)
          retold by Williams
Santa, Mud Pies & Billy Boo – Jesse
Two in a Tub – Jesse
An Easy Primer – Burnett
The Phrase Readers Bk. 1 – Lay & Jones
Story of Spot
Jack and the Bean Stalk
The Story of Ned, Fred & Ted
Little Dot
Tot and the Cat
Blackie's Easy to Read Books (1 set)
Work-a-Day Doings – Serl
Second Story Primer – Gadsby
Sunny Stories for Tiny Folks
Little Stories for Little People
Animal Stories for Tiny Folk
Nature Stories for Tiny Folk
Lucky Dip Series (7) – Blackie
The Child's Hiawatha – Lee
Water Babies – retold by Davidson
Little Playmates
Bible Stories (6)

Briar Rose
Tom Thumb
The Fox & the Grapes
Tom-Tit-Tot
John Hassell Series (12) – Blackie
Little Children of the Great Round World
Famous Canadian Stories
Little World Children
Heidi
Peter Pan & Wendy – retold by Byron
A Dog of Flanders
Little Gray Coat
Kitty Carroll
Put to the Proof
A Little Hero
Table Talks & Table Travels
Golden Budget for Boys
The Lucky Girls' Budget
The Lucky Boys' Budget
Mother Nature Stories
Heroes & Heroic Deeds of the Great War
Builders of History
War Trail of Big Bear
By Star & Compass
The Story of the Great War
Famous Explorers
Canada's Story
This Canada of Ours - Cochrane & Wallace

1.3 Texts for Indian schools ordered from J. M. Dent & Sons, Toronto (publisher), August 1932

100 copies	*Classroom Plays from Canadian History*
100 copies	*Classroom Plays from Canadian Industry*
300 copies	*Silent Study Reader, Pupils Book 1*
300 copies	*Silent Study Reader, Pupils Book 2*
200 copies	*Silent Study Reader, Pupils Book 3*
100 copies	*Silent Study Reader, Pupils Book 4*
100 copies	*Silent Study Reader, Pupils Book 5*

100 copies	*Silent Study Reader, Pupils Book 6*
100 copies	*Children of the Pioneers*
100 copies	*Toy Shop Tales*
100 copies	*Black Canyon*
100 copies	*Pelts & Powder*
100 copies	*With the Birds for Little Folk*
100 copies	*Reading Exercises, Grade III*
100 copies	*Reading Exercises, Grade IV*
100 copies	*Reading Exercises, Grade V*
50 copies	*Reading Exercises, Grade VI*
200 copies	*Work Books in English Usage & Composition, Grade III*
200 copies	*Work Books in English Usage & Composition, Grade IV*
100 copies	*Work Books in English Usage & Composition, Grade V*
100 copies	*Work Books in English Usage & Composition, Grade VI*
100 copies	*Work Books in English Usage & Composition, Grade VII*
100 copies	*Work Books in English Usage & Composition, Grade VIII*
300 copies	*Number Work Book for Beginners*
300 copies	*Reading Work Book for Beginners*
50 copies	*Canadian History Work Book*
50 copies	*English History Work Book*
100 copies	*Nature & Language Work Books, Grade I*
100 copies	*Nature & Language Work Books, Grade II*
100 copies	*Canadian Junior Geography*
100 copies	*Geography Work Book*, B. C. edition
100 copies	*At the Top of the Hill*

1.4 List of Books Considered Suitable by the Department for Supplementary Reading ordered from Blackie & Sons (publisher), October 1932

50 copies each of:

John Hassall series

Puss in Boots
Little Boy Blue
Little Bo Peep
Hansel & Gretel
The Travelling Musicians
Jack & Jill
Peter Piper
Hey Diddle-Diddle
John Gilpin
Red Riding Hood
Aladdin
Beauty and the Beast

Crusoe of the Frozen North

The Story of Aenaes

The Golden Key

Blackie's Pinnacle Library series
Little Gray Coat
Kitty Carroll
Put to the Proof
A Little Hero
The Kitchen Cat
Two Little Mice

The Airman and His Craft

1.5 List of Books Considered Suitable by the Department for Supplementary Reading ordered from Blackie & Sons (publisher), October-November 1933

50 copies each of:

Popular Nursery Stories
Easy Story Book
Nannie's Big Story Book
By Road, Rail, Air & Sea (Hall)

Great Exploits in the Air
Black Beauty (Sewell)
Tanglewood Tales (Hawthorne)
Grimm's Fairy Tales
Little Women (Alcott)
Treasure Island
Kidnapped
Robinson Crusoe
The Heroes (Kingsley)
Water Babies (Kingsley)
Silver Skates

25 copies each of:

Cousin Sara
Giannetta
Narcissa's Ring
Our Sister Maisie

1.6 List of Books Considered Suitable by the Department for Supplementary Reading, January 1934

from Thos. Nelson & Sons (publisher)
50 copies each of:

> *Happy Hours*
> *Baby Animals*
> *Animal Friends*
> *Tales from the Arabian Nights*
> *Robin Hood*

from Macmillan Publishing Co. (publisher)
30 copies each of:

> *Little Black Sambo* (Bannerman)
> *The Little Pigs*
> *The F-U-N Book* (LaRue)
> *Under the Story Tree* (LaRue)
> *In Animal Land* (LaRue)

Little Indians (LaRue)

from Ginn & Co. (publisher)
30 copies of:

Wigwam Stories

from J. M. Dent & Sons (publisher)
25 copies of:

The Golden Forest

1.7 List of Books Considered Suitable by the Department for Supplementary Reading ordered from Blackie & Sons (publisher), November 1936

30 copies	*Tireless Wings*
30 copies	*His First Ship*
30 copies	*A Popular School Girl*
30 copies	*Through the Air & the Jungle*
30 copies	*Four Little Mischiefs*
30 copies	*Margery Dawe*
50 copies	*My Very Own Book*
30 copies	Tales & Talks – *A Book About Animals*
30 copies	*Little Children of the Great Round World*
30 copies	*Peggy & Joan*
30 copies	*The Party Book*
50 copies	*Animal Playmates*
50 copies	*My Lovely Pictures*
100 copies	Easy to Read – *The Magic Duck*
100 copies	Easy to Read – *Three Bad Pups*
100 copies	Easy to Read – *Jill on the Farm*

1.8 Requisition for School Supplies, Mount Elgin Institute, Muncey, Ontario, October 1937

No.	Title	Author	Publisher
ENGLISH			
1	*The Improvement of Reading*	Gates	Macmillan
1	*Reading Activities in the Primary Grades*	Storm & Smith	Ginn
SOCIAL STUDIES			
1	*History of Geographical Discovery*	Baker	Clarke-Irwin
2	*Discovers and Explorers*	Hamer-Jackson	Nelson
1	*A Book of Discovery*	Synge	Nelson
1	*The World We Live in and How It Came to Be*	Hartman	Macmillan
NATURAL SCIENCE			
1	*Science in the Elementary Schools*	Croxton	McGraw-Hill (New York)
ART			
1	*The Child and His Pencil*	Russell	Nelson
1	*The First Steps in Art and Handwork*	Dobbs	Macmillan
ENTERPRISES			
2	*The Activity Programme*	Melvin	Reynal & Hitch-cock (New York)
2	*Adjusting the School to the Child*	Washburn	Gage

1.9 New titles approved by the Department for Supplementary Reading Books, 1917-1938

1917   #3 Writing Course

1931   Teacher's Manual to accomp. Beacon charts

1932   *Class Room Plays for Can. Industry*
        Maps of Ontario

1933   *Oral Arithmetics* – C. C. Golding

1934   LaRue – *In Animal Land*
        Beautiful Bible Pictures
        Stories of Daniel and Elijah
        Little Black Sambo
        The O'Shaughnessy Girls (Catholic)
        Bailey's Writing Course – Teacher's manual

1935   *Edinburgh after Flodden*
        John Gilpin

1936   *Old Curiosity Shop*
        Four Little Mischiefs
        Popular School Girl
        His First Ship
        An Exciting Term
        Madcap of the School
        Margery Dawe
        Through the Air and Jungle
        Tireless Wings
        How Jack Found His Fortune
        Story of Delicia
        The Party Book
        comb. *Robinson Crusoe, Swiss Family Robinson, and
                Gulliver's Travels*

1937   *Dwellers of Marsh Realm*
        Bird Stories from Burroughs

Wishing Owl
Pud, Pringle, Pirate
Paddle Wheels
Green Elf and Golden Elf
Temple Poetry Book VI or G
Book of Wonders
Laugh and Learn
Billy Bork
Two Years before the Mast
Pictureland
Spotty
Song Trail
Shenshoo – The Story of the Moose
Ring – The Story of a St. Bernard Dog
Felicity's Fortune
Marigold Makes Good
Jill Jolliest School
Trouble in Tatters
Canadian West
Old Abe – The Story of the Lincoln Sheep

1938   Maps of the Province of Quebec
        Twilight Tales

Notes

1. As reported in: NAC RG 10, Volume 6032, File 150-41, part 1, Reel C-8149, Headquarters – Supplementary reading books for Indian schools, 1931-1942.

Appendix 2

Day School Libraries, 1943[1]

2.1 Reported Collection Sizes of Indian Day School Libraries

PRINCE EDWARD ISLAND

Lennox Island	–

NOVA SCOTIA

Afton	104
Bear River	–
Eskasoni	109
Indian Cove	108
Malagawatch	–
Middle River	116
Millbrook	103
Salmon River	111
Shubenacadie	105
Sydney	71
Whycocomagh	114

NEW BRUNSWICK

Big Cove	–
Burnt Church	110
Eel Ground	100
Eel River	102
Kingsclear	99
Oromocto	101

Red Bank	112
St. Mary's	113
Tobique	106
Woodstock	107

NORTHWEST TERRITORIES

Fort Simpson C. E.	–
Fort Simpson R. C.	118
Fort Smith	117
Hay River	–

YUKON

| Moosehide | – |
| Selkirk | – |

MANITOBA

Berens River R. C.	128
Berens River U. C.	123
Big Eddy	124
Black River	–
Bloodvein River	–
Brokenhead	132
Chemawawin	–
Cross Lake U. C.	–
Ebb & Flow Lake	–
Fairford	120
Fisher River	138
Fort Alexander	119
Grand Rapids	–
Hollowwater River	–
Island Lake R. C.	–
Island Lake U. C.	–
Jackhead	134
Jack River C. E.	–
Jack River R. C.	133
Lake Manitoba	–
Lake St. Martin	–
Little Saskatchewan	–

Nelson House U. C.	–
Nelson House R. C.	135
Oak River Sioux	121
Little Grand Rapids U. C.	137
Little Grand Rapids R. C.	136
Orford House	–
Pas	122
Peguis Centre	139
Peguis North	125
Peguis South	115
Pekangekum	–
Pine Bluff	–
Poplar River	–
Red Earth	131
Rossville	130
Shoal Lake	126
Shoal River	–
Split Lake	129
Swan Lake	140
Waterhen River	–
York Factory	–

BRITISH COLUMBIA

Ahousaht	–
Alert Bay	85
Bella Bella	–
Bella Coola	90
Boothroyd	7
Campbell River	94
Cape Mudge	80
Chehalts	–
Fort Babine	97
Gitladamicks	96
Glen Vowell	–
Gwinoha	87
Hartley Bay	–
Hazelton	–
Homalco	–

Inkaneep	–
Katzie	–
Kincolish	86
Kingcome Inlet	–
Kispiox	93
Kitamatt	95
Kitkatla	84
Kitsegukla	–
Kitselas	83
Kitwancool	–
Kitwanga	72
Klemtu	–
Koksilah	78
Lakalsap	–
Mamalillikulla	–
Massett	89
Metlakatla	–
Moricetown	–
Nanaimo	–
Okanagan	–
Pemberton	74
Penticton	91
Port Essington	75
Port Simpson	12
Quatsino	–
Rocher Deboule	6
Sannich	–
Seabird Island	77
Seton Lake	88
Shulus	–
Skidegate	–
Skwah	–
Sliammon	8
Songhees	92
St. Catherine's	79
Tsartlip	73
Ucluelet	81

QUEBEC

Brennan Lake	–
Caughnawaga (Bush)	–
Caughnawaga R. C. (3)	66
Caughnawaga (St. Isidore)	–
Caughnawaga U. C.	65
Chenail	–
Chetlain	64
Congo Bridge	82
Cornwall Island East	59
Cornwall Island West	141
Fort George	–
Hunter's Point	–
Lorette	63
Maniwaki	–
Maria	–
Oka Country	–
Oka Village	61
Pointe Bleue	–
Restigouche	60
Rupert's House	–
St. Frances R. C.	–
St. Regis Island	–
St. Regis Village	68
Temiskaming	62

ONTARIO

Albany River	–
Alnwick	–
Back Settlement	26
Batchawana	19
Bear Creek	42
Birch Island	20
Buzwah	1
Cape Croker	17
Christian Island U. C.	71
Christian Island R. C.	23
Dokis	–

French Bay	15
Fort Hope	–
Garden River C. E.	30
Garden River R. C.	24
Garden Village	–
Georgina Island	27
Gibson	11
Golden Lake	–
Goulais Bay	–
Grand Bay (McIntyre Bay)	–
Gull Bay	–
Kaboni	–
Kettle Point	142
Lake Helen	43
Lower French River	21
Manitou Rapids	38
Mission Bay	–
Mississauga River	46
Mobert	–
Moose Deer Point	–
Moose Fort	–
Moraviantown	143
Mud Lake	22
Muncey	–
New Credit	–
Oneida No. 1	5
Oneida No. 2	40
Oneida No. 3	39
Pic	–
Port Elgin	76
Rabbit Island	37
Rama	18
River Settlement	10
Ryerson	–
Sagamook	–
Saugeen	39
Scotch Settlement	44
Seine River	–
Serpent River	33
Shawanaga	34

Sheshegwaning	–
Sidney Bay	127
Six Nations No. 1	–
Six Nations No. 2	41
Six Nations No. 3	–
Six Nations No. 4	–
Six Nations No. 5	31
Six Nations No. 6	–
Six Nations No. 7	2
Six Nations No. 8	35
Six Nations No. 9	–
Six Nations No. 10	14
Six Nations No. 11	29
Spanish River Prot.	47
St. Clair	28
Stoney Point	–
Sucker Creek	16
Tyendinaga Central	–
Tyendinaga Eastern	25
Tyendinaga Mission	–
Tyendinaga Western	–
Walpole Island No. 1	9
Walpole Island No. 2	32
West Bay	13
Whitefish Bay	–
Whitefish Lake	–
Wikwemikong	70

SASKATCHEWAN

Ahtahkakoops	–
Assiniboine	54
Big Island Lake	50
Big River C. E.	–
Big River R. C.	48
Cote's	–
Day Stars	–
Fishing Lake	49
Fort a la Corne South	–
Frog Lake	–

James Smith's	–
John Smith's	57
Keys	–
Kinistino	–
Little Pines	53
Little Red River	51
Long Lake	–
Ministikwan	–
Mistawasis	–
Montreal Lake	52
Red Pheasant	56
Stanley	–
Sturgeon Lake	55
White Bear's	58
Whitecap Sioux	45

ALBERTA

| Sarcee | 69 |

Notes

1. As reported in: NAC RG 10, Volume 6035, File 150-83, part 1, Reel C-8150, Headquarters - Day Schools - Listings of Library Books, 1943.

Bibliography

Primary Sources

George Barnley fonds. National Archives of Canada.
MG 40-Q 31, British and Foreign Anti-Slavery Society and Aborigines
    Protection Society fonds. Oxford University, Rhodes House
    Library [National Archives of Canada, microfiche reels A-1647
    to A-1650].
RG 10, Indian Affairs. National Archives of Canada.
RG 2-42, Ministry of Education. Archives of Ontario.
James Evans collection. J. J. Talman Regional Collection, D. B. Weldon
    Library, University of Western Ontario.
Angus McGill Mowat collection. J. J. Talman Regional Collection, D. B.
    Weldon Library, University of Western Ontario.

Published Primary Sources

Ahenakew, Edward. "Cree Trickster tales." *Journal of American Folklore*
    42 (1929).
————. "Little Pine: an Indian day school." Edited by Ruth Matheson
    Buck. *Saskatchewan History* XVIII.2 (1965).
————. *Voices of the Plains Cree*. Edited by Ruth M. Buck. 1973.
    Regina: Canadian Plains Research Center, 1995.
Canada. Department of Citizenship and Immigration. *Reports of the
    Indian Affairs Branch*. Ottawa: Queen's Printer, 1953-1956.
Canada. Department of Mines and Resources. *Reports of Indian Affairs
    Branch*. Ottawa, 1940-1943.
Canada, Dominion of. *Annual reports of the Department of Indian Affairs*.
    1880-1916.
Central Auxiliary Society for promoting Education and Industry among
    the Indians and Destitute Settlers in Canada. *The Second annual
    report of the Central Auxiliary Society for promoting Education
    and Industry among the Indians and Destitute Settlers in
    Canada: submitted to the Public Meeting held in the Masonic
    Hall Hotel, Montreal, April 8, 1829*. Montreal: Montreal Herald

and New Montreal Gazette Office, 1829.

"Christianity in the Longhouse: the educational problems of the Confederacy about 1810." *The Valley of the Six Nations: a collection of documents on the Indian lands of the Grand River.* Ed. Charles M. Johnston. Toronto: The Champlain Society for the Government of Ontario and the University of Toronto Press, 1964.

Church Missionary Gleaner II.2 (February 1852).

Cooke, Charles A. [Thawennensere]. *A-de-rih-wa-nie-ton on-kwe-on-we neh-ha: a message to the Iroquois Indians.* Trans. by Charles A. Cooke. Toronto: Baha'i Publishing Committee, 19??.

————. "Iroquois personal names–their classification." *Proceedings of the American Philosophical Society* 96.4 (1952).

Cooke, Charles A., ed. *Onkweonwe* 1.1 (October 25, 1900). Ottawa: F. X. Lemieux, 1900.

Copway, George [Kahgegagahbowh]. *Recollections of a forest life: or, the life and travels of Kah-ge-ga-gah-bowh, or George Copway.* Second Edition. London: Charles Gilpin, 1851.

Copway, George. *Running sketches of men and places, in England, France, Germany, Belgium and Scotland.* New York: J. C. Riker, 1851.

————. *The Traditional history and characteristic sketches of the Ojibway nation.* London: Charles Gilpin, 1850.

Holliwell, Mrs. "Holiday musings of a worker: no. II - the love of reading." *British American magazine: devoted to literature, science and art* II (1864).

Jacobs, Peter [Pahtahsega]. *Journal of the Reverend Peter Jacobs, Indian Wesleyan missionary, from Rice Lake to the Hudson's Bay Territory, and returning, commencing May, 1852.* New York: Published by the Author, 1858.

Jones, Peter [Kahkewaquonaby]. *History of the Ojebway Indians: with especial reference to their conversion to Christianity.* London: A. W. Bennett, 1861.

————. *Life and journals of Kah-ke-wa-quo-na-by (Rev. Peter Jones), Wesleyan Missionary.* Toronto: Anson Green, 1860.

Jones, William. *The Jubilee memorial of the Religious Tract Society: containing a record of its origins, proceedings and results A. D. 1799 to 1849.* London: Religious Tract Society, 1850.

Kennedy, Dan. *Recollections of an Assiniboine Chief.* Ed. James R. Stevens. Toronto: McClelland & Stewart, 1972.

LeClercq, Father Chrestien. *New relation of Gaspesia: with the customs and religion of the Gaspesian Indians*. Ed. and Trans. William F. Ganong. The Publications of the Champlain Society V. 1691. Toronto: The Champlain Society, 1910.

Legislative Assembly of the Province of Canada. *Report of the Special Commissioners appointed on the 8th September, 1856, to investigate Indian Affairs in Canada*. Toronto: Stewart Derbishire & George Desbarats, 1858.

Maillard, Pierre Antoine-Simon. "Lettre de M. L'Abbé Maillard sur les missions de l'Acadie et particulièrement sur les missions Micmaques." *Les Soirées Canadiennes: recuil de littérature*. Troisieme annee. Quebec City: Brousseau Frères, 1863.

McLean, John. *The Hero of the Saskatchewan: life among the Ojibway and Cree Indians in Canada*. Barrie ON: Barrie Examiner Printing and Publishing House, 1891.

————. *The Indians: their manners and customs*. Toronto: William Briggs, 1889.

National Council of Women of Canada. *Women in Canada: their life and work*. [Ottawa?]: National Council of Women of Canada, 1900.

Native Brotherhood of British Columbia. *The Native Voice*. 1946-1960.

Osgood, Thaddeus. *The Canadian visitor, communicating important facts and interesting anecdotes respecting the Indians and destitute settlers in Canada and the United States of America*. London: Hamilton and Adams, 1829?.

Pitezel, Rev. John H. *Lights and shades of missionary life: containing travels, sketches, incidents and missionary efforts, during nine years spent in the region of Lake Superior*. Cincinnati: Western Book Concern, 1860.

Province of Canada. Indian Affairs. *Report for the half-year ended 30th June, 1864*. Quebec: Hunter, Rose & Co., 1865.

"Report of the Committee on Aborigines." *Parliamentary Papers* 7 (1836).

Stock, Eugene. *Metlakahtla and the North Pacific mission of the Church Missionary Society*. London: Church Missionary House, 1880.

Tucker, S. *The Rainbow in the North: a short account of the first establishment of Christianity in Rupert's Land by the Church Missionary Society*. London: James Nisbet and Co., 1851.

Wellcome, Henry S. *The Story of Metlakahtla*. London and New York: American News Company, 1887.

Wilson, Edward F. *Missionary work among the Ojebway Indians*.

London: Society for Promoting Christian Knowledge, 1886.

Young, Egerton R. *On the Indian trail: stories of missionary work among the Cree and Saulteaux Indians.* Toronto: Fleming H. Revell Company, 1897.

Young, Egerton Ryerson. *Stories from Indian wigwams and Northern camp-fires.* Toronto: William Briggs, 189?.

Secondary Sources

Adamson, Edith. "Public library service to the Indians of Canada." *Canadian Library Journal* 26.1 (1969).

Alia, Valerie. *Un/covering the North: news, media and Aboriginal people.* Vancouver: UBC Press, 1999.

Amadi, Adolphe O. *African libraries: western tradition and colonial brainwashing.* Metuchen NJ: Scarecrow Press, 1981.

Armstrong, Jeannette C., et al., eds. *We get our living like milk from the land: Okanagan tribal history book.* Penticton BC: Theytus Books, 1994.

Aspinali, Jane. "Library self-determination? Ontario Native Task Force backs separate system." *Quill and Quire* 58.2 (1992).

Aveni, Anthony F. *Empires of time: calendars, clocks and cultures.* New York: Basic Books, 1989.

Avison, Shannon and Michael Meadows. "Speaking and hearing: Aboriginal newspapers and the public sphere in Canada and Australia," *Canadian Journal of Communication* 25 (2000): 347-66

Axtell, James. "The Power of print in the Eastern Woodlands." *The William and Mary Quarterly* S3.44 (1987).

Banks, Joyce M. *Books in Native languages in the Rare Book Collections of the National Library of Canada.* Revised & enlarged edition. Ottawa: National Library of Canada, 1985.

—————. "The Church Missionary Society Press at Moose Factory: 1853-1859." *Journal of the Canadian Church Historical Society* xxvi.2 (1984).

—————. "James Constantine Pilling and the literature of the Native peoples." *Bibliographical Society of Canada: Colloquium III: National Library of Canada, 19-21 October 1978.* (1978).

Barber, Katherine, ed. *The Canadian Oxford dictionary.* Toronto: Oxford University Press, 1998.

Barbeau, Marius. "Charles A. Cooke, Mohawk scholar." *Proceedings of the American Philosophical Society* 96.4 (1952).

Barman, Jean, Yvonne Hébert and Don McCaskill, eds. *Indian education in Canada, volume 1: the legacy.* Vancouver: University of British Columbia Press, 1986.

Battiste, Marie. "Micmac literacy and cognitive assimilation." *Indian education in Canada, volume 1: the legacy.* Eds. Jean Barman, Yvonne Hébert and Don McCaskill. Vancouver: University of British Columbia Press, 1986.

Belshaw, Cyril S. "The Struggle for survival." Rev. of *The Struggle for survival: Indian cultures and the Protestant ethic in British Columbia,* by Forrest E. LaViolette. *Ethnohistory* 8 (1961).

Bennett, J. A. H., and J. W. Berry. *Cree syllabic literacy: cultural context and psychological consequences.* Tilburg University Monographs in Cross-cultural Psychology. Tilburg: Tilburg University Press, 1991.

Beynon, Jack. "Publication dates." *The Native Voice* 1.1 (1946).

Bingaman, Sandra Estlin. "The Trials of the 'White Rebels,' 1885." *Saskatchewan history* xxv.1 (1972).

A Blackfoot Winter count. Occasional paper no. 1. Calgary: Glenbow-Alberta Institute, 1965.

Boone, Elizabeth Hill, and Walter D. Mignolo, eds. *Writing without words: alternative literacies in Mesoamerica and the Andes.* Durham: Duke University Press, 1994.

Boylan, Anne M. *Sunday school: the formation of an American institution 1790-1880.* New Haven: Yale University Press, 1988.

Bright, Donna. *The Provision of public library services to Native Canadians living on reserves in Ontario, Manitoba, Saskatchewan, Alberta, and British Columbia.* M.A. Thesis. University of Western Ontario, 1992.

British Columbia Library Association First Nations Interest Group. *Library services for First Nations people: report on a workshop held in Penticton, British Columbia April 22, 1993.* Vancouver: BCLA First Nations Interest Group, 1994.

Brown, Jennifer S. H. "The Track to Heaven: the Hudson Bay Cree religious movement of 1842-1843." *Papers of the Thirteenth Algonquian Conference.* Ed. William Cowan. Ottawa: Carleton University, 1982.

Bruce, Lorne. *Free books for all: the public library movement in Ontario, 1850-1930.* Toronto: Dundurn Press, 1994.

Buller, Grace. "Native peoples and library service in Ontario." *Ontario Library Review* 59.1 (1975).

Calloway, Colin G. *New worlds for all: Indians, Europeans and the remaking of early America*. Baltimore: Johns Hopkins University Press, 1998.

Canada. Department of Citizenship and Immigration. Indian Affairs Branch. *Constitution and regulations for Indian Homemakers' Clubs*. Ottawa: King's Printer, 1951.

Canada. Royal Commission on Aboriginal Peoples. *Gathering strength: volume 3 of the Report of the Royal Commission on Aboriginal Peoples*. Ottawa: Canada Communications Group, 1996.

————. *Looking forward, looking back: volume 1 of the Report of the Royal Commission on Aboriginal Peoples*. Ottawa: Canada Communications Group, 1996.

Carlson, Judith Ann. *Library services for the Native peoples of North America: an examination of existing service in Ontario and recommendations for their improvement*. Toronto: Ryerson Polytechnic Institute, 1980.

Cherwinski, W. J. C. "Honoré Joseph Jaxon, agitator, disturber, producer of plans to make men think, and chronic objector...." *Canadian Historical Review* xlvi.2 (1965).

Chippewas of Sarnia First Nation. *Aamjiwnaang First Nation*. Sarnia: Chippewas of Sarnia First Nation, 2001?

Colyer, Elizabeth. "Library development in the Far North." *Librarianship in Canada, 1946 to 1967: essays in honour of Elizabeth Homer Morton*. Ed. Bruce Peel. Victoria: Canadian Library Association, 1968.

Commanda, Earl. "Indian library and information services." *Ontario Library Review* 62.4 (1978).

Conlogue, Ray. "Burning Sky, blazing trail: a new exhibit captures the forgotten vision and passion of Oronhyatekha, Canada's first Native doctor." *The Globe and Mail* [Toronto] 18 March 2002, Ontario ed.

Cook, Chris. "Communications link between our communities." *The Native Voice* [*Courier-Islander*, Campbell River] 6 October 2001.

Corley, Nora T. *Resources for Native people's studies*. Ottawa: National Library of Canada, 1984.

Corrigan, Philip, and Val Gillespie. *Class structure, social literacy and idle time: the provision of public libraries in England*. Brighton: John L. Noyce, 1978.

Coughlin, Violet L. *Larger units of public library service in Canada:*

with particular reference to the provinces of Prince Edward Island, Nova Scotia, and New Brunswick. Metuchen: Scarecrow Press, 1968.

Coward, Harold G. "The Spiritual power of oral and written scripture." *Silence, the Word and the Sacred.* Ed. E. D. Blodgett and H. G. Coward. Waterloo: Wilfrid Laurier University Press for the Calgary Institute for the Humanities, 1989.

Crooks, Grace. "James Bay Public Library, Moose Factory." *Ontario Library Review* 43.1 (1959).

Cumberland, F. Barlow. *Catalogue and notes of the Oronhyatekha Historical Collection.* Toronto: The Supreme Court, International Order of Foresters, 1904.

Cummings, Stephen Foster. *Angus McGill Mowat and the development of Ontario public libraries, 1920-1960.* PhD. Thesis. University of Western Ontario, 1986. Ottawa: Canadian Theses on Microfiche, 1986.

————. "On the compass of Angus Mowat: books, boats, soldiers and Indians." *Readings in Canadian library history.* Ed. Peter F. McNally. Ottawa: Canadian Library Association, 1986.

Curtis, Bruce. "'Littery merritt', 'Useful knowledge', and the organization of Township libraries in Canada West, 1840-1860." *Ontario History* lxxviii.4 (1986).

————. "The Speller expelled: disciplining the common reader in Canada West." *Canadian Review of Sociology and Anthropology* 22.3 (1985).

Cuthand, Stan. "Introduction to the 1995 edition." *Voices of the Plains Cree.* By Edward Ahenakew. Edited by Ruth M. Buck. Regina: Canadian Plains Research Center, 1995.

Danky, James P., ed. *Native American periodicals and newspapers 1828-1982: bibliography, publishing record and holdings.* Compiled by Maureen E. Hady. Westport CT: Greenwood Press, 1984.

"Death of Joshua Adams." *Sarnia Observer.* Weekly edition 28 December 1906.

DeFrancis, John. *Visible speech: the diverse oneness of writing systems.* Honolulu: University of Hawaii Press, 1989.

Demay, Jöel. "Clarifying ambiguities: the rapidly changing life of the Canadian Aboriginal print media," *Canadian Journal of Native Studies* XI.1 (1991): 95-112.

Dempsey, Hugh A. *Crowfoot: Chief of the Blackfeet.* Edmonton: Hurtig, 1972.

Dewdney, Selwyn. *The Sacred scrolls of the Southern Ojibway.* Toronto and Buffalo: University of Toronto Press for the Glenbow-Alberta Institute, 1975.

Dickason, Olive Patricia. *Canada's First Nations: a history of founding peoples from earliest times.* Toronto: McClelland and Stewart, 1994.

Ditzion, Sidney H. *Arsenals of a democratic culture: a social history of the American public library movement in New England and the middle states from 1850 to 1900.* Chicago: American Library Association, 1947.

Drucker, Philip. *The Native Brotherhoods: modern intertribal organizations on the northwest coast.* Smithsonian Institution, Bureau of American Ethnology, Bulletin 168. Washington: United States Printing Office, 1958.

Duff, Louis Blake. *Amazing story of the Winghamite secretary of Louis Riel.* Western Ontario history nuggets no. 22. London ON: Lawson Memorial Library, University of Western Ontario, 1955.

Edwards, Barry, and Mary Love. *A Bibliography of Inuit (Eskimo) linguistics in collections of the Metropolitan Toronto Library.* Toronto: Metropolitan Toronto Library Board, 1982.

Empowering people through libraries: conference proceedings. Saskatoon: Library Services of Saskatchewan Aboriginal Peoples Conference, 1992.

Erdrich, Louise. *Books and islands in Ojibwe country.* Washington, DC: National Geographic Society, 2003.

————. *Love medicine.* New and expanded version. 1984. New York: HarperCollins Publishers, 1993.

Evans, Karen. *Masinahikan: Native language imprints in the Archives and Libraries of the Anglican Church of Canada.* Toronto: Anglican Book Centre, 1985.

Farrand, Mrs. B. C. *Indians at Sarnia.* 1889. Brights Grove ON: George L. Smith, 1975.

Flood, John, ed. "The Diary of James Evans, July 11 - August 30, 1838: part one." *Northward Journal* 44 (1988).

————. "The Diary of James Evans, September 4 - November 20, 1838: part two." *Northward Journal* 45 (1988).

Friesen, Gerald. *Citizens and nation: an essay on history, communication and Canada.* Toronto: University of Toronto Press, 2000.

Friskney, Janet B. "Beyond the shadow of William Briggs part I: setting the stage and introducing the players." *Papers of the Biblio-*

graphical Society of Canada 33.2 (1995).

―――. *Towards a Canadian "Cultural Mecca": the Methodist Book and Publishing House's pursuit of book publishing and commitment to Canadian writing, 1829-1926.* M. A. Thesis. Trent University, 1994.

Garrison, Dee. *Apostles of culture: the public librarian and American society, 1876-1920.* New York: Free Press, 1979.

Goddard, Ives, and William Fitzhugh. "A Statement concerning America B. C." *Man in the Northeast* 17 (1979).

Goodwill, Jean, and Norma Sluman. *John Tootoosis: as told by Jean Goodwill and Norma Sluman.* Winnipeg: Pemmican Publications, 1987.

Goody, Jack, ed. *Literacy in traditional societies.* Cambridge: Cambridge University Press, 1968.

Grad, Tamara E. *The Development of public libraries in Ontario, 1851-1951.* M. A. Thesis. Drexel Institute of Technology, 1952.

Graff, Harvey J. *The Labyrinths of literacy: reflections on literacy past and present.* London: Falmer Press, 1987.

―――. *The Literacy myth: cultural integration and social structure in the nineteenth century.* New Brunswick NJ: Transaction Publishers, 1991.

Grant, John Webster. *Moon of wintertime: missionaries and the Indians of Canada in encounter since 1534.* Toronto: University of Toronto Press, 1984.

Greenfield, Bruce. "The Mi'kmaq hieroglyphic prayer book: writing and Christianity in Maritime Canada, 1675-1921." *The Language encounter in the Americas, 1492-1800: a collection of essays.* Ed. Edward G. Gray and Norman Fiering. New York: Berghahn Books, 2000.

Greer, Allan. "The Sunday schools of Upper Canada." *Ontario History* 67.3 (1975).

Hall, Anthony J. *The Red man's burden: land, law, and the Lord in the Indian affairs of Upper Canada, 1791-1858.* Doctoral thesis. University of Toronto, 1984.

Hall, Stuart. "On Postmodernism and articulation: an interview with Stuart Hall." Ed. Lawrence Grossberg. *Journal of Communication Inquiry* 10.2 (1986).

Hannum, Nancy. "Do Native people use public libraries?" *BCLA Reporter* 39 (1995).

Hardy, E. A. *The Public library: its place in our educational system.*

Toronto: William Briggs, 1912.

Harris, Michael. "The Purpose of the American public library: a revisionist interpretation of history." *Library Journal* 98 (1973).

Harris, Michael H. *History of libraries in the western world.* Fourth edition. Metuchen NJ: Scarecrow Press, 1995.

Harris, Michael H. and Stanley Hannah. "Why do we study the history of libraries? A meditation on the perils of ahistoricism in the information era." *Library and Information Science Research* 14.2 (1992).

Harris, Roy. *The Origin of writing.* London: Duckworth, 1986.

Hawkes, Terence. *Structuralism and semiotics.* Berkeley: University of California Press, 1977.

Hawthorn, H. B., C. S. Belshaw, and S. M. Jamieson. *The Indians of British Columbia: a study of contemporary social adjustment.* Toronto and Vancouver: University of Toronto Press and the University of British Columbia, 1960.

Heyser, Richard G., and Lotsee Smith. "Public library service to Native Americans in Canada and the continental United States." *Library Trends* 29.2 (1980).

Hills, Gordon H. *Native libraries: cross-cultural conditions in the circumpolar countries.* Lanham MD: Scarecrow Press, 1997.

Hollaran, Susan. "Rural public library service to Native Americans." *Rural Libraries* 10.1 (1990).

Houston, Susan E., and Alison Prentice. *Schooling and scholars in nineteenth-century Ontario.* Ontario Historical Studies Series. Toronto: University of Toronto Press, 1991.

Hovdhaugen, Even. "Missionary grammars–an attempt at defining a field of research." *... and the Word was God: missionary linguistics and missionary grammar.* Ed. Even Hovdhaugen. Münster: Nodus Publikationen, 1996.

Humphreys, Adrian. "Viceroy's goal is to fill empty bookshelves." *National Post* [Toronto] 15 January 2004, A8.

Hutchinson, Gerald D. "Evans, James." *Dictionary of Canadian biography.* Electronic Edition.

"Indian Homemakers' Association of B. C." *BC Institute against family violence newsletter* (Summer 1994).

Ingles, Ernie and Heather Ganshorn. "Alert Bay Public Library and Museum." *Feliciter* 48.4 (2002).

Jaenen, Cornelius J. *Friend and foe: aspects of French-Amerindian cultural contact in the sixteenth and seventeenth centuries.* New

York: Columbia University Press, 1976.

J. H. Beers & Co. *Commemorative biographical record of the County of Lambton, Ontario: containing biographical sketches of prominent and representative citizens and many of the early settled families.* Toronto: The Hill Binding Company, 1906.

Joblin, Elgie E. M. *The Education of the Indians of western Ontario,* Toronto: Ontario College of Education, 1947.

Joseph, Gene. "Library services to First Nations in British Columbia." http://web.ucs.ubc.ca/bcla/fnig/gene2.htm. Vancouver: British Columbia Library Association, 1994.

"Joshua Adams first city mayor to be thrown out by the voters." *Sarnia Observer* 26 August 1995.

Kealey, Gregory S., and Bryan D. Palmer. *Dreaming of what might be: the Knights of Labor in Ontario, 1880-1900.* Toronto: New Hogtown Press, 1987.

Kerri, James Nwannukwu. "Studying voluntary associations as adaptive mechanisms: a review of anthropological perspectives." *Current Anthropology* 17.1 (1976).

Kingston, Rebecca. "The National Library of Canada: a study in the growth of a nation." *Canadian Library Journal* 45.3 (1988).

Kinomägewäpkong: the teaching rocks. Prod. Ontario Ministry of Natural Resources. Dir. Lloyd Walton. Ontario Ministry of Natural Resources, 1987.

Kulchyski, Peter. "A Considerable unrest: F.O. Loft and the League of Indians." *Native Studies Review* 4.1-2 (1988).

Lancaster, F. W., ed. *The Role of the library in an electronic society.* Urbana-Champaign: University of Illinois, 1980.

Lancaster, F. Wilfred. "Whither libraries? Or, wither libraries." *College and Research Libraries* (1978).

Land, Mary. "Double jeopardy: Native libraries face complex mandate with scarce resources." *Quill and Quire* 61.2 (1995).

Landon, Fred. "Selections from the papers of James Evans, missionary to the Indians." *Papers and records.* Ontario Historical Society xxvi (1930).

LaViolette, Forrest E. *The Struggle for survival: Indian cultures and the Protestant ethic in British Columbia.* Toronto: University of Toronto Press, 1961.

Lee, Deborah A. "Academic information needs and library use of a sample of Aboriginal students at the University of Alberta." Diversity Now Conference: people, collections and services in academic libraries. University of Texas at Austin. 4 April 2000.

Leighton, Douglas. "The Compact Tory as bureaucrat: Samuel Peters Jarvis and the Indian Department, 1837-1845." *Ontario History* lxxiii.1 (1981).

Leighton, James Douglas. *The Development of Federal Indian policy in Canada, 1840-1890.* Doctoral dissertation. University of Western Ontario, 1975.

Lévis-Strauss, Claude. *The Savage mind.* Chicago: University of Chicago Press, 1966.

Long, John S. "The Reverend George Barnley and the James Bay Cree." *The Canadian Journal of Native Studies* vi.2 (1986).

MacDonald, Mary Lu. *Literature and society in the Canadas 1817-1850.* Queenston ON: Edwin Mellen Press, 1992.

Mair, Nathan H. *An Account of the deeds of Thaddeus Osgood, beggar.* Doing Good 2. Montreal: Archives Committee, Montreal-Ottawa Conference of the United Church of Canada, 1986.

"Major Jaxon, who's used to it by now, finds himself, at 90, thrown out again." *New York Times* 13 December 1951: 50.

Manore, Jean L. "A Vision of trust: the legal, moral and spiritual foundations of Shingwauk Hall." *Native Studies Review* 9.2 (1993-1994).

McFadden, Isobel. *Living by bells: a narrative of five schools in British Columbia, 1874-1970.* Toronto?: Committee on Education for Mission and Stewardship, United Church of Canada, 1971.

McKenna, M. Olga. *Micmac by choice: Elsie Sark–an island legend.* Halifax: Formac Publishing, 1990.

McKenzie, D. F. "The Sociology of a text: orality, literacy and print in early New Zealand." *The Book history reader.* Eds. David Finkelstein and Alistair McCleery. New York: Routledge, 2002.

McNally, Peter F. "Libraries in Canada: a précis." *Feliciter* 48.2 (2002).

McNally, Peter F., ed. *Readings in Canadian library history.* Ottawa: Canadian Library Association, 1986.

Merrell, James H. *The Indians' new world: Catawbas and their neighbors from European contact through the era of removal.* Chapel Hill: University of North Carolina Press, 1989.

Mignolo, Walter D. *The Darker side of the Renaissance: literacy, territoriality and colonization.* Ann Arbor: University of Michigan Press, 1995.

Millar, W. P. J. "Osgood, Thaddeus." *Dictionary of Canadian biography.* Volume VIII, 1851 to 1860.

————. "The Remarkable Rev. Thaddeus Osgood: a study in the evangelical spirit in the Canadas." *Histoire Sociale-Social History* x.19 (1977).

Miller, J. R. *Shingwauk's vision: a history of Native residential schools.* Toronto: University of Toronto Press, 1996.

Milloy, John S. *"A National crime": the Canadian government and the residential school system, 1879 to 1986.* Winnipeg: University of Manitoba Press, 1999.

Mohawk ideals, Victorian values: Oronhyatekha M. D. Museum Exhibit. Royal Ontario Museum. March - August 2002.

Molholt, Patricia. "Libraries and new technologies: courting the Chesire cat." *Library Journal* (1988).

Moore, Elise. "The Wheat Pool libraries and the 'useful knowledge' movement." History of the Book in Canada Open Conference for Volume III (1918-2000). Simon Fraser University. 16 November 2001.

Mountain Horse, Mike. *My People the Bloods.* Ed. Hugh A. Dempsey. Calgary: Glenbow-Alberta Institute and Blood Tribal Council, 1979.

Murdoch, John. *A Bibliography of Algonquian syllabic texts in Canadian repositories.* Quebec: Project ASTIC, Gouvernement du Quebec, Ministeres des Affaires culturelles, and Direction regionale du Nouveau Quebec et service aux autochtones, 1984.

————. *A Bibliography of Algonquian roman orthography texts in Canadian repositories.* Rupert House PQ: Project ASTIC, 1988.

Murray, David. *Forked tongues: speech, writing and representation in North American Indian texts.* Bloomington: University of Indiana Press, 1991.

Murray, Laura. "The Aesthetic of dispossession: Washington Irving and ideologies of (de)colonization in the early Republic." *American Literary History* 8.2 (1996).

————. "'Pray, Sir, consider a little': rituals of subordination and strategies of resistance in the letters of Hezekiah Calvin and David Fowler to Eleazar Wheelock, 1764-1768." *Studies in American Indian Literatures* 4.2-3 (1992).

Murray, Laura, ed. *To Do Good to my Indian brethren: the writings of Joseph Johnson, 1751-1776.* Amherst: University of Massachusetts Press, 1998.

Muszynski, Alicja. *Cheap wage labour: race and gender in the fisheries of British Columbia.* Montreal and Kingston: McGill-Queen's

University Press, 1996.

Native Information Services Task Force. *Report: empowerment through information*. Toronto: Ministry of Culture and Communications, 1992.

Nichols, John D. "The Composition sequence of the first Cree hymnal." *Essays in Algonquian bibliography in honour of V. M. Dechene*. Ed. H. C. Wolfart. Winnipeg: [s.n.], 1984.

North American Indian Travelling College. *Traditional teachings*. Cornwall Island ON: North American Indian Travelling College, 1984.

Nowry, Laurence. *Marius Barbeau, man of mana: a biography*. Toronto: NC Press Limited, 1995.

Nurse, Andrew. "'But now things have changed': Marius Barbeau and the politics of Amerindian identity." *Ethnohistory* 48.3 (2001).

O'Donnell, Jacqueline P. *The Native Brotherhood of British Columbia 1931-1950: a new phase in Native political organization*. M. A. Thesis. University of British Columbia, 1985. Ottawa: Canadian Theses on Microfiche, 1985.

Olson, David R. "Aboriginal literacy." *Interchange* 25.4 (1994).

―――. *The Word on paper: the conceptual and cognitive implications of writing and reading*. Cambridge: Cambridge University Press, 1994.

Parkes, Debbie. "Kahnawake turns a page." Montreal *Gazette* 5 October 2003, A3.

Patterson, Lotsee. "Native American library services: reclaiming the past, designing the future." *Wilson Library Bulletin* 67 (1992).

―――. "The Work of tribal libraries." Back to the future: a forum on the education and training requirements of First Nations record keepers. University of British Columbia. 17 November 2000.

Peake, Frank A. "Church Missionary Society: policy and personnel in Rupertsland." *Journal of the Canadian Church Historical Society* 30.2 (1988).

Peel, Bruce. "Early mission presses in Alberta." *Alberta Library Association Bulletin* 11.1 (1963).

―――. "How the Bible came to the Cree." *Alberta Historical Review* 6 (1958).

―――. "Rossville Mission Press: press, prints and translators." *Papers of the Bibliographical Society of Canada* 1 (1962).

―――. *Rossville Mission Press: the invention of the Cree syllabic characters, and the first printing in Rupert's Land*. Montreal:

Osiris Publications, 1974.

Pentland, David H. "An Ottawa letter to the Algonquin chiefs at Oka." *Reading beyond words: contexts for Native history.* Ed. Jennifer S.H. Brown and Elizabeth Vibert. Peterborough: Broadview Press, 1996.

————. "The Rossville Mission dialect of Cree." *Essays in Algonquian bibliography in honour of V. M. Dechene.* Ed. H. C. Wolfart. Winnipeg, 1984.

Pentland, David H. and H. Christoph Wolfart. *Bibliography of Algonquian linguistics.* Winnipeg: University of Manitoba Press, 1982.

Phillips, Glen C. *Sarnia: a picture history of the Imperial City.* Sarnia: Iron Gate Publishing, 1990.

Pilling, James Constantine. *Bibliography of Algonquian languages.* Washington: Government Printing Office, 1891.

————. *Bibliography of Eskimo language.* Washington: Government Printing Office, 1887.

————. *Bibliography of the Iroquoian languages.* Washington: Government Printing Office, 1888.

Plain, Nicholas. *The History of Chippewas of Sarnia and the history of Sarnia Reserve.* Sarnia?: the Author, 1950.

Plain, Terry. *"Aabiish-Enjibaayin": Chippewas of Sarnia oral history project.* Sarnia: Chippewas of Sarnia First Nation, 1994.

Poser, William J. *The Carrier syllabics.* Yinka Dene Language Institute, Technical report #1. Vanderhoof BC: Yinka Dene Language Institute, 2000.

Ramsey, Jarold. *Reading the fire: the traditional Indian literatures of America.* Revised and expanded edition. Seattle: University of Washington Press, 1999.

Raudsepp, Enn. "Emergent media: the Native press in Canada," *Canadian Journal of Communication* 11.2 (1985): 193-209.

Rockefeller-MacArthur, Elizabeth. *American Indian library services in perspective: from petroglyphs to hypertext.* Jefferson NC: McFarland & Company, 1998.

Roedde, W. A. "I Drive a bookmobile: the story of the Thunder Bay District Library Co-Operative, Fort William, Ontario." *CLA Bulletin* 13.1 (1956).

Rogers, Shef. "Crusoe among the Maori: translation and colonial acculturation in Victorian New Zealand." *Book History* 1.1 (1998).

Roher, James R. "The Connecticut Missionary Society and book distribution in the early republic." *Libraries & Culture* 34.1 (1999).

Ronda, James P., and James Axtell. *Indian Missions: a critical bibliography*. Bloomington: Indiana University Press, 1978.

Rose, Michael, ed. *For the record: 160 years of Aboriginal print journalism*. St. Leonards NSW: Allen and Unwin, 1996.

Samson Cree Nation. "Plains Cree language website." http://www.wtc.ab.ca/nipisihkopahk . Samson Reserve AB: Samson Cree Nation, 2000?

Sapolsky, Steven. "The Making of Honore Jaxon." *Haymarket scrapbook*. Eds. Dave Roediger and Franklin Rosemont. Chicago: Charles H. Kerr Publishing, 1986.

Sapp, Gregg. *A Brief history of the future of libraries: an annotated bibliography*. Lanham: Scarecrow Press, 2002.

Sark, John Joe. *Micmac legends of Prince Edward Island*. Lennox Island: Lennox Island Band Council & Ragweed Press, 1988.

Schmidt, David L., and Murdena Marshall. *Mi'kmaq hieroglyphic prayers: readings in North America's first Indigenous script*. Halifax: Nimbus Publishing, 1995.

Schneiders, Paul, and Pam Richards. "Some thoughts on the function of library history in the age of the virtual library." http://www.ifla.org/VII/rt8/1997/thoughts.htm. IFLA Round Table on Library History, 1997.

"School in the bush." *Native Reflections*. Prod. Dennis Sawyer and Andy Thompson. National Film Board of Canada, 1996.

Schreyer, Rüdiger. "Take your pen and write: learning Huron: a documented historical sketch." *... and the Word was God: missionary linguistics and missionary grammar*. Ed. Even Hovdhaugen. Münster: Nodus Publikationen, 1996.

Scow, Chief William D. "President's message." *The Native Voice* 1.1 (1946).

Semple, Neil. *The Lord's Dominion: the history of Canadian Methodism*. Montreal and Kingston: McGill-Queen's University Press, 1996.

Sewid, James, and James P. Spradley. *Guests never leave hungry: the autobiography of James Sewid, a Kwakiutl Indian*. New Haven: Yale University Press, 1969.

Shenk, Wilbert R. "Henry Venn's instructions to missionaries." *Missiology: an international review* 5.4 (1977).

Shera, Jesse H. *Foundations of the public library: the origins of the public library movement in New England, 1629-1855*. 1949. Hamden: The Shoe String Press, 1965.

Shewell, Hugh. "'Bitterness behind every smile': community development and Canada's First Nations, 1954-1968." *Canadian Historical Review* 83.1 (2002).

Shipley, Nan. "Printing press at Oonikup." *The Beaver* (Summer 1960).

Skrzeszewski, Stan, et al. "Bookmobile services to Native people: an experiment in Saskatchewan." *The Book stops here: new directions in bookmobile service*. Ed. Catherine Suyak Alloway. Metuchen NJ: Scarecrow Press, 1990.

Smith, Donald B. "Honore Joseph Jaxon: a man who lived for others." *Saskatchewan history* 34.3 (1981).

————. "Right dream, wrong time." *The Globe and Mail* [Toronto] 15 December 2001: F6.

————. "William Henry Jackson: Riel's secretary." *The Beaver* (Spring 1981).

Smith, June Smeck. "Library service to American Indians." *Library Trends* 20.2 (1971).

Smith, Leslie K., and George L. Smith. *Historical references to Sarnia Indian Reserve*. Brights Grove ON: George Smith, 1976.

Smith, Patricia L., and Garth Graham. "Library service north of the sixtieth parallel: the Yukon and Northwest Territories." *Canadian libraries in their changing environment*. Eds. Loraine Spencer Garry and Carl Garry. Downsview: York University, 1977.

Standing Bear, Luther. *Land of the Spotted Eagle*. 1933. Lincoln: University of Nebraska Press, 1978.

Stevenson, Winona. "The Journals and voices of a Church of England Native catechist: Askenootow (Charles Pratt), 1851-1884." *Reading beyond words: contexts for Native history*. Eds. Jennifer S.H. Brown and Elizabeth Vibert. Peterborough: Broadview Press, 1996.

Stevenson, Winona L. "'Our man in the field': the status and role of a CMS Native catechist in Rupert's Land." *Journal of the Canadian Church Historical Society* 33.1 (1991).

Stuckey, J. Elspeth. *The Violence of literacy*. Portsmouth NH: Boynton/Cook Publishers, 1991.

Task Group on Native Library Services. *Report to the Ontario Public Library Review on Native library services in Ontario*. Toronto: Obonsawin-Irwin Consulting, 1981.

Taylor, Allan Ross. "Nonverbal communications systems in Native North America." *Semiotica* 13.4 (1975).

Tehanetorens. *Wampum belts*. Oshweken ON: Iroqrafts, 1983.

Tennant, Paul. *Aboriginal people and politics: the Indian land question in British Columbia, 1849-1989.* Vancouver: University of British Columbia Press, 1990.

Thompson, James. *The end of libraries.* London: Clive Bingeley, 1982.

Titley, E. Brian. *A Narrow vision: Duncan Campbell Scott and the administration of Indian Affairs in Canada.* Vancouver: University of British Columbia Press, 1986.

Townley, Charles. "Encouraging literacy, democracy, and productivity: the current status of American Indian libraries." *Journal of Multicultural Librarianship* 5.1 (1990).

Trimbur, John. "Articulation theory and the problem of determination: a reading of Lives on the Boundary." *Journal of Advanced Composition* 13.1 (1993).

Usher, Jean. "Duncan of Metlakatla: the Victorian origins of a model Indian community." *British Columbia: historical readings.* Eds. W. Peter Ward and Robert A. J. McDonald. Vancouver: Douglas & McIntyre, 1981.

Vastokas, Joan M. "History without writing: pictorial narratives in Native North America." *Gin Das Winan: documenting Aboriginal history in Ontario.* Eds. Dale Standen and David McNab. Champlain Society, Occasional Papers number 2. Toronto: Champlain Society, 1996.

Walker, Willard B. "Native writing systems." *Handbook of North American Indians, volume 17: languages,* Ed. Ives Goddard. Washington: Smithsonian Institution, 1996.

Warkentin, Germaine. "In search of 'The Word of the Other': Aboriginal sign systems and the History of the Book in Canada." *Book History* 2.1 (1999).

Welsh, Dean C. "Colorado River Tribes public library first in the nation." *Indian Historian* 2.1 (Spring 1969).

White, Richard. *The Middle ground: Indians, empires and republics in the Great Lakes region, 1650-1815.* Cambridge: Cambridge University Press, 1991.

Whitehead, Ruth Holmes. "A New Micmac petroglyph site." *The Occasional* 13.1 (1992).

Wiegand, Wayne A. "American library history literature, 1947-1997: theoretical perspectives?" *Libraries & Culture* 35.1 (2000).

Wilson, J. Donald. "'No Blanket to be worn in school': the education of Indians in nineteenth century Ontario." *Indian education in Canada: volume 1, the legacy.* Eds. Jean Barman et. al. Vancouver: University of British Columbia Press, 1986.

Wiseman, John A. *Temples of democracy: a history of public library development in Ontario, 1880-1920.* PhD Thesis. Loughborough University of Technology, 1989.

Wogan, Peter. "Perceptions of European literacy in early contact situations." *Ethnohistory* 41.3 (1994).

Wolfenden, Madge. "Books and libraries in fur trading and colonial days." *British Columbia Historical Quarterly* xi.3 (1947).

Wyss, Hilary E. *Writing Indians: literacy, Christianity and Native community in early America.* Amherst: University of Massachusetts Press, 2000.

York, Annie, Richard Daly and Chris Arnett. *They write their dream on the rock forever: rock writings in the Stein River Valley of British Columbia.* Vancouver: Talonbooks, 1994.

Index

Aamjiwnaang. *See* Chippewas of
    Sarnia
Abenaki, 10
Abishabis (Small Eyes), 52, 53
Abitibi, 52
Aboriginal agency. *See*
    articulation
Aboriginal sign systems. *See*
    writing: Aboriginal
Aborigines Protection Society,
    120n96
Acadia, xiii, 30, 34, 36
Adams, Alfred, 140, 141
Adams, John, 119n78
Adams, Joshua, 101-105, 119n78
Aesop's Fables, 126
Ahenakew, Edward, 137-140,
    157n53
Alaska Native Brotherhood, 140
Albany Post, 52
Alberni, 79
Alberta, 77, 80, 129
Alderville, 60
Alert Bay, 79
Alert Bay Public Library and
    Museum, 160n89
Algoma District, 49
Algonkian, 10, 11, 52
Alnick, Ontario, 150
American Library Association,
    125
American Philosophical Society,
    97, 157n50
Anderson, David, 55, 56
Anfield, F. Earl, 134-136
Anglican Missionary Society, 138-
    139
Anglicans. *See* missionaries:
    Anglican

Anglican Theological School, 137
Angus Mowat Moose Factory
    Library, 150
Arsenault, John (Jean) O., 107,
    108
articulation, xii, xixn14, 6-7, 15,
    44-45, 52, 56, 57, 69n83, 77,
    79, 82, 84, 88-89, 90-101,
    105, 106-107, 108-109, 110,
    112, 135, 138, 139, 140-141,
    142, 144, 145-146, 164, 165-
    166, 167, 168
Ashton, R., 83
Assiniboine, 29, 51
Atahkakohp Day School, 137
Athapascan, 52, 146
Australia, x, 170n10
Aveni, Anthony F., 13
Axtell, James, 58, 70n105

Banks, Joyce M., x, 28, 49, 59-60
Baptists. *See* missionaries: Baptist
Barbeau, Marius, 97, 100, 118n74
Barkerville, British Columbia, 146
Barner, Arthur, 82
Barnes, Skawenniio, 170n10
Barnley, George, 51, 52-54,
    69n89
Barry, Gerald H., 126-127,
    154n15
Bartleman, James, 170n10
Battleford Industrial School, 62,
    78-79, 82, 123, 124
Bay of Quinte, 40, 60, 74
Beaubassin, 34
Bedford, Nova Scotia, 37
Beecham, John, 50
Bella Bella, British Columbia, 136

220   Index

Wogan, Peter, 58, 70n105
Wood, Lady Augusta, 107, 108,
  120n94
A Work Book in British History,
  126
writers: Aboriginal, 88-89, 137-
  140

writing: Aboriginal, 1, 4, 5, 8, 9-
  12, 26, 30-38, 49-57, 82-83,
  146-147, 165
Wycliffe College, 137
Wyss, Hilary E., x, 88

Young, Egerton Ryerson, 49

Zeisberger, David, 78

About the Author

Brendan Frederick R. Edwards is a doctoral candidate in the Department of History at the University of Saskatchewan in Saskatoon, Saskatchewan. He has a Master of Arts in Canadian Studies and Native Studies from Trent University, Peterborough, Ontario, and a Master of Library and Information Studies degree from McGill University, Montréal, Québec.